The Breath of God

The Breath of God

An Essay on the Holy Spirit in the Trinity

ETIENNE VETÖ

Foreword by Ephraim Radner

CASCADE Books • Eugene, Oregon

THE BREATH OF GOD
An Essay on the Holy Spirit in the Trinity

Copyright © 2019 Etienne Vetö. All rights reserved. Except for brief quotations in critical publications or reviews, no part of this book may be reproduced in any manner without prior written permission from the publisher. Write: Permissions, Wipf and Stock Publishers, 199 W. 8th Ave., Suite 3, Eugene, OR 97401.

Cascade Books
An Imprint of Wipf and Stock Publishers
199 W. 8th Ave., Suite 3
Eugene, OR 97401

www.wipfandstock.com

PAPERBACK ISBN: 978-1-5326-8219-3
HARDCOVER ISBN: 978-1-5326-8220-9
EBOOK ISBN: 978-1-5326-8221-6

Cataloguing-in-Publication data:

Names: Vetö, Étienne, author. | Radner, Ephraim, 1956–, foreword.

Title: The breath of God : an essay on the Holy Spirit in the Trinity / Etienne Vetö ; foreword by Ephraim Radner.

Description: Eugene, OR : Cascade Books, 2019 | Includes bibliographical references and indexes.

Identifiers: ISBN 978-1-5326-8219-3 (paperback) | ISBN 978-1-5326-8220-9 (hardcover) | ISBN 978-1-5326-8221-6 (ebook)

Subjects: LCSH: Holy Spirit.

Classification: BT122 .V48 2019 (paperback) | BT122 .V48 (ebook)

Manufactured in the U.S.A.   04/18/19

Scripture quotations are from New Revised Standard Version Bible, copyright © 1989 National Council of the Churches of Christ in the United States of America. Used by permission. All rights reserved worldwide.

Scripture quotations of Deuterocanonical books are from The Catholic Edition of the Revised Standard Version of the Bible, copyright © 1965, 1966 National Council of the Churches of Christ in the United States of America. Used by permission. All rights reserved worldwide.

Cover image: "Celestial Hierarchy," Yves de Saint-Denis, Vita et passio sancti Dionysii, 1317, parchment. Bibliothèque Nationale de France, Paris, MS fr. 2090, fol. 107v. Reproduced with permission.

Contents

Illustrations | vii
Foreword by Ephraim Radner | xi
Acknowledgments | xix
Abbreviations | xx
Introduction: The Otherness of the Holy Spirit | xxi

1 The Holy Spirit *in* and *through* and *around* Others in the Economy | 1

2 Breath (*Ruah-Pneuma*): Naming the Spirit in the Immanent Trinity | 29

3 The Analogical Trinity | 74

4 The Manifestation of the Breath of the Father and of the Son | 101

   Conclusion | 138

Bibliography | 141
Index of Scripture | 149
Index of Names | 153

Illustrations

FIGURE 1. Andrei Rublev, *Trinity*, 1422–1427, icon. State Tretyakov Gallery, Moscow, no. 13012. Reproduced with permission. 103

FIGURE 2. "Trinity at the Altar," *Missale et horae ad usum Fratrum Minorum*, 1380, parchment. Bibliothèque Nationale de France, Paris, MS Latin 757, fol. 229v. Reproduced with permission. 104

FIGURE 3. "Abraham and the Trinity," English Psalter, c. 1270–80, fourteenth century, parchment. St. John's College, Cambridge, MS K.26, fol. 9r. Reproduced by kind permission of the Master and Fellows of St. John's College, Cambridge. 105

FIGURE 4. *Dreigesicht*, 1610, Unterinntal, oil on wood. Tiroler Landesmuseen/Volkskunstmuseum, Innsbruck, no. 20356. Photo Credit: TVKM/Gerhard Watzek. Reproduced by kind permission of the Tiroler Landesmuseen/Volkskunstmuseum. 106

FIGURE 5. "Heavenly Jerusalem and *communio sanctorum*," Augustine's *De Civitate Dei*, 1142–1150, parchment, Olomouc-Prague, workshop of Hildebert and Everwinus. The Archives of Prague Castle, MS A7, fol. 1v. Reproduced by kind permission of the Dean of the Metropolitan Chapter of St. Vitus. 107

FIGURE 6. "Christ's Baptism," *Evangelia characteribus Syriacis exarata* (*Rabula Gospels*), 586, parchment. Biblioteca Medicea Laurenziana, Florence, MS Plut. 1.56, fol. 4v. Reproduced with permission of the MiBAC. Any ulterior reproduction by any means is forbidden. 108

Illustrations

FIGURE 7. "The Fatherland with selected saints," Novgorod School icon, beginning of the fifteenth century. State Tretyakov Gallery, Moscow, no. 22211. Reproduced with permission. 109

FIGURE 8. "Trinity: Two Persons flanking Dove," *Lothian Bible*, c. 1220, parchment, Oxford. The Morgan Library & Museum, MS M.791, fol. 4v. Gift of Philip Hofer, May 1935. Photo Credit: The Morgan Library & Museum, New York. Reproduced with permission. 110

FIGURE 9. "The Trinity with a 'feminine' Holy Spirit," c. 1390, wall painting of St. Jacob's Church, Urschalling, Bavaria. Photo Credit: Berger, Prien. Reproduced with permission. 111

FIGURE 10. Simone Cantarini, *The Holy Trinity (unfinished)*, 1640, oil on canvas. National Galleries of Scotland, Edinburgh, no. NG 42. Presented to the RI by Edward Cruickshank 1844; transferred 1859. Reproduced with permission. 112

FIGURE 11. "The throne of God as a trinitarian image," early fifth century, mosaic of St. Matrona's chapel, San Prisco, Naples, Italy. Photo Credit: Vincenzo Lerro. Reproduced by kind permission of Vincenzo Lerro and the parish of Santa Croce, San Prisco. 113

FIGURE 12. Anselm Kiefer, *Send Forth your Spirit*, 1974, watercolor, gouache, ink, ballpoint pen, and colored pencil on paper. Metropolitan Museum of Art, New York. Purchase, Lila Acheson Wallace Gift, 1995. © 2019 Image copyright The Metropolitan Museum of Art/Art Resource/Scala, Florence. 114

FIGURE 13. Marko Rupnik, "The Hand of the Father and the Descent of the Holy Spirit on the Son," 2004, mosaic of the chapel of the Apostolic Nunciature, Damascus, Syria. Reproduced by kind permission of the Atelier d'Arte e Architettura del Centro Aletti, Rome. 115

FIGURE 14. "Creation of Adam," stained glass of the Good Samaritan, thirteenth century, Cathedral of Chartres. Reproduced by kind permission of the Rectory of the Cathedral of Chartres. 116

Illustrations

FIGURE 15. Etienne Delaune (attributed to), *God creating Adam and breathing life into him*, sixteenth century, pen drawing, ink, parchment. Musée du Louvre, Paris, collection Rothschild, no. 1525DR. Photo © RMN-Grand Palais (musée du Louvre) / Thierry Le Mage. Reproduced with permission.   117

FIGURE 16. "Celestial Hierarchy," Yves de Saint-Denis, *Vita et passio sancti Dionysii*, 1317, parchment. Bibliothèque Nationale de France, Paris, MS fr. 2090, fol. 107v. Reproduced with permission.   118

FIGURE 17. "Throne of Grace surrounded by the Tetramorphus," *Cambrai Missal*, c. 1120, parchment. Médiathèque d'Agglomération de Cambrai, MS B 234, fol. 2r. Photo Credit: CNRS/IRHT. Reproduced by kind permission of the Municipal Library of Cambrai.   118

Score 1. J. S. Bach, *Kyrie, Gott Heiliger Geist (BWV 671)*, third part of the *Clavier-Übung*, Charru and Theobald (eds.), *L'Esprit créateur dans la pensée musicale de Jean-Sébastien Bach* (Sprimont: Mardaga, 2002), 224. Reproduced by kind permission of Philippe Charru.   121

Score 2. J. S. Bach, *Kyrie, Gott Heiliger Geist (BWV 671)*, third part of the *Clavier-Übung*, Charru and Theobald (eds.), *L'Esprit créateur dans la pensée musicale de Jean-Sébastien Bach* (Sprimont: Mardaga, 2002), 225. Reproduced by kind permission of Philippe Charru.   121

Score 3. J. S. Bach, *Kyrie, Gott Heiliger Geist (BWV 671)*, third part of the *Clavier-Übung*, Charru and Theobald (eds.), *L'Esprit créateur dans la pensée musicale de Jean-Sébastien Bach* (Sprimont: Mardaga, 2002), 224. Reproduced by kind permission of Philippe Charru.   121

Score 4. J. S. Bach, *Kyrie, Gott Heiliger Geist (BWV 671)*, third part of the *Clavier-Übung*, Charru and Theobald (eds.), *L'Esprit créateur dans la pensée musicale de Jean-Sébastien Bach* (Sprimont: Mardaga, 2002), 226. Reproduced by kind permission of Philippe Charru.   122

Foreword

The Holy Spirit, within a contemporary perspective, is often viewed in terms of a diffused substratum to reality, a spreading and enveloping energy that constitutes the world itself. Onto this generalized pneumatic screen can be projected a host of human hopes. In our globalized world, the contemporary version of the Spirit funds mostly a kind of uniform sameness that reflects the social values of vast interconnection and manageability. The political results are disturbing.

Etienne Vetö's remarkable book is attuned to this modern trajectory in pneumatology, even if it does not engage it explicitly. He understands both the traditional scriptural metaphors and images that have ordered the grasp after a global Spirit—fluidity, movement, vaporousness. He recognizes as well the interior yearnings that motivate this search. His own constructive path, however, takes all this up and redirects it back towards the particularities and peculiarities of God's life and will, and thus of human purpose. Vetö does this simply, yet with a decisively transformative reach, through a renewed affirmation of the Holy Spirit according to its "proper name." This name is itself particular, scripturally demarcated, and divinely distinct in its trinitarian singularity. Neither gas nor ether nor disseminating power, Vetö insists that the Spirit is quite particularly "Breath," the Breath of God. There is nothing novel in reasserting this truth. The "Breath of God" is, after all, the simple verbal sign that has ever been used to denote the Second Person of the Trinity: *ruah* or *pneuma*. But rather than allowing this word—and Name—to be an allusive springboard to other, more abstracted and projected concepts, Vetö dares to let all pneumatological statements be measured by the name itself. This pneumatological method, if one can call it that, yields surprising and profound results.

The particularity or uniqueness of the Spirit has always challenged Christian trinitarian thinkers. Augustine, for instance, worried over the use

Foreword

of the term *spiritus* itself as a primary designator for the Third Person of the Godhead, since it seemed to indicate a kind of ontological element common to both Father and Son (both, after all, are "spirit" in some sense). Preferring titles like "gift" or "love itself," Augustine felt that he could thereby maintain some common divine link to Father and Son, even denoting some discrete being by such terms. The Spirit as something "common" to Father and Son, however one ended up parsing it, did in fact linger on as a way of thinking pneumatically, and this created difficulties. *Pneuma* was, after all, a well-used Stoic category of natural philosophy, and its deployment in Christian thinking inevitably pressed in certain naturalizing directions with respect to conceptions of the Holy Spirit itself, in a way that percolated through and finally permeated Western theology in particular by early modernity. Just such a naturalized—and de-particularized—Spirit has roamed about the speculations of contemporary pneumatology for some time now.

This is just what Vetö's proposal counters, and it does so by grounding the Holy Spirit's theological conceptualization firmly in the Old Testament name, *ruah*, which provides the normative parameters for interpreting the New Testament's own Greek translation for "spirit," *pneuma*. Each name is properly translated as "breath." And "breath" is not "spirit" in a modern sense. Breath is rather the personal expiration, inspiration, and respiration of living beings, fundamentally of God. However hard it is to delineate, breath is personal. This is Vetö's crucial claim.

"Breath" as a "name" for God roots this claim regarding personhood in the particularity of divine assertion, that is, in revelation, as human beings receive it. Vetö's denominating approach—focusing on a "name"—is ultimately a strict scriptural method, and it goes beyond the traditionally wooden theological program of starting with the Bible, and then moving on to tradition and final dogmatic assertion, as if traversing progressive stages of knowledge. Vetö will engage the latter two categories, certainly, but his concern is with the actual and actually revealed nature of God, trinitarian as it is. His scripturally inductive method is not one of passing through degrees of analytic abstraction, but of inhabiting mutually informing spheres of reflection. The first is that of the divine "economy" (God's revealed life and actions in the world of history, fundamentally given in Scripture). The second is that of the "immanent" life of God as Trinity itself, understood through the logic of human reflection given both within the church's tradition as well as through personal contemplation. While each sphere reciprocally illumines the other, Vetö's interest is not so much to surpass Scripture

Foreword

with abstracted logics, as to allow any human and ecclesial definitions to clarify the scriptural economy which, at root, constitutes our own—and the church's—mode of being.

So, he digs into the naming of the Spirit in Scripture, not to amass ingredients for an analysis, but to identify divine actualities that *are* the Spirit. "[A]n attentive analysis of the mode of being and of acting of the Holy Spirit in the economy illumines a series of irreducibly unique characteristics—interiority, hiddenness, anonymity, insubstantiality or fluidity."[1] These pneumatic characteristics, by the late twentieth century commonly associated with the Spirit, are laid out through a careful scriptural collation. They represent the divine "economy," however, in a way that challenges simple experiential reconfigurations of their imagery, something often done in early modernity, with its host of naturalistic explanations and ontological definitions. For the Scriptures themselves refuse such explanatory frameworks. That is the nature of biblical denomination: it indicates "givens" rather than analyzes mechanisms.

Vetö's scriptural discussion is key to seeing how this analytic refusal works: profusion, variety, anonymity, power, and more—the scriptural descriptions of the Spirit—are not "resolved" by a kind of metaphysical ground, but are instead maintained as absolute particulars by their very scriptural nomenclature, or "naming." The "economy," precisely in its presentation of discrete acts and moments, maintains a firm grasp on the Spirit's insistent "otherness" or unique being. Any metaphysical scheme to which one might wish to appropriate the Holy Spirit ends up being far more anthropocentric (and thus domesticated) than the ontologically desultory words of Scripture itself, whose connection within the scattered and various episodes of pneumatic action is given only, but immovably, in a revealed "name."

It is precisely the specificity of this name—*Ruah* or Breath—that both enables the diversity of the Scripture's witness to the divine Spirit, but also holds that diversity's simple resolution at bay: that God, understood as Father in Vetö's careful trinitarian discussion of pneumatic procession, "breathes" is not an aspect of divine character or some divine ingredient. God's breathing and thus God's Breath, is an identity that marks "who" God is in a way that cannot be further distilled without actually denying God in the first place. That is the consequence simply of the way Scripture works to speak about God. And if speaking truthfully, this scriptural "way" is a revelation of God that cannot be penetrated beyond itself.

1. See p. xxiii.

Foreword

Such a view of Scripture and its divine truth-telling is contested, to be sure, particularly on the basis of claims regarding God's transcendence of human language. Vetö engages this question with a supple understanding of metaphor (following, e.g., McFague), and in particular of the divine metaphors of Scripture. These, he argues, are less descriptors than "indicators" of God. Furthermore, the actual *names* of Scripture's God—Father, Son, and in this case *Ruah*—are indicators in a unique way, such that it makes sense to designate *Ruah/Pneuma* a "proper name" for God. The reality of such "proper naming" permits activities associated with the Spirit to be attached to it essentially, if neither exhaustively nor analytically.

For Vetö, the divine name of Breath leaves the diverse actions of the Spirit, even in certain common features—interiority, energy, fluidity—just what they are, without themselves being tied to a more fundamental and common pneumatic substratum. Each "feature" is real, and each is the Spirit at work in the Spirit's own being and way. But the Spirit is not reducible to the common denominator of their forms. If Vetö speaks of the Spirit's "personality," which he finally does, the emphasis lies on "person," not on the abstraction of the personal*itas*. Again, the emphasis is on "who" not "what," and in a way that, precisely in the particularity of its formal activity, distinguishes the Spirit from other "personalities," even to the point of perplexity.

For the Spirit's activities, as they are scripturally collated, do stand to the side of the kinds of "personal" elements we associate with Father and Son. This distinction, often difficult to line up in some common divine grammar, is what Vetö calls the Spirit's "otherness." Many theologians have remarked on the oddity in applying "univocal" trinitarian categories to the Spirit, as if Father, Son, and Spirit can ever by conceived of as congruently ordered divine categories. Even at their most humanly-imaged metaphorical level, the Spirit stands out as *un*human and formless. In a real way, "the third hypostasis is profoundly different from the other two, it is 'insubstantial' and impersonal."[2] Hence, "facelessness" or "anonymity" have become common characterizations of the Spirit in our day, not so much to demote its divine trinitarian status as to problematize it. And Vetö develops these problematic elements into a creative trinitarian reflection that rightly seeks to reestablish the divine Trinity's mysterious character, its divine, but also asymmetrically ordered, particularity, as in one sense "analogical" all the way down.

2. See p. 71.

Foreword

These sorts of reflections, going to the center of academic trinitarian discussion, are nonetheless critical to Vetö's practical project. The Spirit's oddity—fastened to its scriptural naming—in regard to its "personal" form is not so much an apophatic tool as it is a disclosing one. That is really the key consequence of Vetö's scriptural naming of the *Ruah* and its palpable, if definitionally uncircumscribed, work. If there are divine "differences" between the persons of the Trinity, differences that cannot be reduced to common denominators and that subsist in the very nature of God, they are "perfect differences," such that particularity and singularity—otherness and uniqueness—emerge as the very matter of reality insofar as God constitutes it. Pneumatic "breath" is that unveiling of distinctive reality itself, down to its roots. "The more the Spirit is active in infusing wisdom, dynamism, life, and relations in others, the more it pulls back. It is itself by making others become themselves."[3] This is true for God's self; it is true for the creature who lives from and for God.

Thus, in the first place, Vetö argues that God's own personal form and being as Father and Son is a pneumatic reality. Vetö's rich trinitarian discussions, drawing on patristic, medieval, and modern conceptions, are a carefully ordered exercise in testing the "fittingness" of the Spirit's scripturally given "proper name" as Breath, to our understanding of God's own nature. And just this fitting use of scriptural vocabulary, bound to its divine referent, prevents the kinds of naturalizing or ontologizing of "spirit" that have been the bane of modern pneumatology. His focus on maintaining the scriptural—and later dogmatic—*taxis* or "order" of Father, Son, and Spirit actually puts a brake on the human appropriations of these intra-trinitarian movements, simply because the *taxis* in its almost formally imposed shape is very difficult to "naturalize." Vetö's chapters here are wonderful examples of the value of a truly scriptural "systematic" approach to dogmatic challenges.

The method, however, is important only because it serves a disclosing purpose. In the second place, then, the careful trinitarian discussions of Vetö press ineluctably to his main conviction, now laid out as a kind of argument: the nature of God, trinitarian as it is, is one that establishes human prayer itself as its creative term, not so much as "simply" a pneumatic act, but as the act or life wherein the Spirit's trinitarian personality is itself paradoxically most fully "manifested." Vetö calls prayer "the truest

3. See p. 28.

Foreword

manifestation of the Spirit,"[4] just because in prayer the fullness of God is given over to the life of the creature, just as the Breath is the divine reality that lets the Father's mind and will live within the Son.

It is this trinitarian argument of personal "interiority," by which the Breath is conceived of as the union of the Father's inner life within the Son, that opens up Vetö's rich understanding of the Spirit's founding and unique creative role in human prayer as its crowning work within creation. Vetö shows how the pneumatic association with gift and emotion, scripturally enunciated and traditionally (and experientially) confirmed, is properly grounded in a trinitarian understanding of divine Breath. Vetö locates these elements within the central reality of the Christian's life of prayer as the fulfillment of his or her movement into the most intimate relation and understanding of the Father and the Son. Pneumatic prayer turns out to be a movement back into the scriptural particularities out of which the Spirit's own strange personality is presented, and therefore into the particularities of the Son's Word, by which the Father's life is given to the Christian:

> Bringing the Father and the Son into us means helping us to listen to them, helping us let their words sink into our hearts and minds. To a certain extent, we do not listen to the Spirit itself, but to the Father, who speaks his *Logos*, and, from within, the Spirit turns the ear of our heart towards the Voice of the Father.[5]

As with the very principle of a pneumatology of *Ruah* or Breath, the articulations of the revealed word, of Scripture, end by looming up as transformative and fulfilling terms for the Christian life as a whole.

In a way very different from ecumenical pneumatologies of metaphysical commonality—the Spirit as that which underlies the sameness of the world—Vetö ends with an unusual ecumenical pneumatology of the scriptural word itself, centered in Christ Jesus. Prayer "in the Spirit" takes us to, articulates before us, and enables our reception of the "teaching" of Christ, his words. Pneumatology as *oratio ad Verbum* constitutes a fruitful challenge, indeed a real gift, to Catholic, Protestant, and Orthodox alike. The vision he offers is not one, however, of a potentially shared set of values or projects, ridden on the back of a pneumatic world movement. Rather, if taken up, Vetö's final proposal of a common centering on the word, given through the Breath of God the Father and shared with the Son, takes us

4. See p. xxiv.
5. See p. 129.

Foreword

beyond ourselves into the actual relationship of divine love within the world. Inspired, we pray, read, and learn; we also "breathe out"—respire—in turn, as our prayer is given the form of love for others. We find ourselves with them and are transformed. The unique person of the Spirit, which can itself analogically redefine our own sense of "personhood" that is so contested in our culture, is manifest just here.

Vetö's book can be seen as a prolegomenon to prayer itself, and his final chapter is almost a small primer on the topic, carefully laid out in its trinitarian dynamic and pneumatic consummation. The surprise to this wonderful book is found in just this discovery: prayer is exactly where the Spirit, elusively but consistently, leads us. The book, then, is to be carefully taken up and studied; and then put aside as we turn, renewed and reoriented, to our true vocation. What better way of doing theology?

Ephraim Radner

Acknowledgments

I would like to thank all those whose help and support have made this book possible. I am especially grateful to Ephraim Radner for his constant encouragements and for contributing such a gracious foreword. I am most thankful to Ephraim Radner, François Lestang, and Karen Kilby, who read the manuscript and offered wise counsel directed to its improvement. Though I assume they will find that much still needs to be perfected, their advice helped me greatly. I am most indebted to Fr. Jerome Santamaria, Sr. Marie Mondésert, and especially to Br. Jean-Sébastien Laurent who have assisted me in the often-unrewarding task of preparing the manuscript for publication. I would also like to thank all the members of the Chemin Neuf Community who together have provided such a fertile environment for this book to develop—and for their patience in bearing with me during the sometimes-difficult writing process. They have been an unfailing source of support and inspiration.

Abbreviations

PL   Migne, *Patrologia Latina*
PG   Migne, *Patrologia Greca*
ST   *Summa Theologiae* (Thomas Aquinas)
SCG *Summa contra Gentiles* (Thomas Aquinas)
DH   Denzinger-Hünermann, *Compendium of Creeds, Definitions, and Declarations on Matters of Faith and Morals*

Introduction
The Otherness of the Holy Spirit

Time and again theologians lament the difficulty of understanding the Holy Spirit and thus of giving it its right weight in Christian thought. This is an old melody; as for the procession of the Spirit, "who can explain it?" exclaims Augustine.[6] Even contemporary trinitarian revivals are blamed for slighting the Holy Spirit. In a recent book, E. Rogers regrets that "Spirit-talk in the last hundred years has been ever more evoked, and ever more substance-free."[7] The lament sometimes extends to the difficulty of finding the Spirit's right place in prayer and Christian life: its role is central, no life of prayer or of faith is possible without it, but how to relate to it?

Where is the problem? It appears to me that it boils down to two difficulties. The first one is that we have the utmost resistance in fully acknowledging the Holy Spirit's otherness. Of course, we do bring it to light: the Spirit seems less substantial and less personal than the Father and the Son, since it works deep down inside human beings and creation as a whole. Moreover, while the names of the first and second persons give some idea of who they are, of their "personality," the Holy Spirit's name makes it even less graspable and more mysterious. What is a "holy spirit"? How can a "spirit" be a divine person? Confronted with this otherness the first theological reflex is to fit the Spirit as neatly as possible into a trinitarian mold constructed from the Father-Son relation. This is not surprising. Faced with Pneumatomachians, Anomians, and other negators of its divinity and personhood, the church fathers tended to do all they could to show the Spirit was equal, co-eternal, and consubstantial with the Father and the Son. The aim was always to stress the similarities between them.

6. Augustine, *Contra Maximinum*, II, xiv, 1 (PL 42, 770–71).
7. Rogers, *After the Spirit*, 1.

Introduction

As Pannenberg points out, the understanding Christian tradition has of the Spirit was developed after and on the model of its comprehension of the Father and the Son:

> As a Son Jesus both differs from the Father and is related to him. This fact is the presupposition for the understanding of the Spirit as a third figure, which is distinct from both the Father and the Son and yet closely related in fellowship with them. It is true that the idea of the divine Spirit as a creative force emanating from God had been long familiar to Jewish tradition. But in Christianity the Spirit became a specific figure, distinct from the Father, on the basis of the understanding of Jesus as the pre-existent Son, and in distinction from him.[8]

Because of this, the third person was conceptualized with tools developed for the two other persons. This begs the question: are these tools fully adequate?

The second difficulty is that there is often a crying gap between economic and intra-trinitarian renderings of the Holy Spirit. Economic pneumatologies offer a multiplicity of traits and works—which do correspond to a faithful reading of the Scriptures, but leave the reader with the impression of, if not a certain chaos and confusion, at least an unlimited fecundity and richness, without a general direction. Then the eternal procession, relations, and personal properties of the third divine hypostasis are developed in terms of love between the Father and the Son or of the "resting" of the Spirit on the second hypostasis—to evoke two of the main pneumatological lines, respectively in the West and in the East. It is hard to see the relation between the two spheres. The second question logically is: where does this hiatus originate?

In this light, solving these difficulties implies two simple steps. Firstly, don't be afraid of the otherness of the Spirit, but welcome it fully and develop pneumatology with specific notions and conceptual tools.

Secondly, take Barth, Rahner, and Balthasar to the word when they propose to understand the "immanent Trinity" by starting with the "economic" one. The idea stems from Barth: "Statements about the divine modes of being antecedently in themselves (*zuvor in sich selber*) cannot be different in content from those that are to be made about their reality in revelation."[9] Rahner translates this into the famous *Grundaxiom*: "The 'eco-

---

8. Pannenberg, *Systematic Theology I*, 304–5; see also 269–72.
9. Barth, *Church Dogmatics* I/1, §12, 479. Barth adds: "All our statements concerning

Introduction

nomic' Trinity is the 'immanent' Trinity, and the 'immanent' Trinity is the 'economic' Trinity."[10] Are not the eternal Father, Son, and Spirit precisely the same "persons" as the Father, Son, and Spirit who act and speak in our lives? To this Balthasar adds a further methodological clause: "There is no access to the Trinitarian mystery other than its revelation in Jesus Christ and the Holy Spirit. No claims about the immanent Trinity can afford to lose their footing in the New Testament."[11] This means that pneumatology should always start by considering the works of the Spirit in the world and in salvation history, especially as expounded by the Scriptures, i.e., the economy. It means that this economy is not only the departure point of theology but that all legitimate development about the third person in the *theologia* should be thought out with an eye constantly trained on it, so that the inner-trinitarian understanding truly echoes the New Testament. Of course, one must always purify the images and notions received from the scriptural revelation through a healthy dose of apophatic theology. However, never should the correspondence between the eternal life of God and his action in salvation history be lost.

In fact, from a methodological point of view, the first step will flow from the second. I will argue in the first chapter of this book that an attentive analysis of the mode of being and of acting of the Holy Spirit in the economy illumines a series of irreducibly unique characteristics—interiority, hiddenness, anonymity, insubstantiality, or fluidity.

As such, they lead us finally to take fully seriously the third divine name—*Ruah* or *Pneuma*—as the only word that brings together and expresses all these traits. Of course, breath or wind is a metaphor, but it is the least inadequate one we have and it is provided by the Scriptures. For this reason, the second chapter, the center of this essay, will consist in the exploration of the possibilities offered by the breath-metaphor for a renewed conception of the Holy Spirit in the inner-trinitarian life, as the eternal Breath of the Father and the Son. If this image taken from the economy is apt to be developed also in our comprehension of the immanent Trinity, then it is capable of bridging the gap between *oikonomia* and *theologia*.

---

what is called the immanent Trinity have been reached simply as confirmations or underlinings (*Unterstreichungen*) or, materially, as the indispensable premises of the economic Trinity."

10. Rahner, *Trinity*, 22. See also *Foundations of Christian Faith*, 136–37.
11. Balthasar, *Theo-Logic II: The Truth of God*, 125.

Introduction

However, if the otherness of the Holy Spirit finds a more adequate expression, this cannot but have consequences for trinitarian theology as a whole. This will be the object of the third chapter. If it is difficult to "accommodate" the Spirit in the Trinity because it has been construed on the Father-Son relation, more appropriate tools to think out the Spirit oblige us—and help us—to offer a better comprehension of some aspects of trinitarian theology. If the Spirit is "other" and unique, then so are the Father and the Son, much more so than what is usually perceived. The unique characteristics of the third person thus open the way to understanding the notion of "person" or "hypostasis" in God as analogical, in the sense that they possess modes of being so different that they cannot be articulated by a fully univocal concept. Indeed, the Trinity itself is "analogical": relations, processions, and all that expresses plurality need to be considered as radically unique in each divine person, Father, Son, and Holy Spirit.

Ultimately, however, the aim of developing a renewed comprehension of the Holy Spirit in the immanent Trinity is not to dwell in the contemplation of the eternal relations in God but to be able to turn back to the economy, where the pneumatological and trinitarian insights gained by developing the breath-metaphor should offer a better understanding of the manifestation of the Spirit, as well as of the Father and the Son. The fourth chapter will expound these ultimate and more existential implications of our research. It will focus on our endeavor to represent the Trinity in art and show how adequate or inadequate different pictorial and musical expressions of the triune God can be. It will especially concentrate on prayer, the truest manifestation of the Spirit. If the Holy Spirit is a divine Breath, and if all three persons are unique in their personhood, then the believer's personal relationship to God will be clarified as well. It may well be that the difficulty we have in relating to the Spirit comes from the tendency we have to turn to it in the same way as we turn to the Father and to the Son. Retrieving its otherness can be a key to a renewed life of prayer and of faith, in which our relationship to the Holy Spirit is finally fully specific.

Of course, the infinite fullness of divine life prohibits developing any complete pneumatology or trinitarian theology with one notion or one image only, however legitimate and rich it may be. The breath-metaphor is no exception. I will not presume to be complete but simply to offer a first solution to the two difficulties exposed and show the value of remembering something as simple as the fact the Scriptures do have a concrete name for the mysterious third person: *Ruah* and *Pneuma*.

I

The Holy Spirit *in* and *through* and *around* Others in the Economy

We start with the economy. Though I will sometimes consider spiritual life and make some forays into systematic theology, this chapter will be mainly scriptural, drawing from both the First and the New Testaments. The aim, however, is not to offer a complete investigation of what the Scriptures teach about the Spirit. I will rarely distinguish the contents of the different books as such, or dwell on the historical developments, but rather look for the comprehension given by the broader whole of the Bible, considered as the *locus* of revelation.[1] Neither will I seek to analyze whether the authors of the New Testament presumed the Spirit to be a distinct divine actor or in what way the authors of the First Testament understood its relation to God. The Scriptures present a divine *Ruah* and a

---

1. This approach is set in the framework of "canonical criticism" or the "canonical approach" to the Bible. Although there are as many types of canonical approaches as there are exegetes who practice it—Brevard S. Childs, James A. Sanders, Rolf Rendtorff, Gerald T. Sheppard, and Christopher Seitz, to cite the main names—their common point is to consider the Bible as the sacred Scriptures of the church, to be situated in the single design of God. In no way does this methodology reject historical criticism, but it recognizes the intertextual resonances and relations between the books. It seeks to complete the historical approach by setting the texts into the context of the whole and of a theological interpretation. Canonical approaches do not seek to harmonize the different voices of the Scriptures at all cost, but consider them to be richly polyphonic rather than contradictory. For more on these exegetical schools, see the excellent introduction by Anthony Thiselton, "Canon, Community and Theological Construction," 1–27; see also Pontifical Biblical Commission, *Interpretation of the Bible*, 50–53.

divine *Pneuma*, distinguished from the natural and the human ones. Of the 378 occurrences of *Ruah* in the Hebrew Bible, close to half refer to God's Spirit, while in the New Testament, 275 of the 379 occurrences of *Pneuma* do.[2] This has been the primary source of the church's comprehension of the Holy Spirit and has shaped its doctrine on the third divine hypostasis. By way of consequence, one can say that these texts, as Scripture of the church, should be read also, if not exclusively, in the light of their reception by the community of readers of the church. Moreover, it means that we simply have no surer access to the way in which what we now understand as the third person of the Trinity reveals itself and works in the economy of salvation than the Bible. We need to allow tradition to re-immerse itself in the Scriptures.[3] This means that the precise aim of this chapter is to provide an initial theological interpretation, based on the Scriptures, to identify what makes *Ruah* and *Pneuma* unique as a dimension of divine action or as a divine actor in the economy.

Because the economy is where God acts with saving power, the Spirit of God is essentially presented in its operation and through the gifts it offers—in the wide sense of what it gives and of how it transforms the believers. However, I will argue that most significant is not *what* the Spirit does or gives, but *how* it acts. To echo the Barthian "mode of being" (*Seinsweise*) and Rahnerian mode of "subsistence" (*Subsistenzweise*),[4] the key to the third divine name's specificity is its "mode of acting" or "mode of operating." This will show that the Spirit acts, speaks, and prays *in* and *through*— and in a certain way, *around*—other actors. Only then will it be possible to reflect, in a second phase, on the Spirit's being, or at least its mode of existence in the economy, which is better understood in the framework of its *modus operandi*. The point will be to put into light *how* it is, its specific *modus essendi*, that is its unique type of "self," characterized by its "fluidity." Finally, I analyze some of the Spirit's gifts, in particular inspiration, life, and the relation to the Father and the Son, and show how these reflect both its way of acting and its way of being.

---

2. See Botterweck and Ringgren, *Theological Dictionary of the Old Testament XIII*, 365–402.

3. The attention given to the church as the Bible's community of readers is also a central contribution of the "canonical approach" to the Scriptures. Scripture is formative of the community's faith, it is intertwined with liturgy and life, and a complete hermeneutic asks for a constant back-and-forth movement between the Bible and the church's reading of it (see Thiselton, "Canon, Community and Theological Construction," 6, 27).

4. See Barth, *Church Dogmatics* I/1, §9, 355; Rahner, *Trinity*, 109–13.

The Holy Spirit in and through and around Others in the Economy

"In the Spirit" and "the Spirit in us"

The Spirit of God is clearly a decisive source of action in the Scriptures, but its acting and speaking are almost always related to another person, *in* whom and *through* whom it operates. I will focus on a central New Testament expression: *en pneumati*, "in the Spirit." It witnesses to the fact that people are led by the Spirit, they are empowered by the Spirit, they pray in the Spirit, they are moved emotionally by the Spirit. Sometimes *en pneumati* refers to the pneumatic "space" or "atmosphere" in which one acts, but in the end, this also means that the Spirit, though quite effective, gives *someone else* power and space.

The first meaning of doing something *en pneumati* is to be led or controlled by the Spirit. Jesus, for instance, "was led by the Spirit (*en pneumati*) into the wilderness" (Luke 4:1). In the same way, "guided by the Spirit (*en tô pneumati*), Simeon came into the Temple" (Luke 2:27). Christians are those "who are led by the Spirit of God (*pneumati Theou agontai*)" (Rom 8:14), they are called to "walk in the Spirit (*pneumati peripateite*)" (Gal 5:16 [modified translation]; see v. 18). "To be led," from the verb *agaô*, can have a wide range of meanings, such as letting another open up the way, or being guided—as the people of Israel in the desert—or even being driven by a compelling force to which one has surrendered (see 2 Tim 3:6).[5] So the Spirit does act, with force. Doing something *in* the Spirit essentially means that the Spirit is doing something *in* us. But it acts precisely to make us act; that is, to make another than itself act.

This is why the Spirit is represented as *in*side someone and sometimes as "filling" someone, as exemplified by the Lukan expression, "full of the Spirit": "Jesus, full of the Holy Spirit, returned from the Jordan" (Luke 4:4); "Elizabeth . . . was filled with the Holy Spirit" (1:41).[6] This interior operation of the Spirit serves to give the direct actor the power to do what he or she needs to do. Jesus' ministry is done in the power of the Spirit: "it is by the Spirit of God that I cast out demons" (Matt 12:28). This is probably also the meaning of the expression "finger of God," which indicates God's "hand," i.e., his strength: "If it is by the finger of God that I cast out demons . . ." (Luke 11:20).[7] And this "power from high (*ex hupsous dunamis*)" (Luke 24:49) is promised to the disciples as well.

---

5. See Käsemann, *Commentary on Romans*, 226; Dunn, *Romans 1–8*, 450; Fitzmyer, *Romans*, 499.

6. Thiselton, *Holy Spirit*, 33–34.

7. Thiselton, *Holy Spirit*, 45.

THE BREATH OF GOD

Through its interior presence and operation, the divine Spirit also *inspires* us. It inspires the author of the Psalms: "David himself, by the Holy Spirit (*en tô pneumati tô hagiô*), declared . . . " (Mark 12:36); "How is it then that David by the Spirit calls him Lord?" (Matt 22:43). It inspires ideas and decisions: "Paul resolved in the Spirit to go through Macedonia and Achaia, and then to go on to Jerusalem" (Acts 19:21). In this way, it reveals—as it does to Simeon: "It had been revealed to him by the Holy Spirit that he would not see death before he had seen the Lord's Messiah" (Luke 2:26)— and teaches: "The Holy Spirit will teach you at that very hour what you ought to say" (Luke 12:12).

That the Spirit of God speaks is one of the arguments used by the church fathers to affirm that it also is a divine person.[8] However, it rarely speaks directly but rather it inspires *others* to speak, as professed in the Nicaean Creed: it "has spoken through the prophets." In the early church, some utterances attributed to the Spirit can very well be understood as being expressed through prophecy in worship by the believers themselves: "While they were worshipping the Lord and fasting, the Holy Spirit said, 'Set apart for me Barnabas and Saul'" (Acts 13:2). The Spirit speaks with others and others speak with it. For instance, the Spirit invokes Christ with the church-Spouse: "The Spirit and the bride say, 'Come.'" (Rev 22:17). In the same way, the apostles after the Jerusalem "Synod" affirm: "it has seemed good to the Holy Spirit and to us . . . " (Acts 15:28). In both cases the church is truly co-actor and co-speaker. In fact, in most cases, the Spirit seems more like an intimate inspiring force than like one of a pair of similar independent subjects. Of course, when it guides an individual, as when Peter explains that "The Spirit told me to go with them" (Acts 11:12), it is speaking directly. Nevertheless, it still is an *in*spiration, most probably happening in the human person's heart, through his or her mind and thought processes, rather than in a direct utterance.

B. Sesboüé propounds that the Spirit is actually mute, because it never speaks directly *in person*.[9] In fact, since it speaks through the prophets, through David, through Jesus, through the apostles and through those who pray, the Spirit is quite talkative. Those who are inspired by the Spirit should remember that it is indeed the main "speaker": "it is not you who speak, but the Spirit of your Father speaking through you" (Matt 10:20;

---

8. See Ladaria, *Il Dio vivo e vero*, 128–29; Sesboüé, "La personalità dello Spirito Santo," 24–25.

9. See Sesboüé, "La personalità dello Spirito Santo," 26–28.

The Holy Spirit in and through and around Others in the Economy

Mark 13:11). Nevertheless, the Spirit does not do so directly or alone. "The Holy Spirit says" means that *someone else* than the Spirit says something in its name and under its guiding force. Balthasar points out that this is rooted in the Jewish conception of the Spirit, as developed by M. Buber, for whom "the Spirit needs human beings, in their encounter, in order to put himself into words."[10]

Moreover, *what* the Spirit says is to a certain extent nothing else than the teaching of the Father and the Son: "The Spirit of truth . . . will not speak on his own, but will speak whatever he hears" (John 16:13); it "will remind you of all that [Jesus] has said" (14:26) and "testify on [Jesus'] behalf" (15:26). Its words come from Jesus' words and refer to Jesus.[11] Of course, two objections could be made. In the same Gospel, the Son seems to possess similar traits: he also says what he has seen and heard from the Father (7:16; 8:26, 28, 38); he also receives his authority from the Father. This is true, but the way the Son and the Spirit speak and refer to "another" differs. Jesus shows the Father by showing himself: "Whoever has seen me has seen the Father" (14:9; see 12:45). We could echo this assertion: "He who hears me hears the Father." Conversely the Spirit so to speak disappears behind the "other" he is referring to. In Johannine style, this would be: "I make the Father and the Son heard." What the Father gives the Son is really the Son's (3:35; 16:14), while nothing similar is said about what the Son gives the Spirit to communicate. The second question is that, in the Acts of the Apostles at least, when the Spirit guides the disciples and the church, is it not delivering its own message? Yes and no. Barth points out that the Spirit brings and adapts the universal message of Christ to each individual in history, in his or her time and space: it puts these individuals into motion through the word of Christ.[12] From another perspective, the Spirit is the "universalisor," since it spreads to all humankind what Jesus of Nazareth said in a given moment of history and in a small region of the world.[13] In fact both perspectives point towards the same reality: there is true creativity in the Spirit's *modus operandi*, but in utmost faithfulness and transparency to Christ.

---

10. Balthasar, *Theo-Logic III: The Spirit of Truth*, 144.
11. See Sesboüé, "La personalità dello Spirito Santo," 26–27.
12. See Barth, *Church Dogmatics I/1*, §8, 324–33; §12, 452–53.
13. See Ladaria, *Il Dio vivo e vero*, 120–23.

All these characteristics are particularly true and visible in prayer.[14] Prayer according to the New Testament is very frequently done *en pneumati*. Jesus is made to exult by the Spirit: "At that same hour Jesus rejoiced in the Holy Spirit (*ègaliassato en tô hagiô pneumati*) and said, 'I praise you, Father, Lord of heaven and earth, because you have hidden these things from the wise and the intelligent and have revealed them to infants'" (Luke 10:21). In the same way, a Christian is led to pray and given the capacity to do so by the Spirit: "Pray in the Spirit (*proseuchomenoi ... en pneumati*) at all times in every prayer and supplication" (Eph 6:18; see also Jude 20).

This inner presence and action of the Holy Spirit enables the pray-er to pray, by inspiring him *to whom* to pray: "You did not receive a spirit of slavery to fall back into fear, but you have received a Spirit of adoption, in which (*en hô*) we cry, 'Abba, Father!'" (Rom 8:15 [modified translation]; see also Gal 4:4). Only *en pneumati* do we "have access to the Father" (Eph 2:18). This is probably one of the dimensions of "prayer in Spirit and truth" in the Fourth Gospel: "the hour is coming, and is now here, when the true worshipers will worship the Father in Spirit and truth (*en pneumati kai alètheia*)" (John 4:23). The Spirit leads us to pray to the Father, but it also inspires in us the right relation to the Son: "No one speaking by the Spirit of God (*en pneumati theou*) ever says 'Let Jesus be cursed!'" (1 Cor 12:3).

The Spirit likewise shows the pray-er *what* to pray for and *how* to pray for it, as Paul's rather contorted way of putting it indicates: "The Spirit helps us in our weakness; for we do not know how to pray as we ought (*ti proseuzômetha katho dei, ouk oidamen*), but that very Spirit intercedes with sighs too deep for words" (Rom 8:26). *What* to pray means what to ask for: John Chrysostom explains that we do not know what is truly useful for us and for the church without the Spirit, while Augustine, followed by Aquinas and Calvin, suggest that the "sighs" inspired by the Spirit are directed towards eternal life that we cannot desire fully without the Spirit.[15] As for the *way* we pray, Aquinas underlines that without the Spirit we have no fully "just desires," i.e., desires according to the order of charity.[16]

The analysis of the Holy Spirit's role in prayer also shows its special relation to desire and emotions. The inner, intimate dimension of the action

---

14. The following paragraphs are a synthesis of a more detailed study: Vetö, "'Praying in the Holy Spirit,'" 157–72.

15. See John Chrysostom, *The homilies of S. John Chrysostom*, 251–52; Landes, *Augustine on Romans*, 27; Calvin, *Epistles of Paul to the Romans and Thessalonians*, 177–78.

16. Thomas Aquinas, *Super Epistolam ad Romanos*, VIII, lectio 5.

The Holy Spirit in and through and around Others in the Economy

of the Holy Spirit may explain this, since desires and passions spring from the heart or the bowels, from the deepest most intimate center of one's being.

Indeed, the Spirit is sent into the heart: "Because we are children, God has sent the Spirit of his Son into our hearts (*eis tas kardias hèmôn*), crying, 'Abba! Father!'" (Gal 4:6). It is in the heart that God finds the Spirit: "God, who searches the heart, knows what is the mind of the Spirit" (Rom 8:27). Of course, *kardia* in the biblical sense is not only related to emotions: it is the hidden center of the person, the source of his or her decisions and thoughts. This means that the Spirit will be related to all that is interior, to a human being's thoughts and will.

However, the New Testament sometimes relates the Spirit even more specifically to emotions and desires. We have just seen that in prayer it gives the right desire and the right way of desiring—not only the right thoughts or volitions. The Spirit makes Jesus "rejoice" (Luke 10:21), and in us it "cries" (Rom 8:15; Gal 4:6): these are expressions of strong emotions. The Spirit also "sighs" in us (Rom 8:26): though these "sighs too deep for words (*alalêtois*)" may indicate either silent prayer or prayer in tongues, they also connote an infra-rational dimension, the deep yearning for God and for redemption.[17] In the same way, Paul sometimes distinguishes prayer "with the mind" and prayer *en pneumati*:

> If I pray in a tongue, my spirit (*to pneuma mou*) prays but my mind (*nous mou*) is unproductive. What should I do then? I will pray with the spirit (*tô pneumati*), but I will pray with the mind (*tô noi*) also; I will sing praise with the spirit (*tô pneumati*), but I will sing praise with the mind (*tô noi*) also. (1 Cor 14:14–15)

There is a distinction here between praying with the *nous* and praying with the *pneuma*. The *nous* is the faculty that "makes rational judgments about things and enables a human being to communicate with God."[18] *Pneuma* can be understood either as the divine Spirit itself or as the human spirit, i.e., the theological faculty given to us to enter into relation to God. In this latter case, it is the faculty "that wills and reacts emotionally to things about them and that is open to the influence of the divine Spirit."[19] In

---

17. See Dunn, *Romans 1–8*, 479.

18. Fitzmyer, *First Corinthians*, 516.

19. Fitzmyer, *First Corinthians*, 516. In this case Paul is just opposing praying according to one faculty or the other. I tend to agree with those who underline the distinction Paul is making between "my spirit" and "the spirit"—the first being the human spirit, the

both interpretations, there is an opposition between the rational-decision taking dimension and another more "appetitive" and emotional dimension, which is related directly or by analogy to the Spirit of God.

Though the emotional dimension is intimate, it sometimes leads the pray-er to ecstatic and enthusiastic behavior. Quite significantly, Ephesians compares being drunk and being full of the Spirit: "Do not get drunk with wine . . . but be filled with the Spirit, as you sing psalms and hymns and spiritual (*pneumatikais*) songs among yourselves, singing and playing melody to the Lord in your hearts" (5:18–19). This echo of the pentecostal experience related in Acts 2 is not an exhortation to refrain from being drunk, but means we are to choose the better type of drunkenness.[20]

In fact, the expression "being led" by the Spirit, which we have studied above, may already have had this connotation: *agaô* in Rom 8:14 and *agalliaô* (to find delight) in Luke 10:21 are understood by some exegetes as having ecstatic and enthusiastic overtones.[21] They are close to the vocabulary of the enthusiasts in 1 Cor 12:2 or of compulsion (2 Tim 3:6) and resemble similar constructions in Greek literature, which clearly refer to ecstatic phenomena. This does not primarily indicate an overwhelming emotional state, but rather the idea of being driven and controlled by a compelling force one has surrendered to. It would be more exact to speak of *enthusiasm* in its etymological meaning—divine inhabitation—rather than about emotions: one should not be surprised if surrendering control to the Spirit of God leads to the impression that a superior force moves the pray-er. Letting the Spirit take hold of our being naturally touches all dimensions of the person, including emotions and passions, especially if the Spirit is specifically present in the hidden depths of the heart. These are then integrated into our relation to God, in harmony with sound Christian anthropology, which stresses the unity between body and soul and the fundamental goodness of affect.

Two reflections outside of the field of biblical studies will corroborate this special relation of the Holy Spirit to emotions and passions. In his writings on prayer and spiritual accompaniment, Ignatius of Loyola sees feelings and emotions as the "matter" of the discernment of the spirits.

---

second the divine (see Lémonon, "L'esprit saint dans le corpus paulinien," 230), but the end result is the same for the question we are analyzing.

20. Barth, *Ephesians 4–6*, 582. On enthusiasm in Pauline literature, see also Käsemann, *Commentary on Romans*, 226; Dunn, *Romans 1–8*, 450.

21. See Käsemann, *Commentary on Romans*, 226; Dunn, *Romans 1–8*, 450.

The Holy Spirit in and through and around Others in the Economy

Discerning means applying our intelligence to this matter and then recurring to our will to make decisions, but the locus in the human person where the Spirit can be perceived is the emotions. They are in a way a "sixth sense" that will help us direct the other five.[22] They are not the Spirit itself: it always transcends desire and passion, as it transcends all the dimensions of our humanity. In a way, discerning the Spirit essentially means taking some distance with emotions by applying our intelligence to them and understanding how the Spirit speaks through them. A same inner motion may have different meanings, according to the flow of spiritual life: an uncomfortable "tug" may indicate a spiritual struggle if we are progressing in our relation to God, while it will be an echo of our conscious if we are moving away from God and into sin.[23] In this latter case we should pay heed to it, but not in the first. However, emotions are essential to listening to the Spirit and without them one looses one of the most immediate and concrete connections with it.

Likewise, in her theological reading of Origen, S. Coakley stresses the strong connection between the Spirit of God and desire, as well as the entanglement between desire "in the Spirit" and human desire. This explains some of the fears and diffidence the early church had with the Spirit, since quickening of desire could lead to quickening of sexual desire: "A special commitment to deep prayer in the Spirit (whether 'charismatic' or 'contemplative') came with the concomitant danger of intensification of erotic power and a problematic entanglement of human spiritual and sexual desires."[24] Origen repeatedly compares praying with sexual intercourse, with its drive, union, and fecundity, and shows a certain fear of a "possible confusion between loss of control to that Spirit and loss of *sexual* control."[25] For Coakley, the foundation of this relation between desire, the Spirit, and God, is that God himself is desire and God makes us desire him. This however happens more specifically in the Spirit, who "enables" and "incorporates" the desire for God in created beings.[26] The Spirit quickens and purifies human desire to direct them in the right way: "God the "Father," through the Spirit, both stirs up, and progressively chastens and purges, the

---

22. See Jacob, *Ignatian Discernment*, 8–9.
23. See Ignatius of Loyola, *Spiritual Exercises*, 201.
24. Coakley, *God, Sexuality and the Self*, 102.
25. Coakley, *God, Sexuality and the Self*, 127.
26. Coakley, *God, Sexuality and the Self*, 114; see also Rogers, *Holy Spirit*, 44.

THE BREATH OF GOD

frailer and often misdirected desires of humans."[27] Here also, the otherness of the Spirit means that the human desire will be transformed, but it is necessary to welcome the desire so as to let the Spirit work in it, rather than to push it away.

In the end, the inner work of the Spirit means not only that it acts and speaks through others, but that it does so in all the person's inner thoughts and motions, and in particular the person's emotions and desires.

Acting and praying *en pneumati* mainly refers to the Spirit's way of operating *in us* and rests on the instrumental sense of *en*: *in* the Spirit means *through* the Spirit. However, in some cases the local or spatial meaning of *en* may also be involved: *en pneumati* would then mean that the Spirit of God is the "space" in which one stands, lives, and acts.[28]

Many scriptural expressions of the coming of the Spirit imply this more exterior dimension.[29] Very often the Spirit "comes down upon" (2 Chr 15:1; 20:14; Acts 1:8; 19:16), "catches" (2 Kgs 2:16), "descends" (Matt 3:16; Mark 1:10; Luke 3:22; John 1:32) or "falls upon" (Acts 10:44; 11:15). It does so to inspire, as is the case with Balaam (Num 24:2) or to give strength, as with Samson or David (Judg 14:6; 15:14; 1 Sam 16:13). So far, this means the Spirit comes down to enter into: the two meanings of *en* are very close. However, the Spirit also stays "on" and "around." For instance, it "overshadows" Mary at the annunciation (Luke 1:35) and Jesus at the transfiguration (Matt 17:5; Mark 9:7; Luke 9:34). It also "rests upon": Simeon is introduced as someone upon whom "the Holy Spirit rested" (2:25). The Spirit comes down under the form of a dove on Jesus in the Jordan and remains on him (John 1:32–33), as an echo of Isa 11:2 (LXX): "the Spirit of the Lord shall rest upon him"—and Jesus himself proclaims: "The Spirit of the Lord is upon me . . . " (Luke 4:18). At Pentecost the Spirit fills the upper room and rests on the apostles: "suddenly from heaven there came a sound like the rush of a violent wind, and it filled the entire house where they were sitting. Divided tongues, as of fire, appeared among them, and a tongue rested on each of them" (Acts 2:2–3). This is the accomplishment of the prophecy of Joel announcing that the God will "pour out [his] spirit on all flesh" (Joel 2:28–29). In a similar way, the *Ruah* of God hovers over the primordial waters in the first lines of Genesis (1:2). Sometimes the idea is even more clearly that of being enveloped by the Spirit. In a way the expression "to

27. Coakley, *God, Sexuality and the Self*, 6.

28. As in the parallel Pauline expression "*en Christô*," *en* has more than one possible meanings (see Wedderburn, "Some Observations," 83–97).

29. For the following analyses see especially Rogers, *After the Spirit*, 62–63.

baptize" or "to be baptized in the Spirit (*en pneumati*)" (John 1:33; Acts 1:5) indicates this, since to be baptized is to be plunged into, immersed. The Spirit "clothes (*enduô*)" the disciples with its power (Luke 24:49). Maybe the way it "seizes" Philip and makes him disappear from the eunuch's sight corresponds to the same perspective of the Spirit enveloping and embracing someone. All this is quite specific to the Spirit—it is never said that the Father or the Son come down on, are poured onto, rest upon, or envelop someone—and offers the image of a form of airy presence that rests on someone or an atmosphere someone is in.

Interestingly, the Anomeans, Basil's adversaries, refused the divinity of the Holy Spirit precisely because, while all things happen *ek Patros* and *dia Huiou*, as their source and instrument, they are spatial and temporal *en pneumati*:

> They [the Anomoeans] assign the words "from whom" to God the Father as if this expression was his one special allotment; for God the Son they select the phrase "through whom," and for the Holy Spirit "in which," and they say that this assignment of prepositions must never be interchanged. . . . By the expression "from whom" they wish to indicate the Creator; by "through whom" they mean an instrument of service, and "in which" they use to refer to time or place (*ton chronon è ton topon*). The holy Creator of all things is thus made into a mere instrument, and the Holy Spirit appears to furnish creation with nothing except time and place (*tès topou è chronou*).[30]

Basil goes on to argue that the Holy Spirit's activity is expressed by *en* but also by other expressions, because his intent is to prove its divine nature and full equality with the Father and the Son. For us, however, the Spirit's divinity is unquestionable, so it is easier to take into consideration the actual specificity the Anomoeans had perceived. The Scriptures use *en* in relation to the Spirit as a metaphor of a spatial or temporal "place" where people can dwell, enveloped in its power and where events happen through this power.

Closer to us, Pannenberg expounds in a detailed way the comparison between the Spirit and the idea of force-fields as understood by modern physics: "The Spirit is the force field of God's mighty presence."[31] Already

---

30. Basil the Great, *On the Holy Spirit*, II, §4, 19. See also Sesboüé, "La personalità dello Spirito Santo," 35.

31. Pannenberg, *Systematic Theology I*, 382. Pannenberg asserts that T. F. Torrance is the first to have recognized the theological potential of force fields in *Space, Time and Incarnation*, 71 (see *Systematic Theology II*, 82 n212).

some church fathers, such as Ignatius of Antioch, Theophilus of Antioch, or Irenaeus, were influenced in their pneumatology by the Stoic notion of a *pneuma* that worked in cosmos, but the idea was eventually refused because of its material dimension in Stoicism. Modern physics has taken up the idea again, with an eye to Stoic sources, but with a totally immaterial conception of field: change need not be ascribed to bodies but to force or energy.[32] Pannenberg considers that these common philosophical and theological roots invite us to understand the Spirit along the line of a force field. In fact, he prefers considering the Trinity as the field, and the third person as a singularity of the field that is the divine life and essence. However, the Spirit's operation has more than the two others' the character of the operations of a dynamic field: "It relates to the link and movement that connect the creatures to one another and to God."[33]

This double dimension of *en pneumati* is not surprising: our human notions are inadequate to express the fullness of God, who is in us as we are in him. The interior and intimate dimension of the Spirit's *modus operandi* certainly is important.[34] Nevertheless, a more decisive aspect covers both meanings: whether the Spirit dwells in, inspires, and leads from inside or whether it descends on, envelops, and embraces, it acts powerfully, not however to do something directly in person, but to enable someone else to act and speak and pray. So, if acting and speaking "in the Spirit" truly means letting the Spirit act and speak "in us," letting it act "in us" does make us really act, and do so "in the Spirit."

"Fluidity": A Unique Way of Being

The specific "mode of operating" of the Spirit of God is not without consequences for its way of being, or at least for the way its existence can be perceived in the economy. The Spirit seems less "substantial" or more "fluid" than the Father and the Son. This means that it is more difficult to define the limits between what it is doing and what others are doing. It is more

---

32. See Pannenberg, *Systematic Theology I*, 382 and n101; *Systematic Theology II*, 79, 82.

33. Pannenberg, *Systematic Theology II*, 84.

34. A historical biblical study of the differences between these two meanings of *en* shows that the Old Testament presents the Spirit, and God in general, as less interior and more as an accompanying presence, while the New Testament, without losing this aspect, insists much more on the inner and intimate dimension (see Siffer-Wiederhold, *La présence divine à l'individu*).

The Holy Spirit in and through and around Others in the Economy

difficult to relate to it directly than to the two other divine names. In a way it is less "personal" or more "anonymous" than they are. Of course, each of these notions is inadequate, because it derives from creaturely and human substantiality and personhood, but at least they give a measure that helps define the specificity of the Spirit with regards to the two other divine "names."

The Spirit operates in such a way as to make it sometimes challenging to distinguish who is acting. Quite a few authors underline the fact that Paul often seems to equate the Spirit and Christ: "Now the Lord is the Spirit (*ho de kurios to pneuma estin*), and where the Spirit of the Lord (*to pneuma kuriou*) is, there is freedom" (2 Cor 3:17).[35] They are so intimately bound as to offer some kind of coincidence, without being totally identical, since the Spirit is "the Lord's." Something similar can be said of the Synoptics: though the Spirit is quite active during Jesus' public ministry, Jesus is clearly at the center stage. Biblical scholars debate their respective roles, but most underline the Spirit's "self-effacement."[36] M. Welker suggests that if we are searching for an individual act-center, "we are referred . . . to Jesus Christ. He is the primarily individual human act-center of the Spirit": there is a "personal act-center" and there is the force through which he acts.[37] This is why, historically and heuristically speaking, it is the difference between the Son and the Father that opened the way for becoming aware of an analogous personal distinction between the Spirit and the Son.[38]

In the same way, the activities of divine Spirit and of the believer are so deeply intertwined that they are not easily distinguished. This is once again perceptible in prayer. We know the Spirit is acting from within, from deep inside in the region of the *kardia*, which only God knows: when Paul says that the Spirit utters ineffable sighs but that "God, who searches the heart, knows what the mind of the Spirit" (Rom 8:27), one can understand that the Spirit is hidden in the inner recesses of our mind and emotions to the point that it is hidden from us as well. Moreover, we sometimes wonder who is praying, the pray-er or the Spirit. In Rom 8:15, the pray-er cries in the Spirit, while in Gal 4:6, the Spirit itself cries in our hearts. In Eph 6:18

---

35. See Pannenberg, *Systematic Theology I*, 269; Balthasar, *Theo-Logic III: The Spirit of Truth*, 109.

36. See C. K. Barrett and J. E. Fison and the debate with J. D. G. Dunn, as expounded by Thiselton, *Holy Spirit*, 38–40.

37. Welker, *Gottes Geist*, 287.

38. See the citation of Pannenberg quoted above in the Introduction (Pannenberg, *Systematic Theology I*, 304–5; see also 269–72).

we are to intercede in the Spirit, but in Rom 8:26–27, it is the Spirit who intercedes for us.

This intertwinement implies that, in a way, the Spirit does not only inspire us what to do, but also embraces our human activity and makes it into its own activity. It makes itself almost human, by asking, crying, or sighing. Aquinas, for example, refuses to take this literally: God cannot lack anything, so he cannot ask; and even less can he sigh or groan, as would a "passible creature." So the meaning should be that the Spirit inspires *the pray-er* to sigh and groan. . . .[39] However, Rom 8:26 is crystal clear: the Spirit itself is doing the sighing. Such is the nature of the Spirit that it embeds itself so deeply in our action that it makes its own and "shoulders" our weakness and our desires. Oriental spirituality and theology are particularly sensitive to this dimension, as a prayer to the Holy Spirit from Symeon the New Theologian expresses beautifully: "Come, you who have made yourself my own desire and who have made me desire you."[40]

Nevertheless, the pray-er and the Spirit are not fused together: Paul clearly considers that there are two actors. On the one hand, praying *en pneumati* is not contradictory with human faculties; it involves them, and the more the better. As seen above, according to 1 Cor 14:14–17, praying in the Spirit is good; but praying with the Spirit *and* with our mind (*nous*) is better.[41] On the other hand, the Spirit's transcendence is irreducible. Though we are called to use our minds, we still understand neither glossolalia nor the sighs and intercession of the Spirit in us (see Rom 8:26–27 and 1 Cor 14:14, 16). This is why praying in the Spirit means letting the Spirit pray in us, surrendering to another who acts in us. If we do not know what to ask for or how to ask we are to let go of our perception of our needs, let go of our wishes, and enter into the desire and will of another (divine) person. Congar underlines the fact that to pray is not only to "extend" our request to a superior being more capable than we are to fulfill them, but also to enter into communion with God's will. Likewise, Congar refers to the reflection of J.-Cl. Sagne, theologian and psychoanalyst:

> What is at stake in prayer is, in particular through the non satisfaction of our desire, through confessing to what we lack, . . . to be able to desire God's desire. That is to desire what God desires and let God desire in us. Prayer manifests itself at this point as the

---

39. Aquinas, *Super Epistolam ad Romanos*, VIII, lectio 5, §692.
40. Quoted by Congar, *Je crois en l'Esprit-Saint*, 381 n8.
41. Lémonon, "L'esprit saint dans le corpus paulinien," 230.

The Holy Spirit in and through and around Others in the Economy

mystery of God in us and an event of the Holy Spirit, because it is the role of the Holy Spirit to be the desire of God in God and the desire of God in us. The Spirit educates our desire, expands it and adjusts it to God's desire by giving it the same object.[42]

This reflection adds an indication to what it means to let our emotions and our desire be transformed by the Spirit, as evoked above: entering into the desire of another. The most important point, however, is that to pray in the Spirit and, more generally, to "live in the Spirit" imply that each of our acts has two actors.

There is a paradoxical double movement between the Spirit and the believer, two dimensions that flow into each other: someone who is acting *en pneumati* is driven by the Spirit to whom he or she has surrendered and needs to enter into the Spirit's "desire"; but one surrenders to a divine Spirit who acts not by imposing itself, but by making its own the person's desires and by enabling the person to act. M. Welker underlines that the Spirit acts by "freely retreating," by "making room (*raumgeben*)," and by "working for the development" of the person.[43] In the end, we have a fascinating form of deep and intimate intertwinement of two distinct actors. "It is that very Spirit bearing witness *with* our spirit (*tô pneumati hèmôn*)" (Rom 8:16) underlines that both the pray-er and the Spirit of God act together to bear witness. This is also echoed in the Oriental tradition, as testified, once again, by Symeon the New Theologian: "I praise you for having become one spirit with me, without confusion, without mutation, without transformation, you who are God above all, and for having become for me all in all".[44]

A further example of the difficulty of understanding the Spirit of God in a substantial and personal way is the type of relations the Spirit has with the other divine names and with us. There is no dialogical relationship between the Father or the Son and the Spirit. Father and Son address each other. There are numerous examples of the Son praying, crying out, praising the Father in the Gospels. The Father addresses the Son less frequently, but in Luke the voice from above speaks to Christ directly: "You are my Son, the beloved; with you I am well pleased" (3:22). This is essentially the foundation of our faith in their personal distinction, if we follow Tertullian's profound analysis in *Adversus Praxeam*: "[Our Rule of faith is] that speaker and person spoken of and person spoken to cannot be regarded as

---

42. Sagne, "Du besoin à la demande," 94; Congar, *Je crois en l'Esprit-Saint*, 384.
43. See Welker, *Gottes Geist*, 273.
44. Quoted by Congar, *Je crois en l'Esprit-Saint*, 381 n8.

one and the same."[45] The Spirit also "cries "Abba! Father" (Gal 4:6). It calls to the Son to hasten his coming: "The Spirit and the Bride say, 'Come'" (Rev 22:17). The Spirit, however, is never addressed by the Father or the Son. For Balthasar, this is an expression of the different type of relationship the three divine hypostases have with each other: "In all 'economic' situations, there is no question of an 'I-Thou' relationship between the Son and the Spirit. The Son's only 'Thou' is the Father; and he is this 'Thou' in the Spirit."[46] Balthasar's vocabulary here definitely has a Buberian connotation: the Spirit is not a "You" or "Thou," i.e., a subject of relation, an *alter ego* with his or her complete otherness and specific autonomy, who can be a partner. It remains in the field of the "third person" (from a grammatical point of view), "him/her/they," which for Buber belong to the same sphere as "it." All that is not a "thou" is objectivized. The Son "faces" the Father, says Balthasar, while he (and the Father) are *in* the Spirit, and relate *in* this Spirit. This analysis corroborates on a relational level what has been pointed out above about the "spatial" dimension of the Spirit.

In the same way, our relationship to the Spirit differs from our relationship to the Father or the Son, though in a more subtle way. While we address the Father and the Son, we rarely do so directly to the Holy Spirit. And when we do address the Spirit it is in the form of an invocation, such as the *Veni Creator* or the *Veni, Sancte Spiritus*.[47] We do not adore it and contemplate it, nor share our burden to it, as we would with the Father and the Son: we relate to it as to a force or to the subject of a force, rather than in the framework of an interpersonal relationship. In the same way, when the Spirit addresses us, it does not express its love nor ask us to entrust our lives to it, but it orients us by telling us what to do or not to do. In a radical assertion with the same Buberian overtones, B. Sesboüé says: "The encounter with the Holy Spirit is not a face-to-face encounter. It does not present a *You*, but remains a *Him*."[48] Sesboüé's statement reflects quite well the relationship between the Spirit and the Father and the Son, but is slightly too extreme to qualify our relationship with it, because we do address it directly. However, the fundamental truth expressed here is that neither the Son and the Father nor we are truly in a face-to-face encounter

---

45. Tertullian, *Tertullian's Treatise Against Praxeas*, XI, 144; see also Andresen, "Zur Entstehung und Geschichte," 3–12.
46. Balthasar, *Theo-Logic III: The Spirit of Truth*, 174.
47. See Congar, *Je crois en l'Esprit-Saint*, 155–59, 377–85.
48. Sesboüé, "La personalità dello Spirito Santo," 25–26.

The Holy Spirit in and through and around Others in the Economy

with the Spirit. Coherently with what we have seen so far, the Spirit is much more "in us" (or "around us") than "in front of us."

This difficulty in really distinguishing the Spirit's own action and speech from those it inspires and of entering into an I/Thou relation with it points towards a specific type of "self." I will allow myself to refer here more to systematic theology than to a scriptural analysis, although it will be but an extension of all that has been reflected on above. In a way, the self of the Spirit of God is not a substantial, solid self, an *ad se* with a clear-cut form, but it is so to speak airy, atmospheric, fluid. For the Spirit—in a way which is not necessary for the Father and Son—we need to use dynamic qualifiers, such as "poured," "filled," "blows."[49] In his usual radical manner, Barth insists on the fact that the Spirit cannot be considered as a "self," even less so than the other divine persons, but rather as an "act": "In a particularly clear way the Holy Spirit is what the Father and the Son also are. He is not a third spiritual Subject, a third I, a third Lord side by side with two others."[50] This is because, speaking and acting in and through others, being in intimate communion with others, means that the Spirit *is itself* in and through *others*. This precisely is its self and its identity. Existing *ad se* for the Spirit means "only existing for Father and Son."[51] In a way, the Spirit is a capacity for God of being outside of himself and inside another. C. Ducoq affirms: "[The Holy Spirit] is the indwelling of God where/in which God is so to speak 'out of himself'. . . . It is the *extasis* of God towards what is not God."[52] In a striking turn of phrase H. Mühlen confirms this: "The Spirit is the 'Being-outside-of-[God]self' of God (*das Pneuma ist das Ausser-Sich-Sein-Gottes*)."[53] For this reason S. Coakley compares the experience of the Spirit with sexual ecstasy, i.e., with the capacity of being totally in the other without losing oneself. This sexual dimension is first perceptible through "a certain loss of noetic control to the leading experiential force of the Spirit." Coakley quotes the French feminist L. Irigaray: "Sexual love is not 'egological', not even 'duality in closeness', but a shared transcendence of two selves toward the other, within a 'shared space, a shared breath'. In this relation . . .

---

49. See Thiselton, *Holy Spirit*, 469.

50. Barth, *Church Dogmatics I/1*, §12, 469.

51. Balthasar, *Theo-Logic III: The Spirit of Truth*, 218.

52. "[L'Esprit Saint] est l'habitation de Dieu là où Dieu est en quelque sorte 'hors de lui-même'. . . . Il est 'l'extase' de Dieu vers son 'autre'" (Ducoq, *Dieu différent*, 122; see also Congar, *Je crois en l'Esprit-Saint*, 715, 716 n34).

53. Mühlen, *Morgen wird Einheit sein*, 128 (quoted by Congar, *Je crois en l'Esprit-Saint*, 715, 716 n34).

we are at least three ... you, me, and our creation of that ecstasy of ourself in us (*nous en nous*) prior to any child."[54]

The same can be said if we turn to the local meaning of *en pneumati*: the Spirit's identity is the very fact of being around others and resting on them. We know that in physical terms, space is not an empty container, but that it depends on the bodies that are "in" it. It is in a sense a dimension of these bodies. E. Rogers, for instance, stresses the paradox: though the Spirit is bodiless and insubstantial—but perhaps precisely because of that—it is closely linked to material realities that it covers and penetrates. Rogers explains that while studying Greek and Syriac texts of the early centuries he noticed that "talk of the Holy Spirit seemed ... almost always strictly tied to talk of holy places, holy people, and holy things. It did not float free of bodily existence as it does in modern North Atlantic Christian discourse and worship. Indeed, it was embodied." The illustrations given are striking:

> One locus was baptism, in which the Spirit descended upon a person. Another was the Eucharist, in which it dwelt as fire in consecrated bread and wine. A third was unction, in which "oil is the dear friend of the Holy Spirit", as Ephrem the Syrian wrote. It breathed on the water at creation; it moved in Mary's womb; it animated the churches; it appealed to the senses as light, fire, incense, wine, and song. The Spirit was not merely transcendent; it was immanent in bodily things.[55]

The Spirit "befriends" matter, it "befriends" the body: "To think about the Spirit you have to think materially. 'In the last days God poured out God's Spirit upon all flesh' (Joel 3:1 [in reality Joel 2:28]; Acts 2:17–18)."[56] The atmospheric and fluid quality of the divine Spirit's way of being calls for a more "substantial" material resting place and anchorage.

Perhaps this is why one of the characteristics of the Spirit is that it can be "shared out."[57] Sometimes it is shared out by God directly, as when the

---

54. Coakley, "Living in the Mystery," 48, 50.

55. Rogers, *After the Spirit*, 1–2; see also 14–15.

56. Rogers, *After the Spirit*, 56–57; see also 58, 60–61, 70. In a similar way, B. Sesboüé transfers the Rahnerian paradigm of transcendental and categorial in a (definitely out of context but) thought-provoking way. While the mission of the Son has its own categorial dimension, that of the life and deeds of Jesus, the Spirit's mission is "categorialized" only in Jesus and in those who receive it: "The Spirit is an exceedingly 'subjective' person, so subjective that, to borrow an expression from Rahner, it has no specific categorial dimension" (Sesboüé, "La personalità dello Spirito Santo," 57; see also 51).

57. For the following analyses, see Thiselton, *Holy Spirit*, 5.

The Holy Spirit in and through and around Others in the Economy

seventy elders receive the spirit of Moses: "The Lord . . . took some of the Spirit that was on him and put it on the seventy elders; and when the Spirit rested upon them, they prophesied" (Num 11:25); in the same way Elisha receives a double portion of Elijah's Spirit (2 Kgs 2:9–15). Sometimes the Spirit is communicated by the laying of hands: Moses shares out the Spirit to Joshua in that way (Deut 34:9) as do the apostles with those they pray for (Acts 8:17; 19:6). The "Johannine Pentecost," when the risen Lord breathes on the disciples to send them out (John 20:22), and the creation of Adam through the life-giving breath of God (Gen 2:7) which it echoes, are but further examples of this sharing out. The Spirit is perceived as an inner force, a fluid that belongs to a more substantial figure but that is not tied to it and can "spread out" to others.

This characteristic *modus essendi* of the Spirit of God is particularly testified in the specific type of images and metaphors used by the Scriptures when dealing with it. Father and Son or *Logos* are names and images that belong to the human world. Conversely, the metaphors for the Spirit are overwhelmingly taken from the realm of nature. Its name first of all—*Ruah* and *Pneuma*—means breath and wind. Though it is a name it is also an image and a metaphor, and as such it is the most frequent one in the Bible. Because of its importance and special status I will explore it in greater depth in the next chapter. However, the Spirit is also compared to water: "On the last day of the festival, the great day, while Jesus was standing there, he cried out, 'Let anyone who is thirsty come to me, and let the one who believes in me drink. As the scripture has said, "Out of the believer's heart shall flow rivers of living water."' Now he said this about the Spirit, which believers in him were to receive" (John 7:37–39a). In the same Gospel, Jesus tells Nicodemus that one should be "born of water and Spirit" to enter the Kingdom of God (John 3:5). The expression "water and Spirit" does not indicate two different realties, but it is a Semitic way of underlining the importance of receiving the Spirit through one of its physical symbols. Paradoxically another image used is that of flames: John the Baptist speaks about the baptism "with the Holy Spirit and fire" that Jesus will give (Matt 3:11) and "tongues as of fire" rest upon the heads of the apostles at Pentecost (Acts 2:3). A more corporeal image is used at Jesus' baptism, when the Spirit comes down under the form of a dove (Matt 3:16; Mark 1:10; Luke 3:22)—maybe an echo of Gen 8:8, where the dove is a symbol of new creation. "Force (*dunamis*)" is a more abstract image, but it is a notion that comes from the sphere of physics so it maintains its anchorage in the world of nature. Sometimes the Holy Spirit gives power: "Jesus, filled with the power of the Spirit, returned to Galilee" (Luke 4:14; see also Rom 4:4); "You will receive power when the Holy Spirit has come upon you" (Acts 1:8). Other times the Spirit is the *dunamis* itself: "The Holy Spirit will come upon you, and the power of the Most High will overshadow you" (Luke 1:35; see also 24:49; Acts 10:37–38).

Of course, there are also images from the human world: oil, seal, "gift," and Paraclete. Jesus is "anointed" by the "Spirit of the Lord" to preach the good news and announce a year of grace (Luke 4:18–19), in obvious parallel to the anointment of the priests and kings of Israel (Lev 4:3, 5, 16; 1 Sam 9:16; etc.). Many scholars consider the anointment proclaimed by the First Letter of John to refer to the Holy Spirit as well (1 John 2:20, 27).[58] Though human beings produce oil, it is still very close to a natural substance. Related to the image of anointment is that of a seal: "[God] has anointed us, by putting his seal on us and giving us his Spirit in our hearts as a first installment" (2 Cor 1:21–22); "[In Christ you] were marked with the seal of the promised Holy Spirit" (Eph 1:13). As God's seal, the Spirit marks God's ownership and authority on those who receive it. As such it is also the premise of the eschatological fullness of God and full belonging to God. The image comes from the human world but it is still related to an inanimate, material reality. The same is partly true for "gift." The Spirit of God is the ultimate gift given to those who pray: "How much more will the heavenly Father give the Holy Spirit to those who ask him!" (Luke 11:13). It is the first gift of faith: "Repent, and be baptized every one of you in the name of Jesus Christ . . . and you will receive the gift of the Holy Spirit" (Acts 2:38; see also 10:45; maybe Heb 6:4). The Spirit is also named the "gift of God" (Acts 8:20; see also 11:17; maybe John 4:10), and in a very similar way, it is called the "promise" of God (Luke 24:49; Acts 2:33; maybe Hag 2:5). In all these cases, though related to a giver, "gift" and "promise" refer directly to the object that is given and only indirectly to the people exchanging it.

Paraklètos (John 14:15–17, 26; 15:26–27; 16:5–15) on the other hand is much more personal and human. There is a great amount of discussion about the meaning of the word, but whether it is to be understood as Advocate, Comforter, Exhorter, or Helper, the main point is that another *Paraklètos* will come after Jesus to reveal him and prolong his mission. The Spirit

---

58. See Thiselton, *Holy Spirit*, 136.

The Holy Spirit in and through and around Others in the Economy

is presented in strong parallel and reference to Jesus.[59] Though it definitely has a very personal dimension, its "personality" is inseparable from that of Jesus, in harmony with what we have seen above as being its characteristic way of speaking under Jesus' authority and to show Jesus. The *Paraklètos* is personal, but it is in a way a "person-for-another." It is substantial, but not in an independent manner.

I would like to evoke a last image, a bit more difficult to classify, that of the "Spirit of Wisdom" sung in the deuterocanonical Book of Wisdom:

> In [Wisdom] there is a spirit that is intelligent, holy, unique, manifold, subtle, mobile, . . . penetrating through all spirits that are intelligent and pure and most subtle. For wisdom is more mobile than any motion; because of her pureness she pervades and penetrates all things. For she is a breath of the power of God, and a pure emanation of the glory of the Almighty; . . . she passes into holy souls and makes them friends of God, and prophets. (Wis 7:22–27)

The *Pneuma* of wisdom is a form of insubstantial breath or fluid, capable of penetrating all things, those more substantial but also all minds. It flows down from God and touches what is far from him because of these airy and fluid qualities.

Now this use of images and metaphors is not just a literary procedure. It testifies to a difficulty in presenting and naming the Spirit of God related to its anonymous and fluid qualities. As some authors put it, "the specific difficulty with the Holy Spirit is that it has no face."[60] The Son is the most personal in human terms because he has a human figure and face. Though God the Father is more difficult to apprehend in human terms, the Scriptures do sometimes allude to his "face": no one can see the God's face without dying (Exod 33:20); no one has seen the Father's face but the Son (John 1:18); and the Son can reveal his face and will do so definitively in eternal life, where we will see him "as he is" (1 John 3:2), "face to face" (1 Cor 13:12).[61] It is also

---

59. See Thiselton, *Holy Spirit*, 140–41. "The coming Spirit . . . mediates the presence of the Father and of the glorified Son to the disciples"; "John insists on this historical anchor. The Paraclete's task is not to bring *independent* revelation" (Turner, *Holy Spirit and Spiritual Gifts*, 80, 83).

60. Sesboüé, "La personalità dello Spirito Santo," 25; see also Balthasar, *Theo-Logic III: The Spirit of Truth*, 115; Lacoste, "Zur Theologie des Geistes," 5–6.

61. Sesboüé, "La personalità dello Spirito Santo," 25. Balthasar considers that 1 John 3:2 refers to Christ rather than God the Father (*Theo-Logic III: The Spirit of Truth*, 441–42), but this contradicts the grammar of the verse.

interesting to note that the church fathers were reluctant to use *dunamis* too overtly in their budding pneumatology, precisely because it lacked the traits that would help defend the hypostatic and personal character of the Spirit: too much did it evoke an anonymous cosmic energy.[62]

Moreover, that air, water, and fire—the three elements other than earth—are used, points to the elusive character of the Spirit. These are the elements capable of penetrating into other realities than themselves, without being caught or trapped.[63] They can also surround and embrace another reality, as an atmosphere or an ocean or a burning fire would. Eastern theology stresses the same about the image of oil:

> The chrism symbolizes in the most adequate way possible the fluidity of the Holy Spirit extending into all the parts of the ecclesial organism. He spreads out like an oil, but more especially like a perfume. Whoever receives the Holy Spirit in the Church receives him in the form of a fluid or a fragrance, a breath of life spreading out from him into all the other members of the Church.[64]

Consistently the Spirit of God is shown to have not only a unique *modus agendi*, but also a specific *modus essendi*. Although its uniqueness has many dimensions to it, the notion of "fluidity" synthesizes quite a few of them.

What the Spirit Gives and How the Spirit Gives

The fluid *modus agendi et essendi* of the divine Spirit provides the frame for a better understanding of what it gives in the economy of salvation. Although the Scriptures offer quite a lot of insight about what believers receive from the Spirit, I will not try to be complete, but rather to understand whether the *way* the Spirit gives helps us comprehend *what* it gives. I will single out three "gifts": inspired wisdom and charisms, life, and a transformative relationship to the Father and Son, that is, adoptive sonship. Demonstrating a necessary link between the Spirit's inner working, enveloping presence, and fluidity and these gifts is impossible and not even desirable, but I will

---

62. See for instance Gregory Nazianzen, "The Fifth Theological Oration—On the Spirit," §32 (*Theological Orations*, 213–14).

63. See Balthasar, *Theo-Logic III: The Spirit of Truth*, 115; Sesboüé, "La personalità dello Spirito Santo," 26.

64. Stanilaoe, *Theology and the Church*, 69.

The Holy Spirit in and through and around Others in the Economy

argue that there is indeed a deep coherence. Here also, what counts in the end is not *what* is given but *how* it is given: the Spirit is the one who gives treasures that belong to all three divine names because of who it is and how it is, because it is precisely, in the divine logic, the "giver."

Understandably, since the Holy Spirit works from within and inspires, since it touches the *kardia* and the mind, it gives intelligence and know-how. About the craftsman of the sanctuary God says: "I have filled him with divine spirit, with ability, intelligence, and knowledge in every kind of craft" (Exod 31:3; see also Isa 11:2). The Spirit counsels, as Isaiah asserts, later quoted by Paul: "Who has directed the Spirit of the Lord, or as his counselor has instructed him?" (Isa 40:13; 1 Cor 2:16). As Spirit of Truth it teaches and leads to the fullness of truth (John 14:17; 15:26; 16:13).

Of course, the Spirit inspires prophecy: for example, Balaam, once the "Spirit of God came upon him," uttered his oracle as "one who hears the words of God" (Num 24:2, 4). The New Testament "gifts (*charismata*)" of the Spirit fall in this line of thought. They are given by the Spirit of God, as a fulfillment of the prophecy of Joel: "Then afterward I will pour out my spirit on all flesh; your sons and your daughters shall prophesy, your old men shall dream dreams, and your young men shall see visions. Even on the male and female slaves, in those days, I will pour out my spirit" (2:28–29; Acts 2:17–18). Interestingly, charisms are a prime example of how intertwined human and divine (pneumatic) action are: without the Spirit there are no true charisms, but the person receiving them needs to open his or her mouth and decide to exercise them—freedom to express a charism or not is one of the main criteria that it is from God.[65] Moreover, the pictures and notions used in prophecy, for example, come from the cultural field and personal experience of the prophet.[66]

Another central gift attributed to the Spirit is life. In the First Testament, the vision of the dry bones brought to life by the invocation of the Spirit narrated by Ezekiel is a powerful example of the life-giving dimension of the Spirit of God:

> [The Lord] said to me, "Prophesy to the breath, prophesy, mortal, and say to the breath: Thus says the Lord God: Come from the four winds, O breath, and breathe upon these slain, that they may live." I prophesied as he commanded me, and the breath came into them, and they lived, and stood on their feet, a vast multitude.

65. See Vetö, "Foi et raison chez Thomas d'Aquin," 104–5.
66. See for instance Aquinas (quoting Jerome), ST, II-II, q.172 a.2–3.

The Breath of God

Then he said to me . . . "I will put my spirit within you, and you shall live." (Ezek 37:9–10, 14)

The Spirit as giver of life is also very present in wisdom literature: "When you take away their breath, they die and return to the dust. When you send forth your spirit, they are created" (Ps 104:29–30); "The Spirit of God has made me, and the breath of the Almighty gives me life" (Job 33:4).[67] This is developed by the New Testament as the Spirit giving the new life of the resurrection: "[Jesus Christ] was declared Son of God with power according to the Spirit of holiness by resurrection from the dead" (Rom 1:4); "If the Spirit of him who raised Jesus from the dead dwells in you, he who raised Christ from the dead will give life to your mortal bodies also through his Spirit that dwells in you" (Rom 8:11).[68] This is why the Spirit receives a role in creation, either as breath of life inspired into Adam by God after modeling him (Gen 2:7) or as the wind breathed out by God on the primordial waters (Gen 1:2).[69]

Now why is life especially referred to the Spirit of God? The Scriptures simply reveal this relation and do not try to explain it. However, *how* the Spirit works can give us an indication: if it operates deep inside, if it is the fluid but powerful energy at work in more substantial realities, it presents obvious analogies with life. Life is the inner energy that moves and animates a body; it is what makes the difference between a body and a corpse. Moreover, the images of breath, water, and power (*dunamis*) used for the Spirit relate it to these elements and energies that give life through an inner and fluid presence. With blood, breath is one of the two main "physical" or concrete expressions of life in the Bible: the first belongs to the more material sphere, the second to the more immaterial one.[70] Wisdom literature in particular stresses the link between life and God's breath, as witnessed by the quotations above. To a lesser extent, the image of water also relates the Spirit to life-giving water: when Jesus stands up to proclaim the coming of the Spirit at the great feast he speaks about "rivers of living water" (John 7:38). This passage retrospectively allows for a pneumatological interpretation of John 4:14: "Those who drink the water that I will give them will never be thirsty. The water that I will give will become in them a spring of water gushing up to eternal life." Also, though strength is not exactly

67. See also Thiselton, *Holy Spirit*, 4–5.
68. See Pannenberg, *Systematic Theology II*, 76–77.
69. See Pannenberg, *Systematic Theology II*, 78.
70. See Thiselton, *Holy Spirit*, 7.

The Holy Spirit in and through and around Others in the Economy

equivalent to life, it is not without relation to its energy and dynamic: because the Spirit is the *dunamis theou*, it gives inner strength that interacts with and augments our human forces.

A third type of gift offered by the Spirit is a transformative relation to the Father and the Son. Prayer is once again paradigmatic, since the divine Spirit leads the pray-er to cry out "Abba!": "You have received a Spirit of adoption, in which (*en hô*) we cry, 'Abba, Father!'" (Rom 8:15 [modified translation]). For biblical scholars, the Aramaic expression "Abba" is a direct reference to the prayer of Jesus (see Mark 14:36).[71] Prayer *en pneumati* signals a transfer of his prayer to the Christian: praying means entering into Jesus' prayer, into his relation with the Father. In prayer we are "entering a 'conversation' *already in play*, a reciprocal divine conversation between Father and Spirit."[72] Of course, this entails a relation to the Son, which is provided by the same Spirit, since it is the "Spirit of [the] Son" (Gal 4:6). As Irenaeus will put it very strongly, the Holy Spirit is our "communion with Christ" (*communicatio Christi*).[73]

So far, nothing is particularly original. The real point, however, is to understand why this gift is attributed to the Spirit, or at least to provide some coherency between the Spirit's *modi operandi et essendi* and its action. Now, it seems to me that the relational role of the Spirit of God corresponds here to two of the dimensions I have underlined. Since the Spirit "draws back" to let others take their place, it is quite coherent for it to put us in relation with others. It shows the Father and the Son, it teaches what the Father and the Son teach. Rather than being the addressee or term of the relationship, it facilitates and mediates it. The second dimension is its local or spatial quality: rather than being the object—or subject—we relate to, the Spirit is the open "space" in which the relation takes place. Rather than the object seen, it is the light in which we see: "The human face of God [is] shown and seen in the Spirit of God."[74] If Pannenberg is right to conceive of the Spirit as a force field, then it is the energy field (*dunamis*) that holds us together and in relation one with another. This may be why, especially in the First Testament, the Spirit is quasi-synonymous with God's presence: "Where can I go from your spirit? Or where can I flee from your presence?" (Ps 139:7). In the period of restoration after the exile, when the people need

---

71. See Fitzmyer, *Romans*, 501; Dunn, *Romans 1–8*, 453–54.
72. Coakley, "Charismatic Experience," 80.
73. Irenaeus, *Against the Heresies*, III, xxiv, §1, 110.
74. Balthasar, *Glory of the Lord*, 472.

to be reassured that God is still with them, the prophet assures them: "My Spirit abides among you; do not fear" (Hag 2:5).[75] Because it "atmospherically" encompasses what is distant, but also because of its fluid property that allows it to spread out, the Spirit brings about the presence of God to the point that it is this presence in itself.

Now, these relationships are transformative. Entering into the Son's relation to the Father is not only a new "interpersonal" relationship, but it also makes us adoptive sons and daughters of God, by regenerating us. The Spirit, indeed, is "Spirit of adoption" (Rom 8:15). This happens through a process that is once again quite coherent with the Spirit's way of acting and of being. Not only does the Spirit of God give life, but it makes us into a new, eschatological, creation by transforming the minds and the hearts through its inner working: "a new heart will I give you, and a new spirit I will put within you; and I will remove from your body the heart of stone and give you a heart of flesh. I will put my Spirit within you . . . " (Ezek 36:26–27a; see also Ps 51:10). With the (implicit) background of images of cleansing water or purifying fire, its transformative action entails purification of sin, and is prolonged by the revelation of hidden sin and conviction of sin (see 1 Cor 14:25; John 16:8–12). Sonship also involves abandoning ourselves to the Father, and this is done in dynamics of the Spirit who leads us from within. Though biblical scholars are not unanimous about which *pneuma* is referred to when the letter to the Hebrews asserts that Christ "through the eternal Spirit (*dia pneumatos aiōnou*) offered himself without blemish to God" (Heb 9:14), quite a few do understand it to be the Holy Spirit.[76] In the same way, Christians, through their royal priesthood, can "offer spiritual sacrifices (*pneumatikos thusia*)" (1 Pet 2:5): they can offer themselves and their lives in and through the *Pneuma*. In the end, this is so to speak a re-generation in the generation of the Son. It is deification or divinization. We are plunged into the life of God, "integrated" or "incorporated" into the trinitarian relations—which leads S. Coakley to coin the expression of "an incorporative 'adoption'" into sonship by the Spirit.[77]

Likewise, the Spirit of sonship is a Spirit of "brotherhood," since by making us sons and daughters of the same Father it makes us brothers and sisters of the same "First-born." The Holy Spirit does not only relate us to God but also to others: "Through [Christ Jesus] and in one single Spirit

75. See Thiselton, *Holy Spirit*, 13.
76. See Koester, *Hebrews*, 410–11.
77. Coakley, *God, Sexuality and the Self*, 136.

The Holy Spirit in and through and around Others in the Economy

both have free access to the Father" (Eph 2:18 [modified translation]). "Both" are the people of Israel and the nations, gathered in the "one Spirit" and in the mediation of Christ in a common access to the Father. The Spirit of God is a spirit of unity: "they were all filled with the Holy Spirit. . . . Now the whole group of those who believed were one heart and soul, and no one claimed private ownership of any possessions, but everything they owned was held in common" (Acts 4:31–32). Traditionally, the gift of understanding all languages at Pentecost has been understood as the "anti-Babel," the reunification of humankind by the effusion of the Holy Spirit after its division and dispersion following the construction of the Tower of Babel. Here also, however, what counts is *why* this is so. Essentially, the process is the same as with our relation to the Father and the Son: the Spirit steps aside to put us in relation to the Father and to the Son and all those who surround us. They also are included in the space of relationship, the force field that binds all together. And this certainly supposes an inner transformation of the hearts and minds, an abandoning of ourselves and of all our relationships into divine relations and love.

In the end, it is not so much what the Spirit of God gives that is specific but the way it gives. The Spirit is not more related to truth or wisdom or strength or indeed life than the Father and the Son.[78] However, because it works from within, it communicates these, it enables us to receive them, and it transforms us through them in the process. Strictly speaking it is not more loving or "relational" than the Father and the Son, but its specific way of being a person-in-another and for-another means that it is the one who relates us to them and introduces or incorporates us in their relations and love. More than the gifts themselves, what counts is that the Spirit, inner "gift" of the Father and of the Son, "given" to be truly in us and to be truly ours, is *par excellence* the "giver."

* * *

So far we have expounded on some basic traits of the Spirit of God as revealed in the economy and tried to find a certain coherence and logic. In the Scriptures *Ruah* and *Pneuma* have shown themselves to be quite different from Father and Son: they are atmospheric and fluid, they act and exist in and through and around others. The more the Spirit is active in infusing

---

78. See Augustine, *De Trinitate*, VII, ii, 3 (PL 42, 936); Aquinas, ST, I, q.39 aa.7–8; *SCG*, IV, 12.

wisdom, dynamism, life, and relationships in others, the more it pulls back. It is itself by making others become themselves. These characteristics flow together to give a typical, specific "personality" of the Spirit.

Now, it may be useful to remind ourselves once again how circumspect we should be about using the too familiar terminology of praying, speaking, desiring, or resting, for example, for the third divine name. It is a constant challenge we rarely entirely live up to. However, at the same time, we know that the economic Trinity gives a (limited but) true access to the immanent Trinity. Indeed, there is no safer access. This means it does reveal something of the Spirit as it is. Because of this, paradoxically, the best way of ensuring we are faithful to the otherness of the Spirit will be in fact to develop a comprehension of who it is in the eternal life of God that coheres with its revelation in the economy. Securing its otherness both in the *oikonomia* and the *theologia* is the key, since the first gives the true access to the second, which in turn offers a framework to purify it from its human and spatio-temporal condition. Each pole strengthens the other in our comprehension of God: if our understanding of the immanent Trinity is true to the economy, in fact, it helps maintain the truth of the economy. So the question will now be: what does its unique mode of acting and of existing in salvation history mean for the Holy Spirit's personhood in the Trinity? How is it possible to understand the Spirit in God without ever "losing our footing" in the economy? This is the task of the next chapter.

2

Breath (*Ruah-Pneuma*)
Naming the Spirit in the Immanent Trinity

How can the traits patiently put together so far be a springboard for a comprehension of the Holy Spirit in the inner-trinitarian relations? How can the third divine person be understood in the eternal life of the Trinity in such a way that its economic specificities are taken into account? I will argue that the key to the Spirit in the immanent Trinity is simply the name the Scriptures offer: *Ruah-Pneuma*. I will also argue that this implies resorting to a metaphor, more precisely the metaphor of "breath," in the Trinity itself: to be faithful to the economy, the third hypostasis should be considered as concretely as possible as the eternal Breath of the Father, the Breath he breathes to and into the Son, and that the Son breathes back as well.

I will start with a few preparatory steps, as a first phase, to set the conditions and the framework for this reflection. I will then expound the breath-metaphor proper, in its different dimensions, on an inner-trinitarian level. The third phase will consist in addressing objections: it will be, in a way, a test for the validity of the whole process and the comprehension of the Holy Spirit it offers.

The Breath of God

The True Name of the Holy Spirit: Preparatory Steps

At least three steps, of different nature, are necessary before applying the breath-metaphor to the Holy Spirit. To justify the need for a new conception of the Holy Spirit, I will show how the classical conceptions of the third person, as developed in the West and the East, do not rest in a strong enough manner on the economic revelation of the Spirit in the Scriptures. Our way will necessarily be different. As a second step, I will then present the "key" offered by the Scriptures: the names *Ruah* and *Pneuma*. They are the third person's main name(s), and they echo in a remarkable way many of the traits set into light in the previous chapter. The third step will then be to consider this new "way" from an epistemological point of view: can the recourse to a metaphor be justified in theology?

Classical Latin pneumatology concentrates on two dimensions or "names" of the Holy Spirit: love and gift. The difficulty is that the Spirit as love has little economic foundation. The Spirit does give the love of God: "God's love has been poured into our hearts through the Holy Spirit that has been given us" (Rom 5:5). In the same way, Paul appeals to the addressees of the letter "by our Lord Jesus Christ and by the love of the Spirit" (15:30). The Spirit also gives *koinonia*, "fellowship" or "communion" to Christians (2 Cor 13:13; see 1 Cor 12:4–31), and we have already seen that it brings down the wall between Jews and Gentiles (Eph 2:18). But never is the Holy Spirit explicitly named love in the Scriptures. All three persons love; love is also attributed to the Father (2 Cor 13:13); and the Johannine "definition," "God is love" (1 John 4:8, 16), can be understood as designating the Father or all three persons, but not directly the Spirit as such. In fact, the idea of the Spirit as Love develops historically as a consequence of the—also non-scriptural—Augustinian analogy of mental processions: the Spirit proceeds through an act of will and love, as the Word does through an act of intelligence.[1] It is reinforced by the other Augustinian-Richardian analogy of the social Trinity or its Bonaventurian-Balthasarian declension in which the Spirit is understood as the bond of love between the Father and the Son: since it is common to both it is the fruit of the mutual love of the Father and the Son but it is also their *nexus*, their communion itself. However, it is difficult to hold together the idea that the Holy Spirit is a bond or nexus of love and that he is a third loved and loving hypostatical reality. Moreover,

---

1. See Augustine, *De Trinitate*, XV (PL 42, 1057–98). See in particular section iii for the Holy Spirit as *caritas*.

Breath (Ruah-Pneuma)

this is no more scriptural than the first analogy. Nowhere in the New Testament do we see the Holy Spirit explicitly as bond of love between the Father and the Son, and even less is it presented as the fruit of their love for one another. For this reason, these conceptions of the Holy Spirit became *theologoumenoi* quite late, only in the fourth or fifth centuries.[2]

Conversely, the Spirit as the "gift of God" is clearly attested in the New Testament. The church fathers develop the notion as an expression of the gift of the Spirit itself and the gifts offered by the Spirit in the economy.[3] However, "gift" is more difficult to use on an inner-trinitarian level. Aquinas, for instance, finds the need to base this dimension of the Spirit on love: "Since the Holy Spirit proceeds as love, . . . he proceeds as the first gift."[4] *Donum* is a personal name of the Holy Spirit because all giving has love as its *ratio* and the ultimate gift is love itself. Since the Holy Spirit proceeds as love it is also gift. This brings us back to the analogy of mental processions and love, with the same difficulty as before.

These analogies are not necessarily meaningless. They are a laudable effort of the human mind to make sense of the mystery of the Trinity. However, they are limited and need to be taken together so as to hold together the unity of substance best expressed by the mental processions and the difference of hypostases illustrated by the three co-lovers or the fruit of love.[5] Moreover, such images contain a permanent risk of projection. K. Kilby rightly observes that the authors of social theories of the Trinity seem to have an overly vivid perception of the intimate life of God: "One can form the impression that much of the detail is derived from the individual author's or the larger society's latest ideas of how human beings should live in community."[6] The fact that these analogies are not grounded in the

---

2. See Ladaria, *Il Dio vivo e vero*, 381. It is worth noting that, although it is predominantly a Western theme, the Holy Spirit as love also exists in the East, starting with Gregory Palamas: "The Spirit of the most high Word is like an ineffable love of the Father for this Word ineffably generated. A love which this same Word and beloved Son of the Father entertains towards the Father: but insofar as he has the Spirit coming with him from the Father and reposing connaturally in him" (Gregory Palamas, *Capita physica*, XXXVI [PG 150, 1144 D–1145 A]). See also Orphanos, "Procession of the Holy Spirit," 33.

3. See, for example, Cyril of Jerusalem, *Catecheses*, XVI, 11–12 (PG 33, 931–35); Augustine, *De Trinitate*, V, xv, 16–xvi, 17 (PL 42, 921–24); XV, xvii, 29 (1081); xviii, 32–xix, 36 (1082–86).

4. Aquinas, ST, I, q.38 a.2 resp.

5. See Balthasar, *Theo-Drama III: The Dramatis personae: Persons in Christ*, 526–27.

6. Kilby, "Perichoresis and Projection," 441.

economy of God's own revelation and self-communication and in the authoritative witness given to it by the Scriptures explains why they should be taken with utmost prudence.[7]

The Greek fathers are much more circumspect in their approach to the third hypostasis. Cyril of Jerusalem considers that one should not explore the nature of the Holy Spirit because one should not investigate what is not written in the holy Scriptures: "Let this knowledge be enough for us. You must not be curious to know the nature or the essence of the Spirit.... If something is not written, we should not dare speak of it."[8] For this reason, both Athanasius and Basil underline that the "the ineffability of [the Spirit]'s mode of subsistence (*tropos tès hyparcheos*) is safeguarded,"[9] an assertion which becomes a Greek *theologoumenon*.[10]

Are we then obliged to choose between Charybdis and Scylla, between analogies without economic foundation and silence? In fact, I believe that the Scriptures offer much more than what is often thought. They offer the third divine name: *Ruah* or *Pneuma*. We know already that these are continuously used to designate God's Spirit—more than half of their occurrences refer to God.[11] Because of this there is every reason to believe that they can be the key to understanding the third divine person, not only in the economy, but also in the eternal Trinity. My hypothesis is that they can offer precious indications on the Holy Spirit in itself: if there is a Breath of God in the economy, this means there is something like a Breath in the

---

7. A recent book by Matthew Levering (*Engaging the Doctrine of the Holy Spirit: Love and Gift in the Trinity and the Church*) presses in the direction of rediscovering these two traditional names of the Holy Spirit. It is learned and highly intelligent, but I believe it does not sufficiently take into account the economic grounding of our knowledge of the third person.

8. Cyril of Jerusalem, *Catecheses*, XVI, 24 (PG 33, 953).

9. Basil the Great, *On the Holy Spirit*, XVIII, §46, 73 (modified translation); see also Athanasius, *Epistolae Ad Serapionem*, I, 15-20 (PG 26, 565 C-580 B); *Epistiloa IV* (641 C-645 A).

10. See also: "It is futile to ask what is the distinction between being generated and proceeding; just as the mode is unknown, so is the distinction" (Didymus, *De Trinitate*, I, 8 [PG 39, 281 B]); "[The Holy Spirit] proceeds in his essence from the Father through the generated Son in a way that is ineffable" (Maximus the Confessor, *Quaest. ad Thalassium*, 63 [PG 90, 672]). See also John Damascene, *Expositio Fidei orthodoxae*, I, 8 (PG 94, 821-4); Leontius of Byzantium, *De sectis*, I (PG 87, 1196). Latin fathers also concur on the specific difficulty of defining the difference between the Son's generation and the Spirit's procession: see Augustine, *Contra Maximinum*, II, xiv, 1 (PL 42, 1097); *De Trinitate*, XV, vii, 12 (PL 42, 1065-6).

11. See above, chap. 1, p. 2.

Breath (Ruah-Pneuma)

life of the Trinity. If God breathes in the economy, there is something analogous to breathing in God. If the third person is named breath and wind in the economy, its eternal "personality" should have some similarity to these realities.

Before developing *Ruah-Pneuma* in the immanent Trinity it is necessary to determine its precise meaning, as a name, in the Scriptures.[12] We have studied how the Spirit acts and is present in the economy, but not yet the meaning of these names themselves. The main signification of both *ruah* and *pneuma* is wind and breath. *Ruah* is a verbal noun modeled on the infinitive denoting the action of wind blowing or of breathing—in fact it is difficult in Hebrew to distinguish very clearly between wind and breath. When it is wind it can be a gentle breeze, but it is often a violent and powerful one. When it is breath it is often associated with life and physical vitality: by analogy, since breathing is a sign of life, it comes to mean life itself. *Ruah* is sometimes also associated with "vanity (*hebel*)," and thus denotes insubstantiality.

In both cases, whether it indicates vitality or insubstantiality, *ruah* transcends the corporeal reality of a person, and expresses the idea of what extends beyond the physical and substantial limits of this person: the "living person as 'a unit of vital power' [Johnson], manifesting itself through its activity above and beyond the corporeal limits of the body. This activity is conceived as an 'extension of the personality'; its force field is the locus of the *Ruah*."[13] In a related but slightly different sense, it also indicates something that is "airy" or, by extension, "spacious."

When associated with "soul" (*nephesh*), *ruah* can also have a less material meaning, close to heart or mind—similar to the Latin *spiritus*: "My soul yearns for you in the night, my spirit within me earnestly seeks you" (Isa 26:9). However, while *nephesh* can indicate the whole person, *ruah* is always within—as in the quote from Isaiah. Like the heart it is the interior, spiritual center of the person. Because of this it can also denote a passion—often anger, but also desire or longing—or more generally a virtue, character, or inner strength.

Pneuma, whether in the Septuagint or the New Testament, is very close to *ruah*, since it also basically means wind or breath, and by extension

---

12. The following exposition is mainly based on Botterweck and Ringgren, *Theological Dictionary*, XIII, 365–402 and on Balz and Schneider, *Exegetisches Wörterbuch*, 279–91.

13. Botterweck and Ringgren, *Theological Dictionary*, XIII, 372.

the principle of life and different aspects of a human person's inner life. However, it is slightly less adapted to express inner emotions or forces than *ruah*. There is also a greater tendency for *pneuma* to designate autonomous realities, like angels or impure spirits. In the case of the Spirit of God it is often characterized as "holy (*hagion*)," while in the First Testament *Ruah* is characterized as holy only three times: Isa 63:10; Ps 51:13; Wis 9:17. These evolutions, however, have little bearing on our reflection: all in all the Hebrew and the Greek names of the Spirit are remarkably similar—a further invitation to utilize them to understand who is the third divine person.

Let us also note that the characteristics expressed by *Ruah* and *Pneuma* correspond in a significant way to those of the Holy Spirit in the economy: a reality that works from inside or that surrounds, that pushes forward and that relates to emotions, a fluid—air and water are both fluids—that extends above and beyond the corporeal substances. We will see that the same characteristics will also be surprisingly adapted to determine the Spirit's inner-trinitarian specificity. It is important to always remember, however, that its first meaning for the Scriptures is a reality of nature, rather than a psychological and mental reality or an ontological determination, like the Latin *spiritus* tends too easily to induce.

These "names" offered by the Scriptures, however, are not only and not primarily personal names, since they recall the concrete elements of wind, air, and breath. As such they are images and "similitudes," as the scholastics would say. More precisely, they are metaphors. Janet Soskice offers a rather wide definition of what a metaphor is: "Metaphor is that figure of speech whereby we speak about one thing in terms which are seen to be suggestive of another."[14] She then proceeds to distinguish them from similes: while these are one-for-one comparisons, often of similars, a metaphor can be extended. It has a creative dimension because it brings out similarities in what may previously have seemed dissimilar in a much richer interplay of words and minds.[15] The same is even more true if we compare metaphors to analogies, where the association between the figure of speech and the reality it expresses is adequate from the start and is just being "stretched": truth, goodness, power, do not surprise us when they are used for God and they do not offer new perspectives about him.[16] Indeed all language about God is analogical, because all words and notions need to be stretched to

---

14. Soskice, *Metaphor and Religious Language*, 15.
15. See Soskice, *Metaphor and Religious Language*, 41, 43, 58.
16. See Soskice, *Metaphor and Religious Language*, 65–66.

Breath (Ruah-Pneuma)

express what is beyond their grasp. However, all language about God is not metaphorical. In a metaphor a subject is expressed by the interaction of two thoughts: one that expresses it directly, the "tenor" (in our case, the Holy Spirit), and one that comes from another domain of thought, the vehicle (breath).[17] This has a close bond with the use of models, where we make use of something known to understand something less known and which does not have an immediate connection to it.[18] This initial dissimilarity offers the space for extension, for creativity and newness. Our question is whether this process is justified in theology from an epistemological point of view, so as to use and extend the images of breath and wind to better understand the Holy Spirit.

The first justification of this new way of proceeding is that it is not truly new. Indeed, it fits squarely with the elaboration of trinitarian theology during the first centuries. The early Christian understanding of the first and second persons was developed in reference to the names revealed by the Scriptures: Father and Son or Word. Applied to God these also are images. Now, the church fathers resorted to them and handled them as metaphors by utilizing in their theological reasoning some dimensions of fatherhood and sonship and of uttering a word. It is logical to comprehend God the "Father" as source of a "Son," and to understand the way he is source as a "generation." It is coherent to comprehend God the "Son" as receiving his being from a "Father," as being "generated" by him. When extending the metaphor of thought and speech, it also is logical to understand the Father as uttering or proffering the Word and the Word as coming from the mouth of the Father, as inner word and then outer, expressed word.[19] Expanding the image even further, one can say that the Father conceives himself and all things in the Word and expresses himself in the Word.[20] Thus, the two metaphors intersect, since both a son and a word are "conceived": Augustine, for instance, will play with these notions and use *conceptus, natus,*

---

17. See Richards, *Philosophy of Rhetoric*, 121.

18. "We may use a subject that is reasonably well known to us to explain or provide schematization for a state of affairs which is beyond our full grasp; this happens when one says that God is our father, or that light is waves, or that the human community is governed by natural law. One has a good notion of law, waves, and fatherhood and uses these notions to give form to the more amorphous concepts of society, light, and deity" (Soskice, *Metaphor and Religious Language*, 60; see also 42, 49–51, 55, 99, 101).

19. See Justin Martyr, *Dialogus*, 61 (PG 6, 614); Theophilus of Antioch, *Ad Autolycum*, 2 (PG 6, 1026–27).

20. See Aquinas, ST, I, q.34; Bonaventure, *Breviloquium*, I, 3.

partus both for human words and for the divine *Filius-Verbum*.[21] It seems to me that this same process used to elaborate Christian thought on the Father and the Son can and should be extended to the Spirit.[22]

In fact, the church fathers and the scholastic theologians sometimes hint at the idea that *Pneuma* and *Spiritus* mean "breath." In his treatise on the Holy Spirit, when defending the divine personhood of the Spirit, Basil notes that the third hypostasis "proceeds as breath from the mouth of the Father, and is not begotten like the Son."[23] Cyril of Alexandria interprets the second narrative of the creation of Adam, when God breathes into him his life-giving breath, by explaining that the Holy Spirit comes from the Father as breath comes from the mouth of a human being and that God is giving Adam a participation in his Spirit—in the same way as the risen Lord breathes out the Holy Spirit on the disciples in John 20:22.[24] In the medieval period, Richard of Saint-Victor notes: "The fact that [the Holy Spirit] is called the 'Spirit of God (*Spiritus Dei*)' or the 'Holy Spirit (*Spiritus sanctus*)' was not totally contrary to the principles of similitude. The word 'breath (*spiritus*)' indicates that which proceeds from human beings and without which they absolutely do not have life." He also stresses that the Spirit is similar to breath because it is breathed onto the disciples by Christ after his resurrection: "Did the Teacher of Truth not teach us that the Holy Spirit is the divine breath (*divinum spiramen*) as through a similitude, when, appearing to his disciples, he breathed on them and said: *Receive the Holy Spirit?*"[25] A final witness will be Aquinas himself, in one of the questions on the third person: "The name spirit (*spiritus*) in things corporeal seems to signify impulse and motion; for we call the breath (*flatum*) and the wind (*ventum*) by the term spirit."[26] Aquinas also uses the beautiful

---

21. See Augustine, *De Trinitate*, IX, ix, 14 (PL 42, 968).

22. As often when it comes to contemporary developments in theology, M. Scheeben expressed this thought as an intuition, without fully expounding it: "For although [the names that the Scripture and the church apply to the divine persons] are only analogous, their analogy is so suggestive, so cogent, and so striking, that an understanding of them conveys to us a clear and most resplendent notion of the sublime mystery" (Scheeben, *Mysteries of Christianity*, 114). Scheeben is reflecting here on the Trinity but especially on the Holy Spirit as "breath."

23. Basil the Great, *On the Holy Spirit*, XVIII, §46, 73 (modified translation).

24. See Cyril of Alexandria, *Adversus Julianum*, 55 (PG 76, 584–85); *In Io.*, 9 (PG 74, 257); *De Trinitate*, 2 (PG 75, 722–23).

25. Richard of Saint-Victor, *On the Trinity*, VI, §9, 327.

26. Aquinas, ST, I, q.36, a.1 resp.

Breath (Ruah-Pneuma)

term of *baptismus flaminis*—literally "baptism of breath" (or "baptism of breeze")—to designate baptism in the Holy Spirit.[27]

However, this tradition needs to be epistemologically grounded. A first general consideration is that we need to allow for a plurality of rationalities in theology. Such a plurality exists already, massively, in the history of theology. This is true diachronically, as the conceptions of reason and of science evolve throughout the centuries: Irenaeus, Aquinas, and Barth are not doing exactly the same thing when they do theology. It is also true synchronically: Tertullian, Gregory of Nyssa, and Ephrem the Syrian witness to conceptions of theology respectively based on working with language, on philosophy, and on hymns and poetry. Bonaventure and Aquinas, who taught at the Sorbonne in the same period, display two very different rationalities, Platonic and poetic for the first, Aristotelian and deductive for the second. The same can be said to some extent of Balthasar and Rahner in the twentieth century. Now, resorting to metaphors is legitimate if we consider that symbolic and poetic speech has its own rationality and that this rationality can be articulated with the more deductive type of reasoning that prevails in mainstream Western theology.[28]

Furthermore, I believe that Janet Soskice's study of metaphors offers a more precise epistemological foundation that not only makes these legitimate but indeed indispensable for theology. Soskice explains that there are three theories on metaphors—and maybe three dimensions to most metaphors, which each theory sets into light.[29] A metaphor can be understood as substitutive: it is a didactic tactic which uses figurative speech instead of literal but which can—and eventually should—always be brought back to the literal expression. Metaphor can also be emotive, insofar as it intensifies the emotional reception of an idea by the hearer. However, both of these are weak forms because they offer no more content or meaning than the non-metaphoric and can thus be suppressed without altering the "cognitive content" of the text.[30] Soskice's comprehension is that a true metaphor is "incremental"; that is, it increases knowledge: "The particularity of a

---

27. The expression appears seventeen times in Aquinas's works: see especially ST, III, q. 66 aa.11–12. See also Roussineau, "*Baptismus Flaminis*," 14–20.

28. The same preoccupation explains S. Coakley's intent on introducing a "semiotic" type of reflection in theology to allow for imagination and "embodied" thought (Coakley, *God, Sexuality and the Self*, 49–50). On the urgent need to discover or rediscover the role of imagination in theology and prayer, see also Steeves, *Grâce à l'imagination*, 295–380.

29. See Soskice, *Metaphor and Religious Language*, 24–53.

30. See Soskice, *Metaphor and Religious Language*, 27, 31, 44.

THE BREATH OF GOD

metaphorical description is not that it translates literal thought, but that the very thinking is undertaken in terms of the metaphor. What interests us in metaphor is precisely that we find in it an increment to understanding."[31] Because of the creative dimension of metaphor, what is expressed in it can be conveyed adequately in no other way. The combination of elements it works on brings new meaning and new understanding, and is simply not susceptible to reduction to literal terms. In this case, the models or metaphors cannot be separated nor fully distinguished from the theory they produce.[32]

Of course, one must be clear about the type of knowledge provided by metaphors: they do not define; they refer, or "point to."[33] They are neither exhaustively descriptive, nor even directly descriptive. They aim *only* but *truly* at offering knowledge that Soskice names "reality depicting" or "partially denoting."[34] This type of approach is necessary in intellectual search because it is what allows for our knowledge to grow, by offering revisable views, which will be refined and enriched, or abandoned. It is legitimated by its actual use and fecundity in science and in religion. In science we have plenty of evidence of the predictive and cumulative success of investigations that are model-based. In religion, analogously, models and metaphors have a meaning only if they give a foundation for this meaning: "If these models provide a way of orientating oneself in the world, they can do so only if they also provide reasons for that orientation. If they explain nothing, they provide no basis for any response, religious or moral."[35] When the Synoptics use parables or when John's Gospel speaks about "living water" or Jesus as "door" and "shepherd," they are endeavoring to say something about God, and not only about the state of mind of the believer in front of Jesus. The model of God as father is so central to Christian tradition that it cannot only be meant to signify our relation to God or God's to us: it also says something, albeit indirectly and in a revisable way, about God in Godself.[36] For this reason one may assume a "critical realist" view, which

31. Soskice, *Metaphor and Religious Language*, 25.
32. See Soskice, *Metaphor and Religious Language*, 115.
33. See Soskice, *Metaphor and Religious Language*, 140, 148.
34. Soskice, *Metaphor and Religious Language*, 97–98, 116, 133. Soskice also speaks about a "pictorial dimension" of extended metaphors (see *Metaphor and Religious Language*, 64).
35. Soskice, *Metaphor and Religious Language*, 111.
36. "The Christian theist typically has not taken models like 'God is the father' or 'the kingdom of God' as merely evaluative phenomena or redescriptions of human

Breath (Ruah-Pneuma)

entails that there is a form of knowledge or "epistemic access" that is neither direct access nor pure fiction.

Moreover, all metaphors are not equal. Jesus is better understood as a good shepherd than as a competent poultry keeper. The richest ones are so to say selected and perfected by the community of believers and their writings; they are indeed enhanced by a history of their application, which enriches their meaning. This is particularly true of metaphors taken from the Scriptures, because these are the milieu from which Christian belief arises, and these metaphors have embodied and shaped the believers' comprehension of their faith for centuries.[37] The metaphors of breath and wind for the Holy Spirit clearly fall into this category.

To be complete, one needs to add a third epistemological consideration. When applied to God the names Father, Son, and *Ruah-Pneuma* may not be metaphorical in exactly the same way as human fatherhood or sonship, or again the characteristic of created breath and wind. It would be necessary to develop a complete "theology of divine names" to have a full grasp of the status of the names the Scriptures give to God, but it is far from absurd to consider that these names, although their origin is metaphorical, are revealed as particular names, as sole determinant or designator of identity.[38] "Father", "Son," and "*Ruah-Pneuma*" are "divinely so-called," rather than only good descriptive "nick-names."[39] For this reason they can be immanently true of God and can be considered anchored in the reality of God. What remains strictly metaphorical, on the other hand, is the content we give to this designator, that is the action and "personality" attributed to each name following the created reality that is designated by the same term.

Though I believe all this makes a strong case for using the breath and wind metaphors to reflect theologically on the Holy Spirit, one final epistemological step is necessary, that of ensuring that we are not exceeding the range of what human language and reason can legitimately say and think

---

experience, but as speaking, albeit obliquely, about states and relations which he knows himself not fully to understand but which he takes to be more than simply human states and relations" (Soskice, *Metaphor and Religious Language*, 107).

37. See Soskice, *Metaphor and Religious Language*, 158–59.

38. It would be interesting to verify to what extent the Jewish philosopher Saul Kripke's notion of a "rigid designator" can be taken to a divine level (see Kripke, *Naming and Necessity*, 48).

39. I am grateful to Ephraim Radner for pointing out to me the possible difference of status between the divine names and their metaphorical horizon.

about the transcendent God. We need to make sure that a metaphorical theology can also be an apophatic theology.

Indeed, the authors quoted above, who have seen that the Holy Spirit can be expounded with the vocabulary of breath and air, are also quick to point out the difficulty in using this name, and are thus very reluctant to extend the metaphor. Basil himself feels obliged to reject any possible accusation of anthropomorphism or of giving too little substantiality to the Spirit: "Of course, the 'mouth' of the Father is not a physical member, nor is the Spirit a dissipated breath, but 'mouth' is used to the extent that it is appropriate to God."[40] One solution is to divorce the term "spirit" from the images of breath and wind. Augustine, for instance, understands *spiritus* from an ontological standpoint, as the spiritual, as opposed to the material. However, in this case, it is what is common to all three persons, not what is specific to one. Indeed, Augustine underlines that "Holy Spirit" designates properties shared by the Father and the Son, who are both holy and spiritual.[41] He then deduces from these common dimensions the idea that the third person is what the Father and the Son share, i.e., their mutual love. For him, as we know, if anything is more specific to the Spirit, it is *caritas* rather than *spiritus*. Little by little, especially in the Latin world, the idea that the name of the Holy Spirit cannot be used theologically imposes itself. Aquinas asserts that Word is what he calls a "proper name (*nomen proprium*)," a name which can only be attributed to the Son, because one can distinguish the product, the *Verbum* or the *conceptus*, from the act of conceiving. Conversely, this is not possible for the Spirit of Love, since no distinct words can differentiate the procession by love from the love produced by it. The Dominican master concludes that there are no words to adequately name the product of the second procession: "The Person proceeding in that manner does not have a proper name (*non habet proprium nomen*). . . . 'Holy Spirit' [is only] by the use of scriptural speech accommodated to Him (*accommodatum est, ex usu Scripturae*)."[42]

This difficulty needs to be taken into account. We know that all language applied to God, not only metaphor, is analogical. As with any other word or image, it will be necessary to purify *Ruah* and *Pneuma* from what is too crudely material or anthropomorphic. In fact, the same fathers and theologians do give a clue as to how to use metaphors adequately: to extend

40. Basil the Great, *On the Holy Spirit*, XVIII, §46, 73 (modified translation).
41. See Augustine, *De Trinitate*, V, xi, 12 (PL 42, 918–19); XV, xvii (1079–82).
42. Aquinas, ST, I, q.36, a.1 resp.

Breath (Ruah-Pneuma)

the names of the Father and the Son-*Logos* into theological notions, they "correct" them by making them go through the sieve of negative theology. For instance, the Father-Son metaphor became acceptable once cleared of any spatial-temporal dimension. The Father generates the Son, but there is no time in which the Son was not, so the generation must be understood as eternal. In the same way, the Son is not generated "outside" of the Father: he fully shares the same divine substance. Though the Word is proffered by the Father, the process by which it is conceived and uttered is not temporal, but co-eternal with the Father's being, and it happens in God.[43] All this was assisted by the "ontologisation" of trinitarian theology and Christology: the "generation" of the Son is understood as the communication of the fullness of the substance of the Father, possessed as numerically one by each hypostasis.

Metaphors may need to be purified more than simple words. Paul Ricœur, for instance, stresses that because of the richness of interactions and their creative dimension they tend to take a life of their own.[44] One cannot extend a metaphor indefinitely, because at one point it ends up reflecting the vehicle only and losing its depicting capacity for the tenor: we simply forget the "thing" of which we speak. We cannot extend the model of God's fatherhood so far as to say that he has a wife, for instance.[45] However, even the greatest prudence and the most intense purification should not, and simply cannot, obliterate the fact that the framework and guiding principle of thought here are images and metaphors (offered by the Scriptures). I also tend to agree with Schelling when he stresses that among the different inadequate types of rationalities we possess to speak about God, anthropomorphic reasoning is one of the less inadequate: why would God be better rendered by ontological concepts often inspired by the inanimate world of nature or by human industry, as is the case for Aristotelian metaphysics,[46] rather than by notions that come from the one being created in God's image to become God's partner?[47] Moreover, Soskice convincingly explains that there is an innate potential for apophatism in metaphor as such. As we know, at the heart of metaphorical speech is the distinction between

---

43. See for instance, the way Aquinas purifies the term *processio* from any temporal or spatial dimension (ST, I, q.27, a.1).

44. See Ricœur, *La métaphore vive*, 81–83.

45. See Soskice, *Metaphor and Religious Language*, 23, 123.

46. See Ross, *Aristotle*, 167–76.

47. See Schelling, *Nachlass 8*, 94 [432].

defining and referring or "pointing to." Precisely because it is not seeking to define or to directly describe, but is consciously and methodically speaking about one thing in terms which seem to belong to another, metaphoric theological reasoning is an act of negative theology.[48] It is inherently apophatic, or at least potentially so, and will thus in fact contribute to respecting and protecting apophatism.

Though these epistemological considerations do not constitute a full gnoseological framework but only a few indications, I do believe they are sufficient to allow us to proceed with the breath-metaphor. It is a legitimate type of theological reasoning, indeed a necessary one, which will indirectly but truly increase our knowledge about the Holy Spirit, in a way no other reasoning can. Moreover, *Ruah* and *Pneuma* come from the Scriptures and are to an extent a name of God. We will need to proceed with extreme caution, naturally, but some of the limits and guardrails are in fact inherent to metaphorical speech itself.

In the end, Augustine was partly right to say that the Holy Spirit's name indicates its common nature with the two other persons. He was right as far as the adjective "holy" is concerned: this does designate its divine origin and the nature it shares with God. On the other hand, "spirit," understood as *ruah-pneuma* and not as ontologically opposed to matter, is specific and distinct. As distinct as breath and wind are distinct from a father and his son. Contrary to what Aquinas asserts, there is a *nomen proprium* of the Holy Spirit: *Ruah-Pneuma* express its unique being and activity, on par with the two other "proper names," Father and Son-*Logos*. And this *nomen proprium* will be the key to understanding the eternal person of the Holy Spirit.

The Eternal Breath of the Father (in)to the Son

How can the name *Ruah* or *Pneuma* illuminate our understanding of the Holy Spirit in the immanent Trinity? Since the economy does offer a far from complete but true access to the life of the eternal Trinity, because in it Father, Son, and Spirit are present and at work in themselves, I propose to use the *Ruah-Pneuma*-metaphor inside the Trinity. I will conceive the third hypostasis as literally as possible as the "breath" of God. However, because no assertion about the immanent Trinity should be made without a footing in the economy, I will check step by step the conformity of what

---

48. See Soskice, *Metaphor and Religious Language*, 140–41, 148.

Breath (Ruah-Pneuma)

is discovered in the process with the different traits set into light in the first chapter: this will act as a guardrail and as a confirmation of the validity of the endeavor. Likewise, as I have already started to do above, I will often show how many great thinkers of the past had perceived the importance of understanding the Spirit as a divine breath, but were not able to fully develop its potential.

To speak about *God* breathing is in fact not accurate from a trinitarian point of view, if only because the subject of operations in the Trinity is not the Godhead or an indeterminately monotheistic divinity, but the three divine hypostases. And the first of these, the *fons* or *principium totius divinitatis*,[49] is the Father. So our first step is to consider the Breath of the Father and the breathing-out of the Father.

In the same way as a living creature's breath comes from the depth of its being, the Breath of the Father will come from the deepest intimacy of his being. Interestingly, even a theologian as speculative as Anselm considers the use of the metaphor of breath, for instance in the Johannine Pentecost (John 20:22), as the expression of the Spirit proceeding from the depths and hiddenness of the divine substance and the hypostases that are its source:

"[It is] as if He had said: 'Just as you see that this breath—through which I signify to you the Holy Spirit (imperceptible things being able to be signified by perceptible things)—proceeds from the depths of my body and my person, so you know that the Holy Spirit, whom I signify to you through this breath, proceeds from the hiddenness of my deity and from my person."[50]

Anselm is referring here to the Son but in his Western conception of the procession of the Spirit *Filioque*, it expresses also the spiration by the Father. The Breath that wells up from the innermost dimension of the divine person corresponds well to the type of inhabitation and action of the Spirit in the economy, who acts in and from the depth of the hearts, who *in*-spires and moves from within. Moreover, physiologically speaking, in the act of breathing oxygen molecules are directly received by each individual cell in the body. The Breath of the Father is not to be conceived of as referring to just one dimension of the Father, to a delimited perimeter of his being: just as in the economy the *Pneuma* inhabits the whole being, in God it is co-extensive to all that the Father is. This means that when the Father

---

49. See Augustine, *De Trinitate*, IV, xx, 29 (PL 42, 908–9); *In Iohannis*, XCIX, 8 (PL 35, 1890); ninth Council of Toledo (DH 525).

50. Anselm of Canterbury, *Procession of the Holy Spirit*, 202.

will give his Spirit, he will give something, or better, someone, who comes from his innermost depths and that touches all he is. The Breath will thus communicate not only an aspect of the Father but in fact the whole being of the Father, in its deepest intimacy.

Let us take another step. In living creatures, breath has no substantiality of its own. It is air, it is a fluid. For this reason, it depends on the body of the being to which it belongs to have a *locus* and simply to exist. In the same way, the Breath of the Father takes on another type of substantiality than that of the Father's. Truly, it is "insubstantial" without the Father: it is not the Father but it is nothing without the Father. The Father's action of breathing out makes the Breath exist. The Breath is always related to him and its *locus* is the depths of the Father. In other words, the Breath *is* only as far as it is *in* another (*in-esse*) and *from* another, namely the Father. As such, moreover, it will also be intimately bound with any operation of the Father: it will not have an independent operation of its own, but will accompany the Father's action from within. Now, in the economy, the fluid, airy, and liquid characteristics of the Spirit confirm the present inner-trinitarian reading and are in turn grounded on it: *Ruah* and *Pneuma* are fluid in the economy because they are already so in the eternal depths of God. This is also why, in the economy, the Spirit is always related to a body, to another actor than itself. This is why it always acts in and through the actions of others. We have seen that it is different from the person it helps and inspires, but often difficult to clearly distinguish from him or her.

Of course, breath is not any kind of inner fluid; it is closely related to the life of the being it inhabits. Can this too contribute to comprehending the third divine person? Here also the great authors of the past have approached this idea of the Spirit being closely related to the breath of life of God, without however fully capturing its potential. We have already seen how Richard of Saint-Victor, for example, underlines the fact that in general *spiritus* is comparable with life-giving breath without which the person cannot live.[51] Richard then concludes that a breath exists for as long as the person who lives through it. Because the Father is eternal the Father's Spirit is eternal: "The breath (*spiritus*) proceeds from humans and without it they absolutely do not have life. And so, by calling the Holy Spirit the Breath of God (*Spiritus Dei*), is indicated the fact that he proceeds eternally from he who is eternal."[52]

---

51. See supra p. 36.
52. Richard of Saint-Victor, *Trinity*, VI, 9, 327 (modified translation). Cyril of

Breath (Ruah-Pneuma)

If we try to be even more literal than Richard in understanding the Spirit as the Breath of the Father, we need to admit that the Father cannot "live," that is, cannot "be," without it. Breath is not life itself but it is an essential dimension of life: as an action, breathing is a fundamental dimension of the act of living. In the same way, the Breath of the Father is not his life or existence as such: the Father is the source of the divinity and is not himself produced, because he is ingenerate. However, one of the dimensions of his divine existence and life is to breathe a breath. It is an aspect of the Father's act of subsistence. We will need to come back to this, but in the same way as the Father is not the Father without the Son, he is not the Father without the Spirit—which means he simply *is* not without breathing the Breath. This does not seem to find an immediate echo in the relation between the Father and the Spirit in the economy, but it does relate to the dynamic and moving character of the third person: there is a coherence in the fact that the inner life-giving breathing of the Father manifests itself *ad extra* as mobile, lively, and vibrant.

Latin theology offers a stepping-stone for the use of the breath-metaphor in the immanent Trinity insofar as, since Anselm of Canterbury, it has called the procession of the Holy Spirit a "spiration (*spiratio*)," even when the image of breathing itself is forgotten. *Spiratio* means "expiration," "breathing out." This expression allows us to use the metaphor with fewer qualms. However, conversely, the metaphor also enables to develop the idea of *spiratio* to its full potential. Indeed, persons and processions are intimately bound in trinitarian theology and it is impossible to comprehend the first without the second. Of course, there is a traditional debate about what constitutes the divine persons, whether the processions (Richard of Saint Victor, Bonaventure) or the relations (Aquinas), but even in the latter case, the procession is constitutive of the person, as the *via* towards the relation.[53] In both instances, the procession is a fundamental dimension in the personal identity of Father, Son, and Spirit: one would say either that the Son is Son because he is generated by the Father (Richard, Bonaventure), or that his procession is a generation because he is the Son and the Father is the Father (Aquinas), but there is a clear link between the type of procession and who the person is. Now, if a divine *generation* produces

---

Alexandria also describes the Holy Spirit as the breath that proceeds from a person's mouth. For this reason, the "breath of life" given to Adam in the second narrative of creation is a participation in God's life (*Adversus Julianum*, 55, PG 76, 584–85).

53. See Durand, "Le Père en sa relation," 47–72.

a Son, it is extremely coherent to think that a divine *spiration* produces a Breath. The Holy Spirit, the Breath, is constituted and defined by its being breathed, by its "expirationness," in the same way as the only-begotten Son is by his generation—or the Word by its being proffered.

Breath is not only what is present in the deepest recesses of a person, it is also breathed outward. Despite being insubstantial and needing a body, or precisely because it is insubstantial, it can overcome the limits of the person's body. Interestingly, in biblical Greek, although *pneuma* and *kardia* are almost synonymous, as expressing the hidden intimate depths of the person, they differ insofar as the *pneuma* can be communicated, while the *kardia* cannot. *Pneuma* is so to speak the contents of the *kardia* and thus what can be shared.[54] This coheres with the economic trait by which the Spirit is given and poured out by God: it is the capacity of God to be "outside of himself" (*das Ausser-Sich-Sein Gottes*), as H. Mühlen would say.[55] Better yet, it is the capacity for God to be in another than himself. Likewise, as we know, the Spirit as possessed by a prophet or an apostle can be shared out to others. Of course, in God, there is no spatial exteriority; there are no bodily limits to overcome. Towards where can the Father breathe out? While there is no exteriority, there is alterity, namely, the alterity between the Father and the Son. "Expiring" his Breath, for the Father, means breathing towards the Son. Now, in the Trinity all alterity is relational, so all inner-trinitarian operations are relational as well, and by extension so is the "field" for any action. As a consequence, "breathing out" in God is identical to "communicating" and "sharing with": the Father breathes his Breath into the Son, brings forth the life and dynamism from the utmost intimacy of his whole being and inspires it into the deepest intimacy of the Son.

When the Breath is breathed into the Son, it will present the same characteristics it has in the Father. Entering into the Son, it will enter into "each cell," that is to say, it enters into the fullness of the Son's being and becomes co-extensive with it. It will become "the Spirit of his Son" (Gal 4:6). Co-extensive with the Son's being, it is part of his act of subsistence, as received by the Father. This means that, in the same way as the expiration of the Spirit is part of the act of subsistence of the Father, likewise the communication of being by the Father to the Son constitutes the Son as such. It is "life-giving" in the sense that the Father shares what makes him subsist and what is co-extensive with his being. In other words, the inspiration of

---

54. See Morales, *Dieu en personnes*, 168–69.
55. Mühlen, *Morgen wird Einheit sein*, 128 (already cited above, chap. 1, p. 17).

Breath (Ruah-Pneuma)

the Breath into the Son is part of the generation of the Son. Moreover, in an echo to what we have seen above, although the Breath passes from one hypostasis to another, although it can freely flow out of the Father, it only subsists in the Father and Son: it needs the substantiality of the other two. Indeed, while the Son is generated by the Father by being posited so to say "outside" of him and in front of him, the Breath is ex-pired by being in-spired. It is never fully "out" and "in front."

A first confirmation will come, as it should, from the economy. The Father's "breathing out and on" or "into" the Son is echoed by the Father sending the Spirit upon Christ and filling him at his baptism. It is also attested every time the Holy Spirit inspires Jesus. The Father communicates the fullness of his holiness, power, and wisdom to the incarnate Son because from all eternity he communicates the fullness of his Breath from the depths of his being. And there is a true communication. Indeed, with the Arian crisis the church fathers had more and more difficulty in accepting that the incarnate Word truly needed an outpouring or unction of the Holy Spirit.[56] Augustine expresses it quite forcefully, stressing that the event at the Jordan served only for the church to receive the Spirit.[57] While contemporary theology has less difficulty with this notion, it sometimes still finds the idea of the Son—rather than more specifically his humanity—receiving the Spirit to be a paradox. Balthasar feels the needs to coin the expression of "trinitarian inversion" to designate what seems to be an inversion of the intra-trinitarian *taxis*.[58] This is, however, much less of a stumbling block or a paradox if the intra-trinitarian procession of the Spirit is an eternal communication of the Breath of the Father to the Son. The baptism of Jesus in the *oikonomia* simply mirrors the operation of the *theologia*. Because it is eternally the "Spirit of the Son," in the history of salvation it becomes the "Spirit of Christ" (Rom 8:9), distinct from Christ, but difficult to distinguish, insubstantial in itself but supremely dynamic and life-giving.

---

56. See Ladaria, *Il Dio vivo e vero*, 80–82; Mühlen, *Una Mystica Persona*, 217–51.

57. "Nor, to be sure, was Christ only anointed with the Holy Spirit when the dove came down upon him at his baptism; . . . It would be the height of absurdity to believe that he only received the Holy Spirit when he was already thirty years old—that was the age at which he was baptized by John; no, we must believe that just as he came to that baptism without any sin, so he came to it not without the Holy Spirit" (Augustine, *Trinity*, XV, vi 46).

58. See Balthasar, *Theo-Drama II: The Dramatis personae: Man in God*, 183–91; *Theo-Logic III: The Spirit of Truth*, 181–84.

A second confirmation comes from the understanding of the notion of "procession" by Eastern trinitarian theology—in the same way as Western theology offered a confirmation of the fact that the Father breathes or "spirates" with the notion of *spiratio*. For the East, only the third person is said "to proceed" (*ekporeuèsthai*), while the Son is begotten. D. Staniloae underlines that the Greek word *ekporeuèsthai* contains the idea of a movement with a term:

> The word "procession" . . . does not mean a simple going forth of one person from another, as for the example in the case of being born; it means rather a setting forth from somewhere towards a definite goal, a departure from the one person in order to reach another (*ekporeuomai* = I set out on the way in order to arrive somewhere). When the Spirit proceeds from the Father he sets out towards the Son; the Son is the goal at which he stops.[59]

The Son is "born": he simply goes forth from the Father. The Spirit on the other hand goes forth towards a goal, towards the Son. This corroborates the fact that the Father does not only breathe, but that he breathes *out* and *into* the Son. I will come back to the fundamental difference between the generation of the Son and the procession of the Spirit in the third chapter, but it is noteworthy that the Breath metaphor allows for a clear perception of how different the "coming forth" of the second and third hypostasis are: one is posited "out" and "in front" of the Father, while the other is posited "on" and "in" the second. Let us also note that the intra-trinitarian "resting" of the Spirit on the Son may illumine the economy and find in it a further attestation. For E. Rogers it is another reason that explains why the Spirit in the economy rests on bodies: "The Spirit rests on material bodies in the economy because she rests on the Son in the Trinity."[60] As we know, it rests on the body of Christ at the annunciation and the baptism, on the body of Christ, which is the church, at Pentecost, and on all the dimensions of this body, namely, the baptized and the bread and the wine of the Eucharist. All this is grounded on the fact that the eternal Breath proceeds from the Father towards the Son, in whom it enters, and in whom and on whom it rests.

A third confirmation comes from the second narrative of the creation of humankind, in Gen 2:7: "The Lord God formed man (*Adam*) from the

---

59. Staniloae, *Theology and the Church*, 20–21. This is an ancient tradition among the Greek fathers, and is well documented in Clement, John Damascene, or Gregory Palamas, for instance (see Rogers, *After the Spirit*, 60–62).

60. Rogers, *After the Spirit*, 69.

Breath (Ruah-Pneuma)

dust of the ground, and breathed into his nostrils the breath of life; and the man (*Adam*) became a living being."[61] In reality it is more of a suggestion than a true confirmation, because it means resorting to the image of an image. Indeed, it can be interpreted not only as an image of the creation of man by God but also as a poetic echo of the generation of the eternal Archetype of humankind, the Son (to be incarnate), by the Father: in the same way as God models Adam and then breathes his own breath into him, the Father generates the Son, "models" him, and co-eternally breathes his Breath into him. The reader will choose if this is helpful or not.

The second divine hypostasis is not only called Son, however, but also *Logos*. In this case, too, the breath metaphor can be uncannily fitting. To speak, to utter a word, implies to breathe out at the same time. The breath carries the word outward and toward the addressee. Likewise, when the Father proffers his eternal Word, does he not breathe out his Breath in the same movement? This is in reality only another way to express the same relation between the Father, the Son, and the Spirit that has just been expounded, but it will complete it and corroborate it.

In the First Testament, the word of God and his breath act together, as two forces which proceed from the mouth of God: "By the word of the Lord the heavens were made, and all their host by the breath of his mouth" (Ps 33:6; see also 147:18). This is particularly true of creation, as we see in the first verses of Genesis, where both *Ruah* and *Dabar* are at work, in a form of creative speaking of God.[62] It also is significantly the case when the Word is presented as potent and even violent: "He shall strike the earth with the rod of his mouth, and with the breath of his lips he shall kill the wicked" (Isa 11:4).[63]

S. Bulgakov recalls the way some church fathers understand this intimate bond between God's Word and Breath in the Scripture in a more speculative trinitarian framework, by resorting precisely to the breath-metaphor:

> To characterize the hypostasis of the Holy Spirit the patristic literature likened the Second hypostasis to the lips and the Third to

---

61. To be precise, the breath breathed into Adam is not named *ruah* here, but *nshama*, the "breath of life." Originally *ruah* expresses the dynamic character of breath more than its life-giving potential, but the two words progressively become interchangeable (see Botterweck and Ringgren, *Theological Dictionary*, XIII, 378).

62. See Pannenberg, *Systematic Theology II*, 78.

63. Botterweck and Ringgren, *Theological Dictionary*, XIII, 376. For more on the inseparability of the Son and the Spirit, see Congar, *Word and the Spirit*. The title of the French original is *La Parole et le Souffle*, which literally means the Word and the Breath.

the breath out of the lips, or the Second to the word and the Third to the air moving as the word sounds. . . . This dyadic union is *necessary* for the very realization of the self-revelation: a word that is unspoken does not sound, although it preserves its conceptual content; a sound that does not contain a verbal idea is not a word but only a vibration of the air.[64]

The main fathers to have developed this image are Gregory of Nyssa and John Damascene. Gregory makes the relation between word and breath an argument in favor of the existence of a divine *Pneuma*: "It is not right that God's Word should be more defective than our own, which would be the case if, since our word is associated with breath (*pneuma*), we were to believe he lacked a Spirit. . . . God has a Spirit, which accompanies his Word and manifests his activity."[65] Commenting on Gregory, John Damascene writes: "When we speak a word, this movement of air produces the voice, which alone makes the meaning of the word accessible to others." In an analogous manner, in God too there is a breath, namely, the Spirit "which accompanies the word and reveals its efficacy."[66]

Now, Bulgakov and John Damascene understand this relation on an economic level, but for Gregory of Nyssa it expresses the eternal relation between the second and third hypostasis. I believe, with Gregory, that it is fitting to once again comprehend the immanent Trinity through its revelation in the economy: the Word and the Breath are inseparable in the economy because they come forth together from the mouth of the Father in the depths of the eternal Trinity. Contemporary theologians have evoked this idea. Y. Congar does so in a picturesque way: "There is no Word without a Breath: the Word would stay put in the speakers throat and reach no one. There is no Breath without a Word: the Breath would be without content and would communicate nothing."[67] J. Moltmann is clearly speaking about the immanent Trinity when he asserts: "The Father utters his eternal Word in the eternal breathing out of his Spirit."[68] T. Weinandy does so as well and plainly relates the economic and immanent Trinity:

---

64. Bulgakov, *Comforter*, 179.

65. Gregory of Nyssa, *Address on Religious Instruction*, §2, 273 (modified translation); see also Gaybba, *Spirit of Love*, 56–57; Dragas, "St. Athanasius," 51–54.

66. John Damascene, *Expositio Fidei orthodoxae*, I, 7 (PG 94, 806), quoted by Kasper, *God of Jesus Christ*, 216–17.

67. Congar, "Actualité de la pneumatologie," 25.

68. Moltmann, *Trinity and the Kingdom of God*, 169–70.

Breath (Ruah-Pneuma)

> God's creative and prophetic word is always spoken in the power of the Spirit.... The breath/spirit by which God speaks his creative word at the dawn of creation and his prophetic word throughout history is the same breath/Spirit by which he eternally breathes forth his Word/Son.[69]

Understanding the eternal spiration of the Spirit along the lines of the breathing out of a breath that accompanies the proffering of the Logos confirms quite a few traits already developed. The Breath is almost nothing in comparison with the Word: the Word is the message, it possesses contents and clarity, while the Breath has no contours, no meaning. Its meaning is the Word.[70] The Breath has no form without the Word it conveys: its action is uniquely referred to the Father's and to the Word's. Nonetheless, the Breath is what "carries" the *Logos* out and brings it to its term. If a word can be said to have substance, the Word is the more substantial of the two, but the Breath confers on it dynamism and efficacy. As we see, the Breath is not the Word, but it is difficult to distinguish from the Word itself. All in all, the expiration of the Spirit is in a way part of the act which produces the Logos. The act by which the third person proceeds is interior to the act by which the second is generated.

Let us proceed with the breath-metaphor. If we expand it fully, the second divine hypostasis also should breathe out. The Breath of the Father is the Son's Breath as well, and a life-giving breath needs to be expired as well as inspired. Is this conceivable in the inner-trinitarian relations?

A first answer is that the Son breathes back the Breath to the Father, in a form of response to the Father's life-giving communication of his Breath. The Son receives the Breath, but offers it back as well. An economic confirmation of this exhalation of the Son toward the Father is the moment in which Jesus gives his last breath on the cross, especially in the Gospel of Luke: "Jesus, crying with a loud voice, said: 'Father, into your hands I commend my Spirit.' Having said this, he breathed his last" (Luke 23:46). It would be coherent to understand the committing of the Spirit by the Son to the Father as grounded in the immanent Trinity. This would also offer a foundation for the faculty the risen Lord possesses to breathe on the disciples: "He breathed on them (*enephusèsen*) and said to them, 'Receive the

---

69. Weinandy, *Father's Spirit of Sonship*, 27.

70. "Christ, the incarnate Word, provides, so to speak, the *content* of this revelation; He is the Truth. On the other hand, the Third hypostasis is the Spirit of Truth, the guide to all truth (John 16:13), or, according to the old patristic comparison, the breath of God's lips" (Bulgakov, *Comforter*, 273–74).

Holy Spirit'" (John 20:22). In fact, *enephusèsen* means to breathe into rather than to breathe on. It is also the verb used in the Septuagint version of the creation of Adam: God inspires his life-giving breath into Adam (Gen 2:7). This means that in the same way as the Spirit very specifically proceeds from the Father to and in the Son—and not only "out of" the Father—it always blows out towards and in others: from the Son to the Father, in the immanent Trinity, from Christ to the Father, and to the disciples in the economy.

In the immanent Trinity, however, what meaning can this giving back of the Breath to the Father have? Some contemporary authors affirm that there is a form of "response" of the Son to the Father in the eternity of divine life. F.-X. Durrwell speaks of a "receptive causality" of the generation by the Son: while the Father is the "efficient cause," the Son is the "receptive cause."[71] Balthasar is more affirmative still, since the Son responds to his generation by the Father with a form of eternal gratitude: "The Son's answer to the gift of Godhead (of equal substance with the Father) can only be eternal thanksgiving (*eucharistia*) to the Father, the Source—a thanksgiving as selfless and unreserved as the Father's original self-surrender."[72] This finds an economic echo in the eucharistic offering of Christ to the Father and, more generally, in his praise addressed to the Father. In the Immanent Trinity in particular, "giving thanks" does not entail mere words: in the same way as the Father communicates the fullness of his being to the Son, the Son gives back his own being. This giving back by giving thanks is the way the Son fully cooperates in his begetting by letting himself be generated, and as such it is part of the generation itself.[73] Now if we understand this in the context of an inner-trinitarian Breath, the Son's "collaboration" is to breathe back. His response is to share back the Breath, which was communicated to him by the Father. The generation of the Son entails the gift of the Spirit, by which the Father communicates his life and being to generate another hypostasis, but it also implies the reception and cooperation of the Son, which happens through his gift of the "Spirit of [the] Son" (Gal 4:6) back to the Father: offering his own life and intimacy, he fully abandons himself to the Father's operation.

There is, however, a second dimension to this breathing back of the divine Breath, which makes it a mutually shared Breath. We know that the

71. Durrwell, *Jésus*, 45 n1.
72. Balthasar, *Theo-Drama IV: The Action*, 324.
73. See Balthasar, *Theo-Drama V: The Last Act*, 86–88.

Breath (Ruah-Pneuma)

Holy Spirit is often understood as a bond of communication and mutual giving between Father and Son (and between God and humanity). This is well established in contemporary pneumatology:

> [The Holy Spirit] is the most intimate in God, the unity of a liberty that transcends itself, and at the same time the most exterior to God; it is the liberty and the possibility, in God, to communicate himself in a new way, i.e., in a way outside of himself. The Spirit is thus the bond of unity, both inside of God and between God and creation.[74]

Now, taken as such, as I have explained, this idea has little direct economic foundation. However, the breath-metaphor can help us retrieve this *theologoumenon* and sheds light on it. The Father communicates the fullness of his interiority in breathing the Breath to the Son, and the Son, by breathing back into the Father, shares all he is in the most intimate way possible. Moreover, because it is a shared Breath the third hypostasis is both "inside" and "exterior" to the Father and the Son and through this it is their intimate communion. If ever there can be an *interior intimo meo* in God it is the Breath: the Breath of the Father is intimately interior to the Son, more so in a way than his own being, and the Breath of the Son is likewise interior and intimate to the Father. It is the "interbreath" at the heart of the Trinity.[75]

There is no straightforward economic example of a sharing of breaths between Christ and the Father. Nonetheless, when Jesus exults "in the Holy Spirit" (Luke 10:21), by *giving* thanks, he is so to speak *giving* back what the Father has given him. And it does express the joy of a deep intimacy between Father and Son: "All things have been handed over to me by my Father; and no one knows who the Son is except the Father, or who the Father is except the Son and anyone to whom the Son chooses to reveal him" (Luke 10:22).

Moreover, mystical and theological poetry—and we know that poetry in theology is not only legitimate but is in fact indispensable—does offer an

---

74. Kasper and Sauter, *Kirche-Ort des Geistes*, 34.

75. The expression is from Margerie, *Christian Trinity in History*, 26. Margerie also recalls that linking the Spirit's role as *nexus* between the Father and the Son with its breath-like quality is in fact a classical idea, since it is already expressed by some church fathers, such as Fulgentius of Ruspe: "The Breath (*Spiritus*) always belongs to the one who breathes and is therefore relation (*refertur*) to the Father and the Son" (*De Trinitate*, VI [PL 65, 400], cited by Margerie, *Christian Trinity in History*, 25 [the quote is actually from *De Trinitate*, II, PL 65, 499]).

echo of a mutual sharing of the Spirit that intimately binds Father and Son. Indeed, Bernard of Clairvaux presents the spiration of the Spirit as a kiss between the Father and the Son. Commenting on "Let him kiss me with the kisses of his mouth" (Song 1:2), Bernard explains that this indicates "truly the kiss that is common both to him who kisses and to him who is kissed."[76] Now in the case of God, where we see the Father "embracing" the Son, there is such a kiss: "That mutual knowledge and love between him who begets and him who is begotten—what can it comprise if not a kiss that is utterly sweet, but utterly a mystery as well?" This kiss is not the mouth of the Father or of the Son but what comes from it, so it literally is the Holy Spirit: "If, as is properly understood, the Father is he who kisses, the Son he who is kissed, then it cannot be wrong to see in the kiss the Holy Spirit, for he is the imperturbable peace of the Father and the Son, their unshakable bond, their undivided love, their indivisible unity." This kiss allows the Son to say that he and the Father are one, as "on equally sublime heights, mouth is joined to mouth." This beautiful idea receives a solid foundation in the context of the mutual inbreathing that is part of the breath-metaphor: the exchange of the Breath by the Father and the Son is a form of mouth-to-mouth "suscitation" (rather than resuscitation!), which can easily become a kiss. Indeed, Bernard himself briefly mentions the relation between the two images: "Thus the Father, when he kisses the Son, pours into him the plenitude of the mysteries of his divine being, breathing forth love's deep delight, as symbolized in the words of the psalm: 'Day to day pours forth speech' [Ps 19:2]." The Holy Spirit is the kiss of God, the kiss in God.[77]

In the same commentary, Bernard of Clairvaux extends the kiss of God to the relation between Christ and the disciples: when the risen Lord breathes onto them, he is in effect "kissing" them, "mouth to mouth." Of course, there is no analogous giving back of the Spirit by the disciples to Christ, though they do need to abandon themselves in the Spirit to him to let him act in them. However, the inner-trinitarian breathing out of the Spirit by the Son represents the eternal foundation of Christ's presence in us as *interior intimo meo*: because the Son breathes out the Spirit deeply into the Father, he can do so in us as well, and thus be present in the depths of

---

76. All the quotations are from Bernard of Clairvaux, *Commentary on the Song of Songs*, Sermon 8.

77. The procession of the Holy Spirit which makes it rest on the Son can likewise be conceived of as an eternal embrace of the Son by the Father: "The Spirit proceeding from the Father comes to rest in the Son who is begotten of the father, and, like an arch, unites the Father and the Son in one embrace" (Staniloae, *Theology and the Church*, 23).

Breath (Ruah-Pneuma)

our being. It is the greatest exteriorization of his deepest intimacy and thus the bond of our communion with him.[78]

As such, the third person is revealed as the one who can enter into others, unite them to Christ, and thus unite them one to another in the church. This is exactly the idea developed by Eastern theology when it compares the Spirit to oil or chrism, and it is well expressed by D. Staniloae in a passage partly quoted above:[79]

> The chrism symbolizes in the most adequate way possible the fluidity of the Holy Spirit extending into all the parts of the ecclesial organism. He spreads out like an oil, but more especially like a perfume. Whoever receives the Holy Spirit in the Church receives him in the form of a fluid or a fragrance, a breath of life spreading out from him into all the other members of the Church, binding him to them and thereby sustaining the whole organism and its sobornicity. This fluid provides no foundation for rigid structure; but as Spirit in the most precise sense of that word, that is, a wave diffusing outwards, it overcomes every separation and brings things formerly distinct into union among themselves.[80]

So far, I have only expounded one meaning of *Ruah* and *Pneuma*, namely that of breath. These notions do not only refer to breath, however, but also to wind and air. Does this dimension lend itself to the same metaphoric treatment as breath in the immanent Trinity? It seems to be more problematic still, since wind and air call for space even more than breath: air fills space and wind blows over the surface of the earth. I will argue that these aspects of *Ruah* and *Pneuma*, when related to the breath-metaphor itself, in fact confirm it and add precious insights in our understanding of the third divine hypostasis.

In the Scriptures, air and wind, when they are directly produced by God, are often referred to as his breath. The most ancient biblical authors seemed to have understood wind quite literally as God breathing out or

---

78. Aquinas also understands a kiss to be an exchange of breath, when he comments, "Greet one another with a holy kiss" (2 Cor 13:12): "Here it should be noted that a kiss is a sign of peace. For a man breathes through the mouth with which a kiss is given. Therefore, when men give one another kisses, it is a sign that they are uniting their spirit (*uniunt spiritum*) of peace" (Aquinas, "Commentary on 2 Corinthians," XIII, lectio 3, §542).

79. See above, chap. 1, p. 22.

80. Staniloae, *Theology and the Church*, 69.

blowing out, in the same way as they conceived thunder to be his voice.[81] It can be one interpretation of the Spirit of God hovering over the waters in Gen 1:2: God moves the waters and separates them by blowing on them.[82] As we have already seen there is often a parallelism between God uttering his Word and breathing out: "He sends out his word, and melts [the ice]; he makes his wind blow, and the waters flow" (Ps 147:18). In fact, although it is a minority position, some understand the Tetragrammaton, YHWH, as coming from the Semitic root meaning "to blow": the God of Israel would have been the Storm God of the Canaanite pantheon and his name could thus be translated as "he who blows out," "he who makes the wind."[83] God does not only breathe, he also blows out wind.

Now the first idea given by wind in contrast to breath simply said is that of force and movement. Whether the wind is a light breeze (see 1 Kgs 19:12) or a powerful hurricane that destroys houses, cedar trees, and ships (see Ezek 13:13; 27:26), whether it is moist and life-giving (see 1 Kgs 18:45) or dry and scorching hot, as in the desert (see Isa 14:21; 30:27–33), it acts and propels forward.[84] At an inner-trinitarian level, this is quite helpful for a true understanding of the third person, because it underlines the dynamic quality of the Breath the Father breathes into the Son. It is a Breath that propels the Word out of the mouth of the Father. If it gives divine life, if it truly participates in generating a divine hypostasis, it is certainly more than an intimate and discreet sliver of wind or a light "puff" of air. It is more powerful than the act by which God creates the universe *ex nihilo*. Infinitely more powerful. It is the full power of God. It may be insubstantial but it is far from feeble.

To fully set this into light it is useful to retrieve another forgotten dimension of the Holy Spirit, namely the term *dunamis*: force or power. We know that it was purposefully ignored by the church fathers, such as Gregory Nazianzen, because of its impersonal, cosmic dimension.[85] Moreover, it is used as an attribute of the common divine substance rather than

---

81. "The voice of the Lord is over the waters; the God of glory thunders. . . . The voice of the Lord breaks the cedars. . . . The voice of the Lord flashes forth flames of fire" (Ps 29:3, 5, 7). See Botterweck and Ringgren, *Theological Dictionary*, XIII, 382.

82. See Pannenberg, *Systematic Theology II*, 78.

83. Römer, *I lati oscuri di Dio*, 23 (Römer refers to authors such as J. Wellhausen and E. A. Knauf). Against this position, see Botterweck and Ringgren, *Theological Dictionary*, V, 510–16.

84. See Guillet, "Spirito," 1230.

85. See above, chap. 1, 22.

Breath (Ruah-Pneuma)

as a *proprium* of the Holy Spirit.[86] It can, however, be freed from any physically cosmic connotation or from designating the unity of substance if it is set into the context of the Breath of the Father and of the Son. The Breath is clearly divine and clearly not the divine substance. In this sense, *dunamis* is not really another *nomen proprium* of the third person to be put at the same level as *Ruah* and *Pneuma*, but rather an extension of these, which offers clarifications, but always needs their context to be well understood. It underlines how the divine Breath is a force, analogous to a powerful wind. This is quite manifest in the economy. When Jesus is led by the Spirit in Luke, we know it means he is pushed forward by an immeasurable force, as if he were propelled by the wind blown out onto him by the Father. All "acts of power" of Jesus are done in the same "power of the Spirit" given by God. When the Spirit is given to the disciples the same traits are obvious: it falls with the noise of a powerful wind upon the apostles (Acts 2:2), and it whisks Philip away from the eunuch on the road between Jerusalem and Gaza to the town of Azot (Acts 8:26, 40).

The other specific dimension of wind and air in contrast to breath is precisely the spatial and exterior one. As we have seen, the Hebrew *ruah* sometimes mean "airy" and thus "spacious."[87] Can this dimension also offer some light as to the application of the breath-metaphor to the immanent Trinity? When Pannenberg describes the Spirit as a force field, for instance, he does not conceive of this only in economic terms but truly in the immanent Trinity. One may understand that, in the same way as a powerful being like a storm god can breathe out a wind outside and around itself, as a form of atmosphere, likewise, in the eternal life of the Trinity, the Breath breathed out by the Father can be analogical to a wind breathed out and around the Son. It is not only a Breath breathed *into* the other divine person, but also the air breathed by the Father with the Son *out* and *around* them, which envelops and embraces them. Of course, we know that "space" in God can only be relational. As such, this space or field is created by the

---

86. "If anyone does not confess properly and truly in accord with the holy fathers that the Father, and the Son, and the Holy Spirit [are a] Trinity in unity, and a unity in Trinity, that is, one God in three subsistences, consubstantial and of equal glory, one and the same Godhead, nature, substance, virtue (*virtutem*), power (*potentiam/dunamin*), kingdom, authority, will, operation of the three, uncreated, without beginning, incomprehensible, immutable, creator and protector of all things, let him be condemned" (Council of Lateran [649], canon 1 [DH 501]). In fact, even *pneuma* is used as a divine attribute, when the Fourth Gospel states that "God is spirit (*pneuma ho Theos*)" (John 4:24), but this is a *hapax*.

87. See Botterweck and Ringgren, *Theological Dictionary*, XIII, 368.

fellowship of the Father and the Son: "The idea of divine life as a dynamic field sees the divine Spirit who unites the three persons as proceeding from the Father, received by the Son, and common to both, so that precisely in this way he is the force field of their fellowship that is distinct from them both."[88] We are not far either from Balthasar's image of an intra-trinitarian "distance" produced by the generation of the Son. The Spirit bridges this space and holds it open at the same time: "Proceeding from both, as their subsistent 'We', there breathes the 'Spirit' who is common to both (*atmet der gemeinsame Geist*): as the essence of love, he maintains the infinite difference between them, seals it and, since he is the one Spirit of them both, bridges it."[89] This metaphorically transforms distance into a space in which the divine persons can so to speak evolve and relate to each other.

Such inner-trinitarian "space" offers a confirmation to two aspects of the divine Breath I have expounded so far. On the one hand, it can be conceived of as the vital space, the *milieu* in which a being finds life. As such, it is a precious complement to the idea of life-giving breath. Indeed, as we know, when it comes to God, choosing only one aspect of the preposition *in* is insufficient: God is *in* us and we are *in* God. The Breath of life is in us and we are in the milieu or "sphere" of its life—literally its atmosphere. In the same way, metaphorically speaking, we can understand the Father giving life to the Son by breathing into him but also by breathing out a sphere of life into which he draws the Son. This finds an echo in the economy, if one follows Balthasar's interpretation of the resurrection of Christ by the Father as bringing him into a *milieu*, which is of all eternity his own: "The Spirit is not only the instrument of the Resurrection. He is also the milieu in which the Resurrection takes place: '*zöopoiestheis de pneumati*, he was made alive in the Spirit' (1 Pet 3:18)."[90] In the same way, the Breath of God will envelop us and be the living milieu of our own resurrection.

On the other hand, more deeply, since this space is relational, it is also the space of the Father and the Son's relation. The force field produced by the relation of the Father and the Son is where their fellowship unfolds. In terms of breath and wind, the air blown out by the Father and the Son is a form of divine "atmosphere" where their dialogue takes place. Indeed, relations imply unity and distance, unity in distance. Not only does the mutual expiration and inspiration provide an intimate bond, but also the Breath

---

88. Pannenberg, *Systematic Theology I*, 383.
89. Balthasar, *Theo-Drama IV: The Action*, 324.
90. Balthasar, *Mysterium Paschale*, 211.

Breath (Ruah-Pneuma)

is like a bubble of air produced by the first and second person, where they face each other and dialogue. Not only does the Breath support the Word and propel it as the Father proffers it, but it equally opens a space—it *is* the space—where the Word "resounds." It is the medium of communication between Father and Son.

These two dimensions correspond to some economic traits of the Spirit, and as such, take part in a faithful ascent from the economy to the eternal Trinity. In the economy those who are *en pneumati* are enveloped and embraced by the *Pneuma*: the Spirit is in the pray-er, but the pray-er is also plunged in the Spirit. This, in turn, plunges the pray-er in the divine life and in the process of divinization, and it introduces him or her into the divine relations. As such, the Spirit is the medium of communication with the Father and the Son. Basil compares the third hypostasis to the light in which we see but that is in itself almost imperceptible:

> If we say that worship offered *in* the Son (the Truth) is worship offered in the Father's Image, we can say the same about worship offered *in* the Spirit since the Spirit in Himself reveals the divinity of the Lord. . . . If you remain outside the Spirit, you cannot worship at all, and if you are *in* Him you cannot separate Him from God. Light cannot be separated from what it makes visible, and it is impossible for you to recognize Christ, the Image of the invisible God, unless the Spirit enlightens you. Once you see the Image, you cannot ignore the light; you see the Light and the Image simultaneously.[91]

In a way, the divine Breath is both the atmosphere and the light in which Father and Son relate to each other and in which we relate to them. This explains yet in another way why it is more difficult to apprehend as a substantial and personal reality than the two other hypostases: transparency is its mark and what enables it to play its role.

There still are two final steps to take to retrieve the main traits of the Holy Spirit according to the economy: the Spirit as the "gift of God" (Acts 8:20; 11:17), and the Spirit's close relation to emotions and passions. In both cases, I will argue that we will in fact also be able to recover the classical Latin names of the Spirit, *Donum* and *Amor*, whilst giving them a

---

91. Basil the Great, *On the Holy Spirit*, XXVI, §64, 97 (PG 32, 185 BC). This idea will be repeated by contemporary theologians: "The Holy Spirit is, as it where, the transparent medium in and through which the Logos is seen" (Bulgakov, *Comforter*, 274); "[Der Geist] beleuchtet; aber wer kann in sein eigenes Licht schauen?" (Balthasar, *Skizzen zur Theologie III*, 9).

more solid economic and immanent foundation in the framework of the breath-metaphor.

As exhaled and inspired into the Son by the Father, to be made his by the Son, the divine Breath is a gift of the Father to the Son. As breathed back into the Father by the Son, it is a gift from the Son to the Father. It is a precious gift, since it comes from the intimate depths of each hypostasis, and is related to their life and existence, as part of their act of subsistence. It is a true gift, i.e., truly given, insofar as the Breath inspired by the Father to the Son fully becomes the Son's Breath, the "Spirit of his Son" (Gal 4:6). In a way it is a gift in a more perfect sense than any worldly gift because, although it fully becomes the Son's, it is still continuously *given*, in an eternal and endless act of spiration. It thus conserves, in a permanent way, the dimension of "givenness" and the relation between the receiver and the giver—without ever becoming any less the Son's.

Conceiving the Spirit as gift according to the framework of the exchange of breaths also solves the main difficulty of the *nomen proprium* "Gift" as it is understood in classical Western theology. We have seen already how Aquinas feels the need to relate gift to love. Indeed, it is well attested in the economy, but difficult to account for in the immanent Trinity. Thomas puts the problem in the following terms in an objection: "'Gift' implies a relation to creatures, and so it seems to be predicated of God from a given point in time. But the names of the persons, e.g., 'Father' and 'Son', are predicated of God from eternity. Therefore, 'Gift' is not the name of a person." His answer is that the Holy Spirit is called Gift because it is "givable" in the economy, not because it is indeed given in the eternal life of God: "Something is called a 'gift' not from the fact that it is actually given, but rather insofar as it has an aptness for being possibly given. Hence, a divine person is called a Gift from eternity, even if He is given from a certain point in time."[92] However, if the third person is the Breath eternally inspired by Father and Son one into and around another, then it is clearly the gift of God (to God) from all eternity, and its economic manifestation as a gift to the believers is grounded.

Do the names *Ruah* and *Pneuma* also help understand the strong bond of the third divine person to emotions and passion in the economy? Maybe not as clearly as for its dimension of gift and givenness, but they do offer a few indications. The Breath of the Father and of the Son wells up and out from the depths of their being and of their heart (*kardia*), a

---

92. Aquinas, ST, I, q.38, a.1, obj4 & ad4.

Breath (Ruah-Pneuma)

region associated with emotions in a human person. Its communication is the communication of their innermost intimacy, analogous to the communication of emotions. In the economy, this inner quality of the Breath means that it reaches the innermost being and heart of the believer, where it touches the emotions and brings forth new ones. The Breath is likewise the capacity for the Father and the Son to be outside of themselves—"*ausser-sich*"—and "in-another." This corresponds to the ecstatic and erotic dimension of passions, and is echoed in the economy by the ecstatic, charismatic, and mystical phenomena, which sometimes accompany life in the Spirit. These are grounded in the both intimate and exterior aspects of the Breath in the Immanent Trinity. Another characteristic of the eternal Breath of the Father is its intense power and dynamism, its capacity to propel and push forward—and to do so as an inner gift and *dunamis*. We know that in the First Testament the word *Ruah* sometimes refers to a strong passion, whether love or anger. In the economy the inner push of the Spirit can and should translate into passions that are the believers' way of receiving and appropriating personally the Breath of God, which drives them forward. It "quickens the soul" and may sometimes even seem to be a superior force that one can only surrender to. This is why Ignatian spirituality is right to refer to emotions and "inner motions" as the primary *locus* to discern the Holy Spirit's action.

Precisely speaking, the third hypostasis is not identical to the emotions or passions of the Father and the Son—I do not wish here to enter into a debate about the existence and nature of God's emotions and passions, and it is not possible to ascribe emotions in whatever meaning to one divine person only. Nonetheless, the Breath communicates them and, so to say, "supports" and strengthens them. And it does the same in the economy. Rather than a passion itself, the Breath is a powerful wind, burning with *dunamis*, which fans the flames of emotions. To use the other dimension of the breath-metaphor, that of the atmosphere, the Breath is the atmosphere in which the flames burn, the oxygen without which there is no fire—fire and flames being also an image of the Spirit in the economy (Matt 3:11; Acts 2:3).

Can this special relation to emotions allow us to retrieve the classical Latin name of the Holy Spirit as Love as well? Love and emotions or passions are not so distant. The difficulty, however, is not only the lack of economic traces of the Spirit as love, but also the fact that all three persons love,[93] because love is one of the main attributes of God, if not the main one. Now, as with emotions and passions in general, the eternal Breath is not identical to love, but it does intimately communicate the Father and the Son's love to each other. By contributing to the communication of their being to each other and by so to speak driving them towards each other, it "fans the flames" of their love. This explains why, likewise, in the economy, it does not have a special relation to love in itself: rather, it inspires love, in the same way as it inspires wisdom or strength. Its special relation is not to love, but to the act by which God inspires it. If it seems to be the divine person with the most affinity to love this is because in effect it is the one that *gives* love: "God's love has been poured into our hearts through the Holy Spirit" (Rom 5:5). Moreover, it may be possible to relate the third divine hypostasis more closely to one dimension of love, namely desire, as we have seen S. Coakley do for the economy. Indeed, desire is love according to the aspect by which it moves us forward and toward the loved one. J.-Cl. Sagne considers the Holy Spirit to be inner-trinitarian love under the specific form of desire:

> The revelation of the Gospel teaches us about the existence in God of a pure exchange of love in the mysterious communion of the three persons. The Spirit is the intimate life of God, a life that is pure gift—in other words, love. The Spirit is the inner dynamism of love, which we call desire. The Spirit is in God the desire of God, pure presence turned towards the presence of the other.[94]

The Holy Spirit is the burning, passionate Breath of the Father and the Son, which moves them one towards the other and binds them together. It is the burning Breath that inspires love in the believers, but also a passionate desire of God, with a great release of feelings. In the end, we have not quite retrieved the name of the Spirit as Love, but the breath-metaphor has helped to define in a much more precise way its special relation to the gift of love and even more so with love in the form of desire.

One last comment can be made about the relation between conceiving the third person as a divine Breath and the classical themes of Gift and Love. All three of these names have in common that the third person comes

---

93. See Aquinas, ST, I, q.37, a.1.

94. Sagne, "L'Esprit-Saint ou le désir de Dieu," 93. S. Coakley on the other hand considers desire to characterize God, and not specifically the Spirit. Nonetheless, because the Spirit inspires us, in the economy "the Spirit is the vibrant point of contact and entry into the flow of this divine desire" (Coakley, *God, Sexuality, and the Self*, 24).

Breath (Ruah-Pneuma)

across as less "personal" and less "substantial" than the Father and the Son: rather than the donator or receiver of a gift it is the object which is given. It is a bond or a *nexus*, a common will or feeling. All in all, the notion that the Holy Spirit is the divine Breath flows well with a great part of the tradition and truly illumines the fluid and impersonal dimensions of the third hypostasis as they are expressed in the economy.

Taxis, Filioque, Consubstantiality (Objections, Purifications, Corroborations)

The breath-metaphor has been expounded in detail, and has shown, I hope, its faithfulness to the revelation of the Holy Spirit in the economy and its fruitfulness in offering a better comprehension of the third person in the inner life of the Trinity. It has shown that we do have the word(s) to name and designate the third person, because the Scriptures offer *Ruah* and *Pneuma*. It now becomes necessary to face the difficulties that arise with it. A metaphor, especially when used so extensively as I have done so far, calls for careful and thorough purification. It needs to be submitted to a precise act of negative theology or, as S. Coakley would say, an "'apophatic' corrective reminder."[95] The capacity for this metaphor to withstand such a correction will be a further test of its validity—as it was for the metaphors of fatherhood and sonship during the first centuries. The first, most obvious, form of purification is from time, space, and matter—as we have seen at the beginning of this chapter in the case of fatherhood and sonship.[96] Like the generation of the Son, the spiration of the Spirit is eternal: the exhalation of the divine Breath by the Father is co-eternal with the generation of the Son and even with the existence of the Father himself. The Father does not pre-exist his own Breath. In the same way, the expiration and inspiration of the Spirit cannot mean an *ad extra* procession. As we have seen already, the spatial dimension—the Breath "in the depth" of the two other persons, the Breath breathed "out," "towards," "into," "back to" the other, as well as the "space" or "atmosphere" it "opens"—is in fact relational. It really means that the Breath is produced by, is shared and communicated with, and also that it fosters the relation between Father and Son. All this is quite obvious. There are, however, more thorny issues, that are specific to the breath-metaphor, namely whether the inner-trinitarian *taxis* is respected,

95. Coakley, *God, Sexuality, and the Self,* 197.
96. See Aquinas, ST, I, q.27, a.1.

whether the model is not too unilaterally Latin with regards to the *Filioque*, and whether such a conception of the Spirit is coherent with the fact that it is divine hypostasis, a mode of subsistence of God.

The first problem relates to the order or *taxis* of the persons. Because the Father breathes the Spirit into the Son, it seems as though the Spirit predates the Son and becomes, with the Father, co-generator of the Son. One can also wonder if the Breath of life of the Father does not give life to him as well: the Spirit would become to a certain extent "producer" of the Father. A living creature will in fact breathe in before breathing out, and thus receive its life from outside.

One of the possible solutions would be to renounce to the traditional concept of *taxis*. A few recent trinitarian theologies have put it into question in the name of the equality of the persons and the refusal of any hint of subordinationism, as well as of a trinitarian life built more on the relations than on the processions. They refuse to conceive of a quasi-linear order of processions from the Father towards the Son and the Spirit, because it entails the risk of considering that the Father exists as such "before" and thus "without" the Son, and likewise the Son in regards to the Spirit. For Pannenberg, for instance, the Trinity is a process of auto-differentiation of God, where each person is itself only through the reciprocal auto-distinction from the other two.[97] G. Greshake is also a staunch advocate of this type of view: the Trinity is an interpersonal event of love (*interpersonales Liebesgeschehen*), that should not be understood in terms of the constitution of the persons, but of "mutual play of love."[98] The Father depends as much on the Son and the Spirit as they do on him, and the Son depends on the Spirit as much as the Spirit on him. Some Eastern theologians have also worked in that direction. Evdokimov, for instance, requests that each divine hypostasis be contemplated in its relation to the two others, so that the hypostatic relation always be triune. He thus accepts the *Filioque* since the Spirit relates hypostatically both to the Father and to the Son, but demands that it be completed by a symmetrical *Spirituque*: the Son cannot be without its relation to the Spirit.[99]

The idea of a mutual dependency fits nicely with the use of the breath-metaphor and conceiving of the third divine hypostasis as Breath does

---

97. See Pannenberg, *Systematic Theology I*, 308–19.

98. See Greshake, *Der dreieine Gott*, 188, 205.

99. See Evdokimov, *L'Esprit Saint dans la tradition orthodoxe*, 68–78. See also Bobrinskoy, *Le mystère de la Trinité*, 77–79.

Breath (Ruah-Pneuma)

argue in favor of a less rigid idea of the *taxis*. However, resisting the notion of procession and reducing divine life to relations contradicts what seems to me to be one of the keys of the development of trinitarian understanding in the first centuries.[100] Moreover, it lessens the fecundity of divine life. Of course, the analogy of human relations should always be used with great caution to comprehend the Trinity, but love cannot be reduced to looking starry-eyed at each other: it also calls for giving and receiving (communicating being, in the case of divine giving) and calls for fruitfulness. Besides, although love asks for equality and creates it, relationships are always asymmetrical: one has the initiative, the other responds. This does not impair on equality: on the contrary, asymmetry is the expression of the necessary and healthy difference and personal identity of each partner. As for the notion of inner-trinitarian *taxis*, it is strongly related to the processions, and seems to me to be too well attested in the tradition to be easily discarded.[101] It is also too well grounded in the economy as revealed by the Scriptures: the Father is the one from whom all comes and towards whom all is orientated (see 1 Cor 8:6); he is the one who sends the Son and not vice versa. The *lex orandi* confirms this, as the public prayer of the church is addressed to the Father. In the same way, the Father and sometimes the Son send the Spirit, but the Spirit sends neither.[102]

We thus need to hold together dependency and *taxis*. Let us start with the second question: does the divine Breath give life to the Father? The Father seems to breathe in a pre-existing air before expiring it, and thus receives life from a pre-existing Spirit. However, the metaphor needs to be purified from what is too crudely chronological and anthropomorphic. As first person, as ingenerate, and as *fons totius divinitatis*, the Father does not start by "inspiring" but by expiring. The Father does not breathe in a form of life-giving air, but he breathes out the Breath as a dimension of his existence. In fact, this is not totally unlike the human experience evoked in the metaphor: we do receive life from the air we breathe, but even more so, we are able to breathe because we are alive. A human being's breath is not an active agent because the person is doing the breathing and the breath does not precede him or her. More technically speaking, "ontologizing" the

---

100. See Tertullian, *Adversus Praxeam*, VIII (PL 2, 163 B–164 A); Athanasius, *Oriationes Adversus Arianos*, III, 24 (PG 26, 373); Basil the Great, *On the Holy Spirit*, XVI, §37, 60–61.

101. See the same references from Tertullian, Athanasius, and Basil as in the previous footnote.

102. For more on this point see Ladaria, *La Trinità*, 215–21.

metaphor and setting it in relational terms (in the metaphysical sense), as the church fathers have done with the images of fatherhood and of sonship, will help pick out what can or cannot be transposed in the life of the eternal Trinity. The Father subsists as Father by an active act of being, which comprises two communications of being that produce two other hypostases. For the Father, to subsist as Father means to generate a Son *and* to spirate or breathe out a Breath. The divine hypostasis of the Father *is* this double communication of being, it is *by* communicating being, it *is* generation and spiration. So the divine Breath does not give life to the Father: rather, the Father *is* by breathing out the Breath (and begetting the Son).

In the same way, the Father does not generate the Son through the Spirit or by means of it—he does not inspire a preexistent Breath into the Son, as God breathed his life-giving breath into Adam. Neither does he proffer his Word with the support of a Breath that predates the Word. The Father does not generate the Son by the *Breath* itself, but he does generate his Son by *breathing* out the Breath: "The Father generates the Son *by spirating the Spirit*; . . . the Father spirates the Spirit *on the Son he is generating*."[103] The spiration of the Spirit by the Father, coeternal with the act of generating the Son, can be thought of as contributing to the generation and as an intrinsic part of it. The Breath itself does not "quicken" the Son, but the breathing out of the Breath by the Father "completes" the generation of the Son.[104] The Breath itself does not support the proffering of the *Logos*, but expiring is part of proffering. Indeed, the two processions contribute to one another and are part of each other. The generation of the Son can also be conceived of as being part of the breathing out of the Spirit, insofar as it offers an end, a *terminus* for the Breath to rest on. The uttering of the Logos contributes to the breathing of the Breath because it gives the Breath a "more substantial" hypostasis to rest upon, to be so to speak attached to.[105]

---

103. Morales, *Dieu en personnes*, 124. See also: "[The Spirit] proceeds in the begetting of the Son. . . . He must therefore be this begetting." Durrwell, *Holy Spirit of God*, 140–41.

104. In a slightly different perspective, Weinandy has developed a similar idea. Noting that in the economy, the Son is himself "in the Spirit"—at his baptism, for instance (Weinandy, *Father's Spirit of Sonship*, 28), Weinandy concludes that the Son is begotten by the Father in the Spirit in the eternal life of the Trinity: "The Son is begotten by the Father in the Spirit and thus the Spirit simultaneously proceeds from the Father as the one in whom the Son is begotten" (17). It is in the act of generating the Son that the Spirit is spirated, and the Son is begotten in the act by which the Spirit is spirated: "The Father spirates the Spirit in the same act by which he begets the Son, for the Spirit proceeds from the Father as fatherly Love in whom or by who the Son is begotten" (69).

105. As Rush has it, the Son is generated *"ex Patre cum Spiritu"* and the Holy Spirit proceeds *ex Patre cum Filio (Eyes of Faith*, 34).

Breath (Ruah-Pneuma)

So far, however, I have shown why the Breath of the Father does not predate the Son, but not why the Son still is the second person and the Sprit the third, as defined by the *taxis*. This becomes clear only when we look at the Son breathing back the Breath to the Father. We know that this breathing back is part of the generation of the Son—another aspect of the fact that the spiration of the third person is part of the generation of the second.[106] As is the case with the Father, it is not the Breath as a divine person who gives life to the Son, but the act of breathing back or co-spiring is part of the Son's hypostatical act of subsistence. The spiration is implied, not the person itself. This is quite clearly expressed by the 1995 Document of the Pontifical Council for the Promotion of Christian Unity on the procession of the Holy Spirit:

> The Father only generates the Son by breathing (*proballein* in Greek) through him the Holy Spirit and the Son is only begotten by the Father insofar as the spiration (*probolè* in Greek) passes through him. The Father is Father of the One Son only by being for him and through him the origin of the Holy Spirit.[107]

In the same way, the reception of the Breath of the Son by the Father is part of the Father's being, not because the Breath gives the Father something he does not have, but because this reception is part of the spiration of the Breath and that this spiration is part of the act of being of the Father. Moreover, saying that the Father gives the Breath to the Son and vice versa is not completely exact: one should rather say the Father breathes into the Son, the Son breathes back into the Father, and this produces the Breath. This means that the Son's breathing back is also part of the procession of the Spirit. For the Spirit, to proceed is to be breathed by both the Father and the Son, to be breathed into the Son by the Father, and to be breathed back by the Son into the Father. Only the whole movement constitutes the Breath in its full dimension of a divine hypostasis as such, sharing the divine substance on equal terms with the two others.

In this sense, there is a true reciprocal dependency of the Son and the Spirit—and of both to the Father, but also of the Father to them. Nonetheless, the *taxis* is quite clear as well: the Father is the first hypostasis because he generates the Son and is the first to breathe into him. The Son is the

---

106. "The Son, being begotten in the Spirit, simultaneously loves the Father in the same Spirit by which he himself is begotten (is Loved)." Weinandy, *Father's Spirit of Sonship*, 17.

107. Pontifical Council, *Greek and Latin Traditions*, 15.

second, since he receives the divine essence from the Father and receives "life" through being breathed into by the Father and breathing back to the Father. The Breath is third because it is breathed by the two others and is not itself the origin of a hypostasis. I believe this offers a better balance than rejecting the order of processions or instituting a *Spirituque* on par with the *Filioque*.

In fact, solving the difficulty posed by the breath-metaphor in regards to holding together *taxis* and dependency offers the possibility to shed light on another classical difficulty in trinitarian theology: why is the Father not Father without the Holy Spirit? Why is the Son not Son without the Spirit?[108] That the Father is not Father without the Son, and the Son not Son without the Father, is fairly obvious, because of the fatherhood-sonship metaphor. The generation of the Son and the relations of fatherhood and sonship constitute the two hypostases as such. However, precisely because the hypostases are constituted by the processions and relations, the Father and the Son are what they are also through the breathing of the Breath and their relation to it. Aquinas underlines, without further clarification, that the Father is himself through two relations: "There is a person in God who is related to two persons, namely the Father, who is related to the person of the Son and to the person of the Holy Spirit. . . . We [thus] need to conceive of two relations in the Father."[109] Since the divine person is the relation, the Father *is* his relation to the Son but also to the Spirit. However, if the breathing out of the divine Breath is part of act of subsistence of the Father and is part of his generation of the Son; if the breathing back by the Son is likewise part of his generation and his act of subsistence, then the procession of the Spirit and the Spirit itself are constitutive of the Father's fatherhood and the Son's sonship.[110] Conceiving the third person as Breath offers a key to explaining why each person is constituted by two relations.

---

108. See Ladaria, *La Trinità*, 215–21.

109. Aquinas, ST, I, q.32 a.2, resp.

110. For Weinandy also, the spiration of the Spirit contributes to the fatherhood of the Father and the sonship of the Son; that is, to their being as persons: "The Spirit, springing forth within the Father as his love in or by which the Son is begotten, conforms the Son to be the Son for the Father. Putting it more strongly, hopefully not too strongly, it is by the Spirit that the Father substantiates or 'persons' himself as Father because it is by the Spirit that he begets the Son. In so doing the Father substantiates or 'persons', by the same Spirit, the Son and the Son personally re-acts, and is 'personed' in the Spirit of sonship, as Son of the Father" (Weinandy, *Father's Spirit of Sonship*, 73; see also 17).

Breath (Ruah-Pneuma)

Another possible objection to the breath-metaphor is that it brings about an exaggeratedly Latin conception of the relation between Son and Holy Spirit, which sets the *Filioque* in stone. Indeed, the Son breathes back the Breath into the Father; he clearly takes part in the spiration of the Breath, since the third hypostasis is produced as such once the full expiration-inspiration cycle is complete.

Now I believe it makes sense to keep the idea of the Son making the Breath his own, as "Spirit of his Son" (Gal 4:6), by breathing it back. This is the eternal condition of possibility for the Breath to be the "Spirit of Christ" (Rom 8:9) in the economy and for Christ to participate in sending the Paraclete to the disciples (John 15:26; 16:7). However, the question needs to be addressed at the level of the immanent Trinity. From this point of view, one should not forget that the divine Breath is firstly breathed by the Father, who breathes it into the Son. The Son cannot breathe it without receiving it. He makes it his own as a gift he receives—and we have seen that this gift is given continuously by the Father in the eternal life of the Trinity. This is why the giving back of the Breath by the Son is only a response, made possible by the first breathing, the Father's. It is the echo or boomerang effect of the breathing into him by the Father as a moment of his generation. In fact, even if the Son himself is responding, since this response is part of his sonship, it is also still part of the *Father's act*, the act of generating the Son, or at least a prolongation of it. It is a prolongation of the Father's act of breathing out the Spirit, a participation of the Son in the Father's breathing out of the Breath. In this sense the ultimate origin, the origin in the full sense of the word, is the Father. In a way, Father and Son are "one principle" of the Holy Spirit, as defined by the Second Council of Lyon and the Council of Florence, precisely to alleviate the fears expressed by the Greeks of a double spiration: if the Holy Spirit proceeds from both Father and Son, it does so "not by two spirations," but "by a single and unique spiration."[111]

What seems to be a mutual and reciprocal inspiring of the divine Breath by the Father and the Son contains in fact a strong asymmetry: it is reciprocal but not symmetrical.[112] This asymmetry is grounded on the purification of the anthropomorphic dimension of the metaphor: because the Father does not start by inspiring the Breath from "elsewhere" he is the

---

111. Council of Lyon II, DH 850; see also Council of Florence, Decree for the Jacobites (DH 1331).

112. On the importance of the notion of asymmetry in trinitarian theology, see Lieggi, *La sintassi trinitaria*, especially 47–55, 73–106.

full and ultimate origin of the Spirit, its origin without origin. He does not share with the Son an air he has so to speak "recycled" through his breathing it, but an air that comes from him and only from him. The Son does not breath back an air he has received both from the Father and from "outside," but a Breath he has received from the Father and only from him. In a way, the Son is not truly "co-spirating," as the Latin tradition would have it: he is "re-spiring." In Latin or romance languages to "respire" is the word used for breathing (*respirer, respirare, respirar*): it evokes the idea that the air we breathe out comes from elsewhere. The Son re-spires, while the Father expires but does not re-spire.

Not only does the breath-metaphor maintain a clear priority of the Father in the procession of the Spirit, but I believe it equally addresses another aspect of the fundamental Orthodox uneasiness to the *Filioque*: the risk of not taking into account the hypostatic difference between the persons.[113] It is not because the Son participates in breathing the Breath that his role and position is not fundamentally different from the Father's: he is not a "second Father."[114] Re-spiration is profoundly different from ex-piration. Moreover, the Spirit is not Spirit because it proceeds also from the Son but simply because it is breathed-out. Being breathed-out makes it proceed as Spirit, in the same way as being generated makes the Son proceed as Son.

Though these clarifications may not be sufficient from an Orthodox point of view, they at least conform to the distinction expressed in the document of the Pontifical Council for Promoting Christian Unity on the procession of the Holy Spirit that underlines the difference between the Greek *ekporeuèsthai*, which means to "proceed from the ultimate origin" and the Latin *processio*, which is wider, and simply means to "come from."[115] As such, they are also in line with the Greek fathers who support a procession of the Spirit *from* the Father *through* the Son, as is famously the case for Maximus the Confessor, for instance: "By nature the Holy Spirit in his being takes substantially his origin (*ekporeuomenon*) from the Father through the Son who is begotten."[116]

---

113. See Meyendorff, *Byzantine Theology*, 89–94. Of course, the problem with the *Filioque* is not only theological but also canonical, since it is a unilateral insertion of a change in the Symbol of Faith by the Western Church. However, that is another question.

114. "If the Spirit is possessed in common, in an identical fullness, *he is nevertheless possessed differently*. For the Father begets the Spirit, while the Son is begotten in the Spirit." Durrwell, *Holy Spirit of God*, 142.

115. See Pontifical Council, *Greek and Latin Traditions*, 6.

116. Maximus the Confessor, *Quaestiones ad Thalassium*, 63 (PG 90, 672 C). See also

Breath (Ruah-Pneuma)

A last objection to the breath-metaphor is that it is difficult to understand the Breath as a divine person consubstantial to the Father and the Son. Richard of Saint-Victor recalls the image of breath used by the Scriptures for the Holy Spirit and uses the terms *flamen* or *spiramen* that mean breath, but he stops short of resorting to the metaphor, because he points out that breath is not consubstantial to the human person breathing it.[117] A son shares in the same way the human substance as a father, while breath, though springing forth from a human being, does not share the human nature with the breather. In the same way, it is simple to conceive of Father and Son as divine hypostases or persons, because the metaphor of fatherhood and sonship draws on resources of the human world. It is more difficult to think of the Breath as an individual reality; one, moreover, which shares the divine intelligence and will with the first and second persons. Is the Breath truly an individual "mode of subsistence" of God, on par with the Father and the Son?

In fact, this is precisely my point: the third hypostasis is profoundly different from the other two, it is "insubstantial" and impersonal. The breath-metaphor addresses exactly these dimensions of the Holy Spirit in the economy and tries to provide an inner-trinitarian explanation that is coherent with them. Naturally, the trinitarian dogma asserts that the Spirit is consubstantial with the Father and the Son and that it is a person as they are persons. There are two options here. One can either consider this to be the ultimate limit of the breath-metaphor, the point where it cracks at the edge. A breath can simply not be a (con)substantial individuality. The metaphor has given us food for thought but does not live up to the demands of the doctrine of the Trinity. This would already have a heuristic value: we should never forget that a metaphor is a metaphor and that it can never be directly descriptive. The other option, however, is to take yet another step of negative theology. Considering the Holy Spirit as unsubstantial and impersonal as we have done so far truly illumines many material and anthropomorphic conceptions of substantiality and personhood. Rather than saying that the Breath is unsubstantial and impersonal, could it not be substantial and personal, but in a very different way from the Father and the Son? Indeed, the classical idea of the Spirit as bond of love between

John Damascene: "I say that God is always Father since he has always his Word coming from himself, and through his Word, having his Spirit issuing from him (*ekporeuomenon*)" (*Dialogus contra Manichaeos*, 5 (PG 94, 1512 B; see also 848–49 A).

117. See Richard of Saint-Victor, *Trinity*, VI, §9, 327. We have already seen Basil pose the same difficulty (*De Spiritu Sancto*, XVIII, 46; see above, p. 40).

the Father and the Son hints in this direction: divine love is so perfect, goes the traditional justification, that it is hypostatical. However, this calls for more thought on what "hypostatical" means for the third person. If the fluid and so to speak anonymous Breath of God is a consubstantial person of the Trinity, this implies that we need to elaborate in a new way what it means to be a divine person, in relation to the unique divine substance. Not only does the breath-metaphor remain valid, but also it opens the way for a deeper and more precise reflection on divine personhood and being.

* * *

I have argued that the most adequate, or least inadequate, understanding of the Holy Spirit is to consider it as the Breath of God, eternally breathed by the Father to and into the Son and from the Son back to the Father, in the depths of the life of the Trinity. One may always ask: why is there such a Breath in God? The same can be asked about the Father and the Son. We simply have the testimony of the Scriptures. *A posteriori* it is possible to analyze the divine names as expressions of love, for example: God gives all he is in the Father and receives all he is in the Son; likewise, God communicates even his intimacy in the Breath, by whom the Father and the Son share each other and belong to each other. In this way "God is love" (1 John 4:8, 16). There is no necessity in these arguments, however, just great fittingness. Nonetheless, I believe that in the end the choice of the breath-metaphor has been vindicated from an explanatory point of view. It simply expounds the main name given by the Scriptures to the *Ruah-Pneuma*, in a way, I hope, that has some analogy to the process by which Father and Son became theological notions. It also has much more economic foundation than any other image or notion, since it offers an insight into the third divine person at an inner-trinitarian level that is faithful to its specific traits in the economy—insubstantiality, anonymity, fluidity, presence, and action in the depth of another, relation to emotions—and, in return, helps explain them. It is implausible for all this not to have a foundation in the immanent Trinity. As such, the breath-metaphor truly is "reality depictive" and offers knowledge on the third divine hypostasis. Naturally, utilizing such a metaphor gives rise to valid objections, but these have been confronted and this confrontation has in fact helped purify the whole process. Indeed, the metaphor has proven resilient and has even offered a balance between mutual dependency and *taxis*. It has helped explain how Father and Son are

Breath (Ruah-Pneuma)

themselves only in relation to the Holy Spirit. So far, the breath-metaphor has been confirmed as through fire. The questions still open, concerning the modality of the Breath's consubstantiality and personhood, are no longer strictly pneumatological, but ask for a trinitarian solution—and will bring to light the full trinitarian implications of the metaphor. This will be the task of the third chapter.

3

The Analogical Trinity

How can something as insubstantial as a breath be one of the three hypostases of the tri-une God—especially when one considers that, when it entered into trinitarian reflection, the word *hupostasis* was synonymous with *ousia*, substance? In Latin terms, how can the Breath of God be a divine *persona*? What kind of person can act in and through another, and become so intimate that it is hardly possible to distinguish it from another? Is it not strange that I have consistently called the Breath "it," rather than he or she, while referring to it as the third divine person? The difficulty comes from two sides: "person" is a name the Holy Spirit has in common with the Father and the Son, on the one hand, and with human beings, on the other. Now the divine Breath shows itself to be so different from both that it is challenging to conceive it can share the name with either one.

I will argue that the key to this problem is to recognize that "person" and "hypostasis" are analogical terms in the Trinity. Of course, the analogical dimension of personhood is often stressed when comparing God and human beings, because analogy characterizes the relation between the Creator and creation. Between human and divine person there is a certain similarity—which allows for the use of the common word "person"—but an even greater dissimilarity. Paradoxically, the theological use of "analogy" stresses difference more than similarity.[1] However, I believe that

---

1. The classical definition of analogy is that "between the Creator and the creature so great a likeness cannot be noted without the necessity of noting a greater dissimilarity between them" (Fourth Lateran Council, chap. 2 [DH 806]).

The Analogical Trinity

divine personhood also is analogical. The analysis expounded in the first chapters leads us to understand the Holy Spirit as a unique type of divine person: not only a unique person, but a person in a unique way. This in turn points to the fact that all three, Father, Son, and Spirit, are each unique in their personhood. Comparing them one with another reveals a certain similarity in an even greater dissimilarity. Only if each person as a person is more dissimilar than similar to the others is it possible to understand the divine Breath to be a person on par with the Father and the Son. This innertrinitarian analogy is developed from the classical form of analogy between God and human beings but reflects back on it by helping to better understand the difference between divine and human person. This is especially true in the case of the third hypostasis: because Father, Son, and Holy Spirit subsist in three entirely unique ways, because of the "perfection" of their difference, it is easier to comprehend how a "person" so different from human persons as the Breath may still be named using the same terminology.

Of course, this means that it will be necessary to determine more precisely what divine personhood means. I will do this progressively, in the process of defining how the persons can be so unique. Personhood in God is defined by trinitarian relations and by modes of possession of the one divine substance. This is what is "similar" for all three, but also precisely what each holds in a "dissimilar" way. Personhood in God is also defined, in comparison with human personhood, as a specific relation to speech and action, to intelligence and will. We will see how the divine hypostases possess these "similar" traits in a "dissimilar" way: the divine Breath is generally speaking the most dissimilar to a human person, but, according to different aspects considered, each is more or less similar and dissimilar; that is, more or less "personal," in the sense of human personhood.

If hypostasis or person is analogical in God, most certainly all the other notions that indicate distinction in the Trinity, such as relation and procession, will be as well: none of these can be conceived of independently from the other. A renewed comprehension of one of the divine persons leads to a renewed perception of all three and from there of the Trinity as a whole: the whole Trinity is in a way "analogical." Indeed, the breath-metaphor allows not only for a more precise conception of divine personhood but also for a better comprehension of all classical trinitarian notions. I will start by considering personhood, before turning in a second step to the other trinitarian concepts.

The Breath of God

On Personhood and Analogy

The divine Breath, insubstantial and impersonal as it is, can be considered a person or hypostasis because each trinitarian person is a person in a unique way. The idea that the notion of inner-trinitarian personhood is analogical has been "floated" in trinitarian theology during the past fifty years. Rahner mentions the question in a footnote, insisting on the fact that trinitarian concepts indicate either total numerical unity or true, deep distinction. "Person" falls into the latter category. For this reason it cannot be univocal, it cannot have the same meaning for Father, Son, and Spirit:

> There is something strange here. Every doctrine of the Trinity must emphasize that the "hypostasis" is precisely that in God through which Father, Son and Spirit are *distinct* from one another; that, wherever there exists between the three of them a real, univocal correspondence, there is absolute numerical identity. Hence the concept of hypostasis, applied to God, cannot be a universal, univocal concept, applying to each of the three persons in the same way.[2]

Though he thinks the word person is too much a part of Christian tradition to be abandoned, Rahner is quite reserved about it, because it risks inducing a form of generalization, while it should in fact express the differences between the three divine names:

> [The Concept of "Person"] attempts to generalize once more that which is absolutely unique. When we say: "there are three persons in God, God subsists in three persons" we generalize and add up something which cannot be added up, since that which alone is really common to Father, Son, and Spirit is precisely the one and only Godhead, and since there is no higher point of view from which the three can be added as Father, Son, and Spirit.[3]

Pannenberg also evokes the question, precisely about the Holy Spirit's difference in personhood from the seemingly more "personal" Father and Son: "As a field, of course, the Spirit would be impersonal." It is a person only insofar as we understand that the term person possesses a specific meaning for each one of the divine names: "The trinitarian persons are differently defined as persons."[4]

2. Rahner, *Trinity*, 11 n6.
3. Rahner, *Trinity*, 104.
4. Pannenberg, *Systematic Theology I*, 383–84.

The Analogical Trinity

Balthasar touches on the question a few times in the last volumes of the *Trilogy*: "Let us not forget that in God there can be no genus to subsume a univocal concept of person or that the application of 'three' to him has nothing to do with what can be counted quantitatively."[5] This is particularly true of the third person, because it is "faceless" and because the Scriptures use images of fluid rather than solid elements for it:

> Is it not indicated, as far as the Spirit is concerned, in the very fact that in Scripture he has no face? Above the earth, which stands firm, the Spirit is symbolized by the three other elements: storm, wind, tempest, flaming fire, flowing water poured forth, all these images express his elusive nature.[6]

According to Balthasar, rather than simply "person," the Holy Spirit should be named a "personal type of being," because "the New Testament gives no clear statement of 'personhood', with regard to the Spirit, that would be equal to that of the Father and the Son."[7] This does not mean that the Spirit is less personal but that it is a "meta-person (*Überperson*)." In the end, one must admit: "The way in which the Spirit is Person is beyond our grasp."[8]

The most systematic approach to this question was made at a congress held at the Jesuit University of Naples in 1997 under the lead of B. Sesboüé, also with a special attention to the Holy Spirit.[9] Sesboüé analyzes the history of the Creed to show that many Symbols were binitarian. Ignatius of Antioch, Polycarp, Irenaeus, and Tertullian find it difficult to give space to the Spirit. Even the Nicene Creed of 325 is totally unbalanced in favor of the Father and the Son.[10] This is not because of a resistance in accepting the divinity of the Spirit, since the Jewish heritage of *Ruah* and *Pneuma* made that point obvious, but because of a difficulty in fitting it as a third individuality on par with the two others. As such, the Spirit is the "unknown God"

---

5. Balthasar, *Theo-Logic II: Truth of God*, 146; see also *Theo-Logic III: The Spirit of Truth*, 148.

6. Balthasar, *Theo-Logic III: The Spirit of Truth*, 115.

7. Balthasar, *Theo-Logic III: The Spirit of Truth*, 110–11.

8. Balthasar, *Theo-Logic III: The Spirit of Truth*, 144.

9. See Tanzarella, *La personalità dello Spirito Santo*.

10. For a more complete documentation of this question, see Sesboüé, "La personalità dello Spirito Santo," 29 n14–17. The New Testament also has binitarian professions of faith: 1 Cor 8:6; 1 Tim 2:5–6; 6:13.

THE BREATH OF GOD

and it seems "anonymous."[11] As Sesboüé asserts, echoing Balthasar, "the Holy Spirit is a trinitarian Person, in the special mode of a Meta-Person."[12]

The idea that Father, Son, and Spirit are hypostases in a unique way is not only a modern idea. It may already be inchoately present when Basil explains that each one should be named separately, without being "conumbered" as if they were a group of similar realities, because each one is the one God:

> There is one God and Father, one Only-Begotten Son, and one Holy Spirit. We declare each Person to be unique (*monachôs*), and if we must use numbers, we will not let a stupid arithmetic lead us astray to the idea of many gods. . . . The Holy Spirit is one, and we speak of Him as unique (*monadikôs*).[13]

More clearly, one of the reasons why Augustine was ill at ease with the notion of *persona* was because it was the only *ad se* (absolute) notion to be used in plural form in the Trinity. It is better to speak of Father, Son, and Spirit than of three persons. Unfortunately we need to concede the term person to be able to speak about what these three are: "It is now generally agreed to use the plural with other names besides those signifying relationships, as required by the necessities of argument, in order to have a name to answer the question 'Three what?' with, and so to say three substances or persons."[14] Aquinas himself stresses the fact that *persona*, applied to God, designates the singular as such. Since in God there is no genus it is not a common name in the sense of a genus or of something universal. For this reason it is common only in reason and not in reality: "The commonality [of the name person applied to the three divine persons] is conceptual and not real."[15] Used as a common name it just indicates an *individuum vagum*, not the divine person as such.

So far we just have an agreement among important thinkers on the analogical dimension of personhood in the Trinity in general. I will try to bring the reflection one step forward, by showing how well this is grounded in the notion of trinitarian hypostasis or person, whether one considers the person as *relatio subistens*, as in the Thomist tradition, or as "mode of

---

11. These expressions, used by Sesboüé, come respectively from Dillard's *Au Dieu inconnu*, and Boulnois, *Le paradoxe trinitaire*, 443.
12. Sesboüé, "La personalità dello Spirito Santo," 56.
13. Basil the Great, *On the Holy Spirit*, XVIII, §§44–45, 72.
14. Augustine, *Trinity*, VII, iv, 12; see also VIII, pr.
15. Aquinas, ST, I, q.30 a.4 ad3.

The Analogical Trinity

being" or "mode of subsistence," following Barth and Rahner. Never do we have something that is indistinctly common to all three persons: as far as they are persons, their distinction touches all that they are and makes them radically different from each other.

Aquinas defines the divine person as a "relation as subsisting."[16] The distinction between the persons is determined by their relation of origins. In this regards, when compared to the divine substance, each person is identical to it. On the other hand, if they are compared one with another, the persons are distinct, according to their opposite relations.[17] This means that from the point of view of relations, each person is fully what "opposes" it to the other, that is, what relates it to but also makes it different from the other. The Father is only and fully Fatherhood, as Hilary of Poitiers said beautifully many centuries before: "God does not know how to be ever anything else than love, nor to be anything else than the Father. He who loves does not envy and he who is a Father is at the same time wholly a father ... Hence, in so far as He is the Father, He must be the whole Father in all His own attributes."[18] Likewise, the second person is only and fully Sonship. It follows that the third will be only and fully what relates it to the Father and the Son, in other words what they give to each other and share. It *is* interiority; it *is* shared-ness. The fact that from another point of view each person is identical to the divine substance does not limit the differences, on the contrary: it points out that each one is not an individual of a common species or genus—the divine nature—but a unique way of being this nature in its totality. It is not a subdivision of the substance but the totality of the substance. This is precisely why they are only and fully their relation. This points towards an analogical conception of divine personhood rather than to the differentiation of a univocal notion.

The same is true if one adopts the Barthian or Rahnerian understanding of the trinitarian person. Echoing the Cappadocian fathers' *treis tropoi tès huparxeôs*, Barth opts for three "modes of being (*Seinsweisen*)": "God is One in three ways of being, Father, Son, and Holy Ghost. . . . The one God, i.e., the one Lord, the one personal God, is what He is not just in one mode

16. Aquinas, ST, I, q.29 a.4 resp.

17. "In God essence is not really distinct from person; and yet that the persons are really distinguished from each other. For person . . . signifies relation as subsisting in the divine nature. But relation as referred to the essence does not differ therefrom really, but only in our way of thinking; while as referred to an opposite relation, it has a real distinction by virtue of that opposition" (ST, I, q.39, a.1 resp.).

18. Hilary of Poitiers, *Trinity*, IX, §61, 383 (modified translation), (PL 10, 330).

but ... in the mode of the Father, in the mode of the Son, and in the mode of the Holy Ghost."[19] Because "mode of being" may be interpreted in a modalist way and because he wishes to stay closer to the traditional language of trinitarian doctrine, Rahner prefers "mode of subsistence (*Subsistenzweise*)": "The one God subsists in three distinct manners of subsisting."[20] In both case, however, the idea is that God is not a unique substance with three dimensions, and even less a substance with a common core and some peripheral differences, but a substance that *is* or *subsists* in three uniquely different modes.

The Father, then, is the fullness of the substance, subsisting in the mode of an origin without origin or of gratuitous self-giving. He is only and fully *fons ergo ipse et origo totius divinitatis* and *plenitudo fontalis*.[21] Subsisting, or being a "person" for him means to give and to give freely, because no other principle obliges him to do so.[22] The Son is the fullness of the substance as receiving—and in some accounts giving back in thanksgiving, but never without having received both his subsistence and his capacity to give back. Because he is also *Logos*, the second mode of subsisting of God is likewise the divine substance as being-conceived and locus of conception (Augustine, Aquinas), expressivity (Bonaventure, Balthasar), and auto-communication (Rahner). Quite naturally, the third person will be a unique, fully different mode of subsisting of the one divine substance. The characteristics gathered from the economy and the specific *modus operandi* and *essendi* do not simply imply a specific role for a reality that also has many points in common with two others, but they point truly to a mode of subsisting of the divine substance. The Breath is the substance as subsisting in and through, the substance as being-shared. Of course, the words we have to express this are inadequate, but while the first and second hypostases subsist in a way "outside" of each other, or better yet, "in front of each other" and "face-to-face," the eternal Breath subsists inside the other

---

19. Barth, *Church Dogmatics* I/1, §9, 359; see also 348.

20. Rahner, *Trinity*, 109; see also 114.

21. See Council of Toledo XI (DH 525) and Bonaventure, *Sententiarum*, I, d.27, pars 1, art. unicus, q.2, ad.3. Rahner insists that the one substance does not "predate" the Father: "The first manner of subsisting at once constitutes God as Father, as unoriginate principle of the divine self-communication and self-mediation. Hence no 'God' should be conceived behind this first manner of subsisting, as previous to this distinct subsistence and having first to assume it" (Rahner, *Trinity*, 112).

22. See Richard of Saint Victor, *Trinity*, V, 4, 296; XVII, 310–11.

The Analogical Trinity

two. This is not only a specific activity of being that otherwise subsists in the same way as they do: it is fully a mode of subsistence.

Of course, the three persons have a point in common: they are modes of the same substance. All three "subsist"; that is, they share an act of subsistence. However, the Father subsists-as-giving, the Son subsists-as-receiving, the Breath subsists-as-being-shared. This marks and gives an orientation to the whole of each act of subsisting. They are not subdivisions of that substance, but an unrepeatable way of being it in its totality. The divine nature is never neutral. Once again, it is not a "common core." But, as Balthasar puts it, God's nature is totally fatherhood, sonship, or breath: "[The divine essence] would never exist except as fatherly, sonly, or spirit-ually."[23] This implies that every dimension, every operation, every thought or volition of each person—if we may think in these terms for the divine hypostases—is totally paternal for the Father, filial for the Son, pneumatic for the Breath, totally marked and orientated by its personal difference.

A final comment may be useful: analogy and differences need not be a sign of imperfection, on the contrary. If God is perfect, then differences in God will also be perfect. They will be, in a way, more radical than in the created world. In the Trinity, all is either perfectly one—numerically identical—or perfectly unique. The divine Breath is not less a person, it is not a person "notwithstanding all": it is another way of fully being the one divine substance. In truth, although I have sometimes suggested the opposite in the first steps of the reflection, the Spirit is no less substantial or personal than the Father or the Son. As Basil puts it, the Spirit, though it is a breath, is not "a dissipated breath, . . . the Spirit is the essence of life and divine sanctification."[24] It truly is a mode of subsistence, but it is another way of subsisting, and of doing so "personally." As such, the Holy Spirit extends our knowledge of what personal subsistence means for God.

As we see, the fact that the divine Breath is so different from the Father and the Son does not prevent it from being a hypostasis or person: all three are profoundly distinctive and this is precisely part of what being a *relatio subsistens* or *Subsistenzweise* is all about. However, the difficulty in understanding the third divine name as a person does not only stem from its uniqueness in relation to the Father and the Son but also from its difference

---

23. Balthasar, *Theo-Logic II: The Truth of God*, 137; "That essence is forever 'given' in the self-gift of the Father, 'rendered' in the thanksgiving of the Son, and 'represented' in its character as absolute love by the Holy Spirit" (Balthasar, *Mysterium Paschale*, viii).

24. Basil the Great, *On the Holy Spirit*, XVIII, §46, 73 (modified translation).

from a human person. For the church fathers, the grounds for attributing personhood to the Holy Spirit was that it speaks and acts.[25] This seems to be the minimum required to still name it a person: can we attribute speech and action to a *Ruah* or a *Pneuma*?

I believe that the analogous dimension of divine personhood as such is also the key to understanding humanly personal traits such as speech and action in a differentiated enough way to attribute them to a divine Breath. To do so, we need to consider God's intelligence and will. Traditionally speaking, speech and action are considered as a sign of these spiritual faculties that any person, human, angelic, or divine, must possess to be named a person. The Holy Spirit is a divine person because it shares with the two others the fullness of divine intelligence and will, and the breath-metaphor will prove itself valid only if it is compatible with this teaching. In a way, this criterion offers a form of "negative theology": it leads to a purification of what is too literal in the breath-metaphor to adequately define the third divine hypostasis as a hypostasis. However, the analogical dimension of divine personhood provides an understanding of intelligence and will that is compatible with its possession by a Breath—or at least, in a way that would offer the least degree of incompatibility. This type of apophatism will also purify our conceptions of divine intelligence and will by opening them to different dimensions and help us comprehend in a more precise way what it means for a trinitarian person to share an aspect of the unique substance with the two others.

Indeed, three modes of subsistence mean not only three modes of possessing or "subsisting" the one substance of God but also, by way of consequence, three modes of possessing the one intelligence and the one will of God. In classical trinitarian theology, intelligence and will are held as dimensions of God's nature and as such are numerically identical in the Trinity.[26] This does not imply, however, an undifferentiated possession. The Father is the source of the intelligence and will: he possesses them as their origin and wellspring, and as what he gives gratuitously to the Son and the Spirit. The Son partakes in the very same intelligence as receiving it. As Word, he is the *locus* of the Father's thought and its end product. If we may allow ourselves a comparison with the human thought process, the Father

---

25. See Ladaria, *Il Dio vivo e vero*, 128–29; Sesboüé, "La personalità dello Spirito Santo," 24–25 (see above, chap. 1, p. 4).

26. See Council of Rome, *Tomus Damasi* (DH, 172); see also DH, 501, 542, 545–46, 572, 680, 851.

The Analogical Trinity

is closer to the gushing forth of creative thought and the Son to the receptive dimension of perception and understanding—even if these categories are deeply inadequate for God.

Likewise, the Son fully shares the same will as the Father, but as receiving its power and volition rather than producing them. It is wholly his own, but as a will-received. This explains, for example, how it is possible for the incarnate Son to obey the Father, from his childhood to Gethsemane, though they share the same numerical identical will. Traditionally, the obedience of the Son to the Father is interpreted as obedience of the Son's humanity to his divinity.[27] However, this leads to a form of quasi-schizophrenic double subject in Christ. Of course, obedience—and a certain form of tension between the Son and the Father, as in Gethsemane—is possible in and through the human nature the Son has assumed. It is, however, truly the Son who obeys (in his humanity), not his humanity *per se*; and he obeys the Father, not his own divinity. Now this is conceivable once one understands that the Father and the Son each possess the one and only will according to a deeply different and specific mode. Because in the eternal Trinity the Father's will is originating while the Son's will is a will-received, in the economy the Son is liable to obey the Father—although they share the same will.[28]

How does the divine Breath enter into the picture? We are at the limits of human language and conceptualization, but I will offer a hypothesis: the Breath is the intelligence and will of the Father and the Son as shared. It is the intelligence and thought of the Father as inhabiting the intelligence and thought of the Son; it is the will and volition of the Father as inhabiting the will and volition of the Son. The Breath is the subsistence of the one divine intelligence and will in the mode of mutual interiority. If I may allow myself once again to use a human comparison, the Breath is what makes the thought of the other interior to my thought. It is what makes me understand "from inside": literally it is the *in*tuition of God. In the same way, the divine Breath is what makes the will of one interior to that of the other. The Breath makes Father and Son will-with-each-other in the strongest sense of the word. In the human world, to desire someone already makes the other inhabit so to speak in our will. In the human world, love conforms our will to the other, whether to another human person or to God. This happens between children and parents (sometimes!), when a child stands close to its

27. See for example Aquinas, ST, III, q.20.
28. See Vetö, *Du Christ à la Trinité*, 435.

parents to see and do as they do, or does so with its elder siblings. It happens in a happy loving relation. The eternal Breath of God does this in an infinitely more perfect way: it makes the will of the Father part of the will of the Son and interior to it, and the will of the Son part of the will of the Father and interior to it. Let us add that in the human world an exchange of thought and volition tends to give dynamism to the process of knowledge and desire. Likewise, it is not impossible to think that the divine Breath energizes the unique divine operation of thought and will, makes it fertile and superabundant.

Of course, this may exceed what we are truly able to know about the inner-trinitarian relations, but it conforms to the personal traits manifested in the economy by a Spirit which does speak and act, albeit only in and through the speech and operation of others, by inspiring them and giving fecundity to their thoughts and acts. And in the end, whichever way the Breath of the Father and the Son does partake in the divine intelligence and will, the point is that it is perfectly coherent to conceive of three very different modes of knowing and willing in God.[29] It is also consistent that these modes be quite different from what we know of human thought and volition, without ceasing to be truly personal traits.

Even though the answer to the problem of attributing speech and action and thus intelligence and will to the Breath in God allows for a broader conception of divine personhood and confirms its analogical dimension, it further entrenches the fact that the third person seems less substantial than the Father and the Son. We know that each is fully the divine substance so that there are no *degrees* of substantiality between them, only different *modes* of subsisting. However, when compared to material reality and human beings, the Spirit seems more fluid and atmospheric. Are the first and second persons more "personal"? Do they have a clearer-cut figure than the third? One may still believe that the notion of hypostasis or person is more fitting for the Father and the Son.

In fact both the Son and the Father present some degree of "insubstantiality" and "impersonality." For instance, the Son is also the Word. If this dimension of the second hypostasis is underlined, we then have a "substantial" and "personal" Father proffering and breathing out two much more

29. In less traditional terms, Rahner asserts that there is one self-consciousness in God, possessed in three modes: "There are not three consciousnesses; rather, the one consciousness subsists in a threefold way. There is only one real consciousness in God, which is shared by Father, Son, and Spirit, by each in his own proper way" (Rahner, *Trinity*, 107).

The Analogical Trinity

fluid realities, a Word and a Breath. The church fathers were sometimes accused of considering the second person as a simple *flatus vocis*, proffered by God. Hilary defends himself by asserting: "This Word is a thing, not a sound; a nature, not simply an expression; God, not a voice."[30] Of course, the Word is as fully substantial as the Father, but the fact that he is a Word does imply another type of subsistence. This is echoed in the way Irenaeus presents the Son and the Spirit as the "two hands" of the Father: "[The human being] molded by His Hands, to wit, by the Son and the Holy Ghost: unto Whom also He said, 'Let us make Man.'"[31] The Father is the main actor, the Creator, while the Son and the Spirit are in a way "appendixes," "members" of his "body," who assist him: "For there are ministers to [the Father] in all that is His, His Progeny and the Image thereof, i.e., the Son and the Holy Ghost, His Word and His Wisdom."[32] Bulgakov also is in this line when he explains that the Father is the center and actor of an auto-revelation he accomplishes through the Son and the Spirit: "The First hypostasis is the One that is Revealed, while in relation to this hypostasis the other two are its bihypostatic Revelation.... In this trinitarian mode of love, according to its meaning, there is only one *subject*, the *center of the revelation*."[33] Of course, this introduces a certain monarchy of the Father, but it seems to me that a "relative monarchianism"[34] is quite coherent with an analogical conception of personhood in God. Priority according to the *taxis* is quite compatible with a strict equality of the persons according to their possession of the divine essence and is not necessarily subordinationist.

The paradox is that the Father also has some traits that make him less substantial and personal than generally imagined. Barth stresses that the Father does not have a "form" and only "takes form" in the Son: "God reveals Himself as the Father.... God the Father is God who always, even in taking form in the Son, does not take a form."[35] God the Father is Sovereign and no form can fully contain him. In the same way, Balthasar explains that

---

30. Hilary of Poitiers, *Trinity*, II, §15, 47–48 (modified translation), (PL 10, 61); see also VII, §11 (207–8). See also Tertullian, *Adversus Praxean*, VII.

31. Irenaeus, *Against the Heresies*, IV, pr.4, 310; see also V, i, §3, 451–52; v, §1, 458–59; vi, §1, 460–61; xxviii, §4, 517.

32. Irenaeus, *Against the Heresies*, IV, vii, §4, 326–27.

33. Bulgakov, *Comforter*, 149.

34. The expression is from Sesboüé, whom I thank for an inspiring discussion on this question. Ladaria also thinks along the lines of a "relative priority" of the Father (Ladaria, *La Trinità*, 215–21).

35. Barth, *Church Dogmatics* I/1, §8, 324.

the Father, like the Spirit, is "meta-personal" rather than "personal." Since he makes the Son and the Spirit well forth from himself without needing another ground than himself, the Father is the perpetually gushing forth and immeasurable source of the divinity. He is "depth," "unfathomable origin," "bottomless origin of love," "abyss," or "abyss of love."[36] As such he also has no face,[37] or at least his face is not perceptible, because he "dwells in an unapproachable light" (1 Tim 6:16). He is the Holy God of Israel, the "invisible God" of the First and of the New Testaments.[38] In this configuration, the Son is the most personal and substantial: he is the one who takes flesh, and this expresses an eternal, inner-trinitarian disposition. His personhood is the model of human personhood, as it is predisposed to take on a human nature, so it is coherent to understand his personhood as the less different from human personhood. From a paternal source without origin gush out a more substantial Son and an airy, atmospheric Breath.

These models of relative substantiality and personal characteristics of the three persons show that divine personhood is and should be, from a certain point of view, more fluid than human personhood. Insofar as it is a mode a subsistence of God, identical each time with the divine substance itself, it is naturally supremely substantial. But since a divine person is also totally a relation, it is also infinitely more "unsolidified" than a human person. Of course, the divine Breath is the less humanly substantial and the most "anonymous" of the three persons, since it mainly has the traits related to fluidity. However, this just means that the Breath of God shares this common characteristic of divine personhood but expresses it in the most radical way possible—in a unique way, as it were. Indeed, from another point of view, that of personhood as relational, it could also be considered the most personal of the three, because it is interior to the Father and the Son in a special way.[39]

36. See Balthasar, *Mysterium Paschale*, 254; *Theo-Logic III: The Spirit of Truth*, 441–45.

37. Balthasar, of course, knows the Johannine verse that announces a full vision of God: "When he is revealed, we will be like him, for we will see him as he is" (1 John 3:2). He interprets "him" as indicating the Son, because we are conformed to Christ—even if this is incompatible with the grammar of the text (see *Theo-Logic III: The Spirit of Truth*, 447–48). See above, p. 21n61.

38. See Balthasar, *Theo-Drama V: The Last Act*, 403–5; *Theo-Logic II: The Truth of God*, 23, 66, 92–93.

39. "The Holy Spirit is the hidden or unnamed person or 'who' because the very nature of his subjectivity as a subsistent relation is to illuminate or, more deeply, to substantiate or person (sic) the Father and the Son for one another. It could even be said that the Holy Spirit is the most personal of the trinitarian persons, and the most relational

The Analogical Trinity

In the end, the analogous dimension of divine personhood is the key to the analogous dimension of personhood in general: it is legitimate to use the notions of hypostasis or person for the Breath of God, however different it may be from human beings, not only because God and humans are infinitely different, but because Father, Son, and Spirit are profoundly unique. On the one hand, the difference of nature between God and humans trumps the inner-trinitarian differences, of course, but on the other, the divine hypostases are more perfectly different from each other than any inner-worldly differences and, from a certain point of view, from the difference between Creator and creature. Once the degree of *dissimilitudo* in the notion of divine hypostasis or person is acknowledged, then all other types and degrees of differences can be assimilated.

The analogous dimension of divine personhood in itself and in regards to human personhood explains why I have consistently called the third person "it." This is not intended as a sign of an "infra-personal" dimension. Rather, it underlines how different and unique the divine Breath is in comparison with the Father and the Son and with human beings. This brings up the question, however, of using "she" as a way of expressing the Spirit's difference at least with the first and second divine persons. In the context of rising gender-awareness, quite a few pneumatologies—in the English-speaking world at least—have chosen to express themselves in the feminine.[40]

However, I believe the neutral form is more respectful of the biblical use of *Ruah* and *Pneuma*. *Ruah* is generally feminine in the Hebrew Bible, but it can occasionally be masculine.[41] *Pneuma* on the other hand is always neutral in the LXX and the New Testament. *Paraklètos,* which is as close to a personal name of the Spirit as it happens, is masculine. Furthermore, there is a difference in grammar between Hebrew and English: Hebrew qualifies many non-human and even non-gendered realities as masculine and feminine, while English reserves masculine and feminine to gendered realities, especially human—the exceptions, like "ship" or "church," for example, are instances of personification. To qualify Breath in the feminine in

---

in his subjectivity, because he is the most translucent and transparent. Through him the Father and the Son eternally gaze upon one another in love" (Weinandy, *Father's Spirit of Sonship*, 84).

40. Let us note, however, that the feminine dimension of the Spirit is quite traditional and can be found in very different cultural spheres: see, for instance Congar, *Je crois en l'Esprit-Saint*, 720–32.

41. See Botterweck and Ringgren, *Theological Dictionary*, XIII, 372.

English would give it a much stronger gender orientation than the original Hebrew. And it would not render the other possibilities: the neutral form expresses in a more exact way what is signified by the feminine, neutral, and sometimes masculine qualifications of the Spirit of God.

Of course, we do lose something in the passage from the Hebrew (mainly feminine) to the Greek (neutral), and then to the Latin *spiritus* (masculine). There may be a maternal dimension of the divine *Ruah* that I have not fully taken into account, expressed, for instance, by the Spirit "swept over the face of the waters" (Gen 1:2) and echoed by the *Pneuma* "overshadowing" Mary (Luke 1:35) at the annunciation. Some of the traits I have set into light for the Spirit may be considered typically maternal and feminine: the intimate, interior dimension, or the propensity of letting the other be, of inspiring without taking the forefront, or the specific relation to life, and even to emotions and passion. However, to characterize these traits as feminine depends to a certain extent on stereotypes of what it means to be feminine or female. This would mean opening another chapter with a fundamental reflection on these issues, which cannot be done in the limits of the present essay.

All things considered, there certainly is a "feminine" dimension of the Spirit, but the most vivid feature to emerge is that the third hypostasis can be all three, which means that it cannot precisely be gendered.[42] This offers a further confirmation of the fact that it is a person in a unique and fluid way.

These impersonal traits of the divine Breath and the different modes in which Father, Son, and Holy Spirit are persons may also be helpful to better understand human personhood. Obviously, we must proceed here with even greater caution than when reflecting on divine personhood in itself: the risk is to project into the Trinity our conceptions of personhood and then, inverting the process in an illegitimate way, to retro-project them back into the human person.[43] I will simply offer some musings in a few brush-strokes that need to be taken *cum grano salis*.

Each mode of subsisting as a person in God illuminates a fundamental dimension of human personhood. A person is person by positing himself or herself. It accomplishes itself by acting and by producing, by

---

42. Jerome already underlined that the fact that the Spirit is feminine, neutral, or masculine according to different languages is a sign that God is not gendered (see *Commentarium In Isaiam*, XI, 40 [PL 24, 405 A]).

43. See Kilby, "Perichoresis and Projection," already referred to above, chap. 2, p. 31.

The Analogical Trinity

giving itself as selflessly as possible, and by expressing itself, as the Father does. Secondly, a person is also a person by receiving and giving back, by "giving thanks," as the Son does—not only in relation to God but also to others. Barth, expounding his conception of the human person with Jesus-Christ as a model, considers "thanksgiving" to God to be a fundamental, constitutive characteristic: to be oneself is to respond to the gift of God.[44] I believe this can be transposed accordingly to the relation between human persons. Following the second mode of subsisting as person, a human person is fully person only when acting with others and with what it has received from others, by inserting oneself in a tradition and a common history. It is called to express not only itself but others as well. But, finally, a person is certainly also a person, in an essential way, by inspiring others, by acting with them in such a close way as to let the other become himself or herself, by drawing back to let others exist, as does the divine Breath. A person is a person by entering into the intimacy of the other and being itself in the other, through thought, emotion, and sexuality. A person is a person through bringing others together and enabling their communication. In other words, a (human) person is a person when it is fluid and transparent. Though heuristically speaking our notion of divine personhood is analogical to the human person, which is the starting point of our knowledge, on an ontological level, divine personhood is the archetype and it allows us to uncover the true richness of its human "analogies." Each divine person offers a paradigm for an essential aspect of personhood, and the mode of subsisting of the divine Breath completes the full picture of human personhood in an original and often underestimated way.

The analogical quality of the notion of divine person in general also points towards the fact that each human person is unique. Strictly speaking, one probably cannot go as far as to say that the notion of human personhood is analogical. Balthasar, who insists on the analogical quality of the divine person, makes this a distinguishing factor between divine and human personhood: while "'Person' in God cannot be used . . . as an apparently univocal concept," this is possible "in the secular, or at least human, sphere."[45] Rather than speak about a certain similarity in a greater dissimilarity, one would need to consider a certain *dissimilitudo* inside of a *maior similitudo*. Nonetheless, each human person is a mystery and is such because of his or her unrepeatable and incommunicable personhood. Each

---

44. See Barth, *Church Dogmatics* III/2, §44, 181–90.
45. Balthasar, *Theo-Logic III: The Spirit of Truth*, 115.

person contains the human nature in a specific way, and relates to others and to the whole of the universe from a specific, unrepeatable perspective. This must be taken into consideration much more for humans than for other forms of individuality in the material world. Furthermore, the uniqueness of each human person most certainly grows with its response to his or her vocation, to the unique, unrepeatable design God proposes to each. Balthasar distinguishes between the "natural" individuality each human being receives at his or her conception and the more radically unique personhood that is acquired in response to God's vocation and by conforming oneself in a personally specific way to the person of Jesus Christ.[46] In another vein, in the created world, angels may be the beings that are the closest to being analogical in regards one to another: indeed, scholastic thought developed the idea that each angel was a species to itself.[47] All in all, the analogical dimension of divine personhood offers a model of perfection for all types of personhood and should inspire us to take ever more into account the uniqueness of each human being.

In the end, we need to continue to say "person" or "hypostasis" with the same reluctant acceptance as Augustine or Rahner.[48] The best would be to be able to use only the scriptural names of Father, Son-*Logos*, and *Ruah-Pneuma*. Since we do need a general term, however, knowing to what extent it is analogical, in itself and in comparison with human persons, helps us use it better, or at least less inadequately.

All That Is Common Is Identical
—All That Is Different Is Unique

So far I have explored the type of trinitarian personhood that corresponds to what we discover about the third person if we expand the breath-metaphor, and thus how this metaphor enriches the comprehension of the whole Trinity. It is impossible, however, to reconsider one of the notions involved in our understanding of the triune God without taking a fresh

---

46. See for example Balthasar, *Theo-Drama III: Persons in Christ*, 163–73.

47. See Aquinas, ST, I, q.50, a.4. This is also true in Jewish thought, especially in the Kabala: "An angel is a spiritual reality with uniquely specific essence, qualities and characteristics." Each is the expression of a type of "emotion" or energy: "An angel is in an absolute way the manifestation of a unique emotional essence" (Steinsaltz, *Thirteen Petalled Rose*, 13–14).

48. Augustine, *De Trinitate*, V, ix, 10 (PL 42, 917–18); Rahner, *Trinity*, 103–15.

The Analogical Trinity

look at all the others. If hypostasis or person is analogical, then all the terms that express differences will be analogical as well, namely procession and relation. Let us once again echo one of Rahner's trinitarian axioms: all that is common in God is simple and numerically identical, but all that is different is unique. In the end, only the substance and its attributes are one: "That which alone is really common to Father, Son, and Spirit is precisely the one and only Godhead, and there is no higher point of view from which the three can be added as Father, Son, and Spirit"; for the rest, one should not try "to generalize one more time that which is absolutely unique."[49] However, perhaps even the one substance and its attributes are brought into a new light: that which is numerically identical, if it is possessed by three different modes of subsistence, will carry the mark of the rich diversity of the Trinity. Simply said, all dimensions of the triune God can be revisited. Accordingly, in this section I will start by exploring the analogical dimension of trinitarian processions and relations. I will then proceed with the main notions that express God's unity, the one substance and the perichoresis of the divine persons.

There is a common aspect to the two trinitarian processions, called generation and spiration in the West, namely the communication of the divine substance from one person to another, the production of one "mode of subsistence" by another. This does not justify, however, the spontaneous view that both are a more or less equivalent communications of being, with only accidental differences to distinguish them. If they produce two uniquely different persons from a unique first person, then it makes sense to understand generation and breathing-out to be as unique and analogical as the persons themselves. The Eastern tradition, indeed, does not refer to one concept—procession—containing two sub-concepts—generation and spiration; it uses two distinct words—generation and procession—with no truly common notion to unify them. Bulgakov is quite adamant about refusing any general notion that would unify generation and procession under one *genus*:

> Does this generalization (*duae processiones*) have any basis in Scripture, in direct Revelation? Can we find anywhere in Scripture the linkage of the generation of the Son and the procession of the Spirit as two forms of origination, *duae processiones*? Indisputably, we cannot. There is no Biblical justification for counting and accepting them as two variants: one *and* one. On the contrary, they

49. Rahner, *Trinity*, 104.

THE BREATH OF GOD

should be examined in their particular concrete quality, which is not subject to abstract numerical generalization and the identification contained in the latter.[50]

The church fathers have already pored over the question of how to distinguish the production of the Son and of the Spirit. Though they conclude that the procession of the third hypostasis is a mystery, the Cappadocians at least agree that the distinction between the Son and the Holy Spirit arises from the different ways in which they come from the Father. We have previously evoked Basil's idea that the Spirit "proceeds as breath from the mouth of the Father, and is not begotten like the Son."[51] For Gregory Nazianzen the Holy Spirit is the "unbegottenly proceeding or going forth."[52] The difference with the Son, who is begotten, is stressed doubly: not only are the terms generation and procession distinct, but Gregory underlines the fact that the Spirit is "unbegotten." There is nothing lacking in the Spirit which explains why he is different from the Son and the Father, but simply a difference of relation between the hypostases: "The very fact of being unbegotten or begotten, or proceeding, has given the name of Father to the first, of the Son to the second, and of the third, him of whom we are speaking, of the Holy Ghost."[53]

In Western thought, Augustine expresses the uniqueness of each *processio* when he notes that both Son and Spirit proceed from the Father, but that the Spirit is not a Son, neither of the Father, nor of both Son and Father. He concludes in apophatic mode:

> As for the distinction between being generated and proceeding, in connection to the Most High, who could explain it? Not everything that proceeds is generated, even if everything that is generated proceeds.... Both of them are ineffable—as the Prophet says of the Son: "Who can tell his generation?"—so it is equally right to say of the Spirit: "Who can tell his generation?"[54]

---

50. Bulgakov, *Comforter*, 133.

51. Basil the Great, *On the Holy Spirit*, XVIII, §46, 73 (modified translation); see above, chap. 2, p. 36.

52. Gregory Nazianzen, "The Fourth Theological Oration," §19 (*Theological Orations*, 190).

53. Gregory Nazianzen, "The Fifth Theological Oration," §9 (*Theological Orations*, 199).

54. Augustine, *Contra Maximinum*, II, xiv, 1 (PL 42, 770–71).

The Analogical Trinity

This puzzlement in regards to divine communications of being that are so different as to produce two different persons is echoed by Anselm of Canterbury: "The Holy Spirit is not from God *His* Father but only from God who is Father. . . . The Holy Spirit, with respect to the fact that he exists from God, is not the Father's son; nor is the one from whom he exists *His* Father."[55] He also concludes that the Spirit proceeds "*quodam inerrabili modo*" from the Father and the Son.[56]

In the end, none of these church fathers and theologians are able to determine what is the difference between the generation of the Son and the procession-spiration of the Spirit. They simply agree on their dissimilarity. In the West, the disparity between the two processions will gradually be explained by the number of persons at their origin: generation is the procession which has only one person, the Father, at its source; procession or spiration is the one which has two persons, Father and Son. This will by the way entrench even more strongly the Western defense of the *Filioque*: the Spirit must proceed also from the Son, or else it is not possible to distinguish between the Son and Spirit.[57] This brings about an even greater risk of not distinguishing the processions in themselves but only through their "situation." The same general communication of being happens in two different situations, because their sources differ. However, if they produce two persons that are so unique as to be more dissimilar than similar, should their difference not run deeper? Should it not be a difference of *type* of communication of being?

The breath-metaphor may be helpful to give some inner determination to the difference of processions. Indeed, one of the difficulties we have seen is that the second procession has often been for the better and for the worse modeled on the first procession, the generation of the Son. Generation, however, is another metaphor: it is essentially a communication of substance by an individual reality that aims to produce another individual reality, which will be an image of the first. For this reason, the third *nomen proprium* of the second person, after Son and Word, is Image.[58] As Lévinas notes about human paternity and filiation, nothing knits tightly together

---

55. Anselm of Canterbury, *Procession of the Holy Spirit*, 184–85.

56. Anselm of Canterbury, *Monologion*, 57.

57. "It is necessary to say that the Holy Spirit is from the Son. For if He were not from the Son, then there could be no way of distinguishing them as persons" (Aquinas, ST, I, q.36, a.2 resp.).

58. See Aquinas, ST, I, q.35.

difference and similarity as does the father-son relation. Though a son is another being altogether from his father, no other being will be as similar to a father as his son.[59] Now, the second procession, the breathing-out of the Father into the Son and of the Son into the Father does nothing of the kind. It does not produce a likeness or an image. To breathe-out is to produce something very different from the source. And even if it is a full communication of substance that allows for a third mode of subsistence, this other subsistence subsists, once again, "in" and "through" the subsistence of the other two. It is a "sharable" subsistence. While generation is a movement that goes "out" from the source, breathing-out is also a breathing-*into*. While generation produces a reality that is in a way "exterior," "in front of," and "face-to-face" with its origin, breathing-out wells up from deep within and communicates a reality that is shared by the origin and the other. All this calls for taking as literally as possible the unique difference between generation and spiration, according to the metaphors they are based on.

Of course, the breathing out of the Breath does take place through the Son, so in the end we do retrieve the Western idea of the difference being a difference in a number of sources. However, one must think it out the other way around. Rather than the number of sources, what is foundational is the type of communication of being. Producing an image or an expression goes well with a one-to-one relation. Conversely, sharing out the deepest of one's being with another so that it becomes the other's, to the point the other can share it back, logically brings together the sources and thus "multiplies" them. Breathing-out-and-into allows for and asks for a sharing of the operation of communication the divine substance.

One further difference distinguishes the generation of the Son and the breathing-out of the Breath, especially if one does accept the idea that the Son breathes back the Spirit: while generation gives the Son the capacity to co-spire the Spirit and is prolonged so to say by the Son's participation in another procession, the Breath's spiration ends with the Breath itself. In chapter 1 we have explored how the Spirit in the economy rests on people and things, and evoked in chapter 2 how the Eastern tradition underlines the inner-trinitarian resting of the third hypostasis on the second: "When the Spirit proceeds from the Father he sets out towards the Son; the Son is the goal at which he stops."[60] In the West, this "resting upon" is understood

---

59. Lévinas, *Le Temps et l'Autre*, 85–86.

60. Staniloae, *Theology and the Church*, 21. See also Bobrinskoy, "*Filioque* Yesterday and Today," 144.

The Analogical Trinity

as the fact that the Holy Spirit stops and, in a way, goes no further: it reposes itself on the Son and thus puts to rest the dynamic of the inner-trinitarian processions.[61] The divine Breath is not without fruitfulness, however, since its being breathed out, as we have seen above, is part of the generation of the Son. However, this means that, in the eternal life of God as in the economy, its fruitfulness is expressed inside the Father and the Son's operation, as belonging to it. Both *ad extra* and *ad intra* the Spirit is immensely creative but this creativity is never only its own. Being Father means to be the ultimate principle without principle of processions and thus to exercise one's own fecundity. Being Son—according to the Latin tradition—means being the co-principle of a procession, exercising a received fecundity. Being Breath implies being creative and fruitful inside the Father's and the Son's fruitfulness. Even the fecundity of the Trinity is analogical. This, by the way, corroborates and gives added weight to what has already been seen about the *Filioque*: since the Son is not the ultimate source of the Spirit and only breathes it back and since everything the Son is and does is profoundly unique in regards to what the Father is and does, the Son is in no way source of the Breath as the Father is. The *co*-spiration is deeply different from the *spiration* and is not truly comparable to it—so it should not infringe on the Father's quality as only *fons et origo totius divinitatis*.

In a way, there is nothing truly new in this reflection on the difference between the generation of the Son and the procession-spiration of the Holy Spirit. It is simply important to fully realize to what extent the notion of trinitarian procession is analogical. If the hypostases are as uniquely different as I have argued, their procession, as foundation of their distinction, will likewise be unique—not only a unique production but a unique type of production, either by generation or by breathing-out.

With procession, relation is the other main notion that indicates distinction in the triune God. The theological tradition that coined the definition of the person as *relatio subsistens* insists on the full identity of person and relation: the Father is Fatherhood, the Son is Sonship and the Holy Spirit is (passive) procession or spiration.[62] Logically, if *persona* is analogical, so too will be *relatio*. Because of the identity between relation and person, what I have developed above about personhood should suffice to affirm the specificity of each relation and there is no need for a detailed exposition on this point. Indeed, rather than consider one concept—relation—and

61. See for example Aquinas, *De potentia*, q.10 a.4 ad18; *I Sent.*, d.11, q.1 a.1 ad2.
62. See Aquinas, ST, I, q.40, a.1.

its sub-concepts—paternity and filiation, active and passive spiration—we should understand each of the latter as a fully singular type of relation.

However, this analogical dimension is brought into light in a unique way in the case of trinitarian relations by the difficulty tradition has had in naming the relations that characterize specifically the third person. Generation implies two relations, which are named differently according to the procession they are grounded on. Communicating the fullness of divine substance in order to produce a perfect Image or expression establishes a relation of Fatherhood or Paternity. Receiving the substance founds a relation of Sonship or Filiation. We thus have three words: generation, Fatherhood, and Sonship. Strangely, however, the relation established by the procession called spiration is named spiration as well. Moreover, this same word, spiration, is used to express both the relation of the Father (and the Son) to the Spirit, and the relation of the Spirit to the Father (and the Son). They are often distinguished by being qualified as active spiration (parallel to Fatherhood) and passive spiration (parallel to Sonship)—but the name is the same. We could coin other words, such as "Expiration-Respiration," "Breathhood," or simply "Breathing-out" on the one hand, and Breathship or "Being-breathed-out," on the other, but the first are simply English translations of *spiratio*, and the latter are awkward and most probably too artificial. Indeed, the point is not to find a new terminology, but to underline that each relation is truly unique and cannot be constructed, linguistically speaking, the same way, at least in English: Father*hood*, Son*ship*, and spi*ration* or breath*ing-out*, are different types of words. Their very difference expresses the fact that each of the trinitarian relations are one-of-a-kind. As such, the inadequacy of the word spiration shows itself to be, in the end, (apophatically) extraordinarily adequate.

We can continue to explore the analogical dimension of other aspects of the triune God, even those that are related to God's unity. The divine substance is one. However, we have already seen how the one substance, intelligence, and will of God are possessed in a fully different mode by each person: they are always already paternal, filial, and pneumatic. The three modes of subsistence of the numerically identical substance are unique: the notion of "mode of subsistence" is analogical in the Trinity. This is obvious because it is synonymous to "person" or "hypostasis," but we need to realize that this implies that the substance is never neutral. Nothing in God is neutral.

The Analogical Trinity

In this regard, it is possible to reconsider each of the attributes traditionally understood to belong to the divine substance.[63] These attributes characterize the one substance and thus express the unity of the Trinity. However, they are attributes of a substance that subsists only according to three modes and never "out" of these. This implies that each attribute has three modes and is always according to a mode. Let us just take one example: God is omnipotent. However, if the Father communicates his substance to the Son without any reserve, omnipotence is immediately qualified as given and shared—categories that are not habitually considered part of omnipotence. Moreover, the Son receives the Father's power: the Son is truly and fully omnipotent but he so to say "depends" on the Father as permanent source of being and power. Now, a received or dependent omnipotence seems to be a contradiction in terms. And the Holy Breath brings us one step further: not only do the Father and the Son share the divine attribute of omnipotence, but in the Spirit they share the personal power of the other, as such. The power *of the Father*, as such, is interior to the Son, who can wield it as his own, the power of the Son, as such, is interior to the Father, who can wield it as his own. It is, so to say, a "communal omnipotence." All these qualifications offer a profoundly renewed vision of omnipotence—a truly divine one at that. They allow God to be first and ultimately the criterion of what power truly is.[64] They allow God to be conceived of as God. The most important, however, is that this happens because the divine substance is not understood prior to and independently from its triple possession by the Father, the Son, and the Breath. Omnipotence in God is always and only paternal, filial, and pneumatic. It is given, received, and communal, and as such it has no neutral mode.

Let us note that in no way does the triple possession of the substance alter its perfect unity and simplicity. The analogical dimension of the modes of possessing God's substance and of its attributes brings no more—and no less—distinction than the trinitarian processions, relations, and persons. This is simply what the distinction of the persons truly implies. God is absolutely simple—but God's simplicity is incredibly rich and plural.

In the same way, it is worthwhile to take a fresh look at the classical doctrine of perichoresis, the mutual inhabitation of each person of the

---

63. Other authors have experimented with renewed conceptions of the traditional divine attributes: see Barth, *Church Dogmatics* II/1, §29; Balthasar, *Theo-Logic II: Truth of God*, 138–49. However, I believe they have not stressed the trinitarian dimension of these attributes as much as they could have.

64. See Barth, *Church Dogmatics* IV/1, §59, 186.

Trinity in the two others: "Because of this unity [of essence] the Father is entire (*totus*) in the Son, entire in the Holy Spirit; the Son is entire in the Father, entire in the Holy Spirit, the Holy Spirit is entire in the Father, entire in the Son."[65] Now, if each person is truly unique, each will inhabit the others and be inhabited by them in a unique and unrepeatable mode. The Father is in the Son and the Breath as their eternal and continuous source. Moreover, he is in each according to a specific mode, either through generation or through breathing-out. The Son-*Logos* is in the Father as the hypostasis, which is eternally and continuously conceived and expressed by him; and he is in the Breath as its eternal and continuous *re*-spirator. The Breath is in the Father and the Son as the eternal and continuous sharing to the other of each one's most intimate being, which binds them together.

In fact, the analogous dimension of their personhood allows not only for a distinct position but also for a distinct *role* inside the perichoretic unity of the Trinity. The Father, as source of the Godhead, holds together all he produces through a unity of origin—and according to some theologians, through being a focal point of unity.[66] He is in the others through his operation. The Son is in the Father as the product of the Father's operation and in the Breath through his own (received) operation. He may also operate a form of "mediation" in the life of the Trinity, by receiving and giving back the Father's gift. The unity given by the Spirit is the unity of mutual interiority and intimacy. It is a more "personal" or "hypostatical" type of unity ("hypostatical" is to be understood here not in the christological meaning, but in the sense of what pertains to one of the divine hypostasis). It is "personal" in one sense because breathing-out-and-into communicates not only the substance of the Father and the Son but (in another way) their person, because it communicates their "heart" and "desire." It is "personal" in another, more radical, sense, because it is the gift of another person, that of the Breath itself. There may seem to be another paradox here, since the Breath was found to be one of the "less personal" of the three divine names. However, it is also the most personal, from the point of view, not of the substantial dimension of personhood, but of its transparency, its "sharedness," and "relationality." As such, the Spirit adds a form of "hypostatical seal" on the more substantial type of unity of the Father and the Son. The perichoretic sharing of the one divine substance in the Trinity operates

---

65. Council of Florence, Decree for the Jacobites, 1439 (DH 1331); see also Durand, *La périchorèse des personnes trinitaires*.

66. See Durand, *Le Père, Alpha et Oméga de la vie trinitaire*, 245–74.

The Analogical Trinity

according to different modes, as source, exchange, and personal gift—or in other words we are more familiar with, as paternal, filial, and pneumatic. Although the Breath is not more related to unity than the Father or the Son, it does play a unique and defining role in this unity.[67] Notwithstanding the fact that God subsists in three profoundly different and unique modes, indeed because of this, God is endowed with a unity that surpasses all conceivable unity and simplicity.

* * *

This can lead to some concluding comments to the present chapter on the trinitarian implications of the breath-metaphor. On the one hand, the metaphor is but a metaphor: it needs to be put into perspective and critically balanced by the tradition of the church concerning trinitarian faith. This helps keep in mind that the eternal Breath of God is a divine hypostasis on par with the Father and the Son, consubstantial to them and truly "personal," in the sense of a specific mode of subsistence of the one God. It knows and wills and participates in the divine self-consciousness. On the other hand, the breath-metaphor has helped us stretch the boundaries of the traditional trinitarian concepts: by illumining the uniqueness of personhood of the Spirit in comparison to the Father and the Son, and by showing how each is "differently different" from human persons, it has opened the way for an analogical conception of divine personhood. In this light, every common term that designates plurality in the Trinity—person, relation, procession—proves to be analogical as well. In fact, not even the common terms which express unity are neutral: neither the one essence, nor the divine attributes—glory, power, intelligence, will—nor the perichoretic inhabitation of the persons in each another, can be understood outside of their unique possession by each person.

Now, this comprehension of the Trinity is the conceptual framework in which the breath-metaphor can be worked out and received. Only then does it fully make sense. However, it is precisely through the metaphor that this understanding can be reached. Most of the established inner-trinitarian

---

67. Although he does so along different lines than I do, Weinandy also expounds an active conception of perichoresis where each person acts according to its *proprium*, and in which the Spirit is the key factor (Weinandy, *Father's Spirit of Sonship*, 79–80). In a more general sense, R. Kendall Soulen shows that the Scriptures offer a plurality of models of unity in the Trinity: based on the Tetragrammaton, on the relation between Father, Son, and Holy Spirit, and on the multiplicity of divine names (Soulen, *Divine Name(s)*).

notions are based on the Father-Son relation, but do not "operate" as well when taking the Spirit into account. Considering the third person for itself and in itself and staying as close as possible to the specific traits of the *Ruah-Pneuma* as revealed in the economy, "breaks open" the classical system and obliges to re-elaborate it in new terms. The breath-metaphor has a precious heuristic value insofar as it keeps open the perception of the differences in God.

In the end, in the same way as the unity and simplicity of the triune God are perfect and surpass all worldly unity and any conception of unity we may have, his plurality and the distinctions that are also part of his being are "perfect" as well. In God even differences and otherness surpass anything we can conceive of from our worldly experience. Indeed, both unity and alterity are the conditions of love—and both are the fruit of love. As usual the bottom line and criterion of all trinitarian thought is the simple assertion found in the First Letter of John: "God is love" (4:8, 16). Trinitarian theology has spent much of its energy working out how "one" the Trinity is: rightly so, and it must continue to do this with great energy and determination. The God of Jesus-Christ is the one God of Israel. However, the other path is just as crucial: the rich and fruitful differences of the Trinity should be made to appear and flourish.

4

The Manifestation of the Breath of the Father and of the Son

Ascending from the economy to the eternal Trinity is not an aim in itself. Of course, understanding the triune God is a source of joy and delight, however poor our comprehension may be. Nevertheless, the ultimate goal of trinitarian theology is to be able to discern the Father, the Son, and the Breath in the concrete lives of the believers and nourish their relationship to the triune God. The movement of ascension finds its fulfillment when one "descends" back to the economy to decrypt it with a deeper and more precise understanding gained in the immanent Trinity.

To do this, I will concentrate on two types of manifestations of the Breath in its relation to the Father and the Son: the endeavor to represent the Trinity through art and the trinitarian dimension of prayer. Art offers by its nature a representation of our theological understanding, which is too often forgotten or considered as secondary. Representation is in fact an integral part of the thought process. Resorting to metaphors, as I have done throughout this essay, is but one aspect of this: we also need to confirm and to complete theology through art and sometimes even ground it in art, and, more generally, in imagination.[1] Prayer was one of our starting points—prayer *en pneumati*—and it is the main embodiment of the Breath in the economy. Of course, other fields of investigation would certainly be fruitful as well: the life of the church—obviously—and human existence

---

1. For more on this, see for instance S. Coakley or N. Steeves (see above, chap. 2, p. 37n28).

THE BREATH OF GOD

and activity both benefit from a pneumatological perspective and, in return, enrich pneumatology. Exploring them in the light of our reflection on the Holy Spirit as Breath would be an excellent test of how effective such a pneumatology can truly be. However, both would ask for a rather long exposition of ecclesiology and anthropology, which could not fit in the limits of this essay. Moreover, prayer offers access in a nutshell and in a concentrated form to the work of the Spirit in the lives of the believers.

Representing the Triune God

After our reflection on the "analogical Trinity" in the previous chapter it is impossible not to see that the whole representation we have of the Trinity has shifted. If each person is person in a unique way, how should we represent the triune God? Is it even possible to represent the eternal Breath, which exists (only) in and through the Father and the Son? How can it be depicted if it has no "face" and is substantial and personal in such a different way? I will mostly focus on iconography and painting,[2] but will conclude with a quick foray into the realm of music, which offers what is perhaps the less inadequate expression of the Breath.

In fact, a large part of Christian iconography, and even some of its most famous illustrations, simply do not correspond to the renewed comprehension the breath-metaphor has led us to. We tend to represent the Trinity as three human persons—as in the beautiful and inspiring icon of Rublev, depicting the three angels who visited Abraham and Sarah by the oaks of Mamre (Gen 18:1-15) (figure 1). Representing the divine persons with angels portrayed in human traits is inadequate, but that is obvious and fully acceptable. What is more problematic in the light of all that has been said about the uniqueness of each person is the pronounced similarity between the three: ascribing a personal name to each is quite difficult and open to interpretation. The angels are virtually identical and differ from each other only through their clothing and gestures.

A characteristic manuscript example from France (figure 2) shows even more similarity, since even the gestures are identical. Even poorer in this regard are the depictions of the Trinity as a body with three heads (figure 3), or one head with three noses and mouths (and beards, since all three

---

2. I am greatly indebted to Coakley's excellent chapter, "Seeing God: Trinitarian Thought and Iconography," in *God, Sexuality, and the Self,* 190-265, for the present section, as well as to Boespflug, *Dieu et ses images.*

The Manifestation of the Breath of the Father and of the Son

are male) but four eyes and one forehead (figure 4). Of course these insist on the unity of substance and avoid misrepresenting divine personhood along the lines of human persons, but the risk is to imagine a common neutral substance with three "outgrowths." The divine persons are then less distinct between each other than are human beings—while the opposite is true.

Figure 1—"The Trinity," Andrei Rublev, 1422–1427, State Tretyakov Gallery, Moscow.

The Breath of God

Figure 2— "Trinity at the Altar," Franciscan Missal, 1380, Bibliothèque Nationale de France, Paris.

The Manifestation of the Breath of the Father and of the Son

Figure 3—"Abraham and the Trinity," English Psalter, c. 1270–1280, St. John's College, Cambridge.

Figure 4—Trifrons Trinity, 1610, Tiroler Volkskunstmuseum, Innsbruck.

Other types of representations are more faithful to the analogous dimension of the divine hypostases in so far as they underline the differences between the persons. As we have seen above, each person may be depicted with varying degrees of substantiality and of resemblance to the human person. In some cases, the centrality of the Father—source of the Godhead and of the life of the Trinity—is quite clear, as in the Trinity with two medallions found in Prague (figure 5). A very large Father holds two small medallions, one with the Lamb of God in his right hand, and one with the

The Manifestation of the Breath of the Father and of the Son

dove of the Holy Spirit in his left hand. It seems like an echo of Irenaeus's understanding of the Son and the Spirit as the two hands of the Father. Only the Father is represented with the traits of a human person, while the lamb and the dove are turned towards the Father, making him in effect the absolute center of the Trinity.

Figure 5—"Heavenly Jerusalem and communio sanctorum," Augustine's De Civitate Dei, 1142–1150, St. Vitus Library, Prague.

Other forms of iconography will give a more central role to Christ, as is the case in the depiction of his baptism, where the Father is only a hand and the Spirit a dove, while the second person is, obviously, a human figure, who looks at the spectator and commands his or her attention (figure 6).[3] Through his incarnation the Son is the most human of the three: Father and Spirit are so to speak "faceless." Though Christ is kenotically plunged in the

---

3. Let us note that the *Horos* of the Council of Nicaea II allows for representations of the Son with the traits of a human being, not of the Father nor of the Holy Spirit (see DH 600). The Father is depicted with specific human characteristics only from the twelfth century on, while before that he was represented with traits taken from the representation of Christ (see Boespflug, *Dieu et ses images*, 186).

THE BREATH OF GOD

waters of the Jordan, and seems quite small in comparison with the towering presence of John the Baptist, he is the most solid and substantial person of the Trinity. This corresponds to one aspect of his personhood, if we consider the Father to be perpetually gushing forth and to need the Son to have a form.[4] The Son is in effect the most visible and tangible, since he is the one who reveals the Father and the Holy Spirit. Of course, this is a representation of the Trinity in the economy of salvation, as befits the incarnate Son. The Transfiguration, or any of the mysteries of the life of Jesus would follow the same model. We know, however, that it expresses one aspect of the eternal relations between the persons.

Figure 6—"Christ's Baptism," Rabula Gospels, sixth century, Biblioteca Medicea Laurenziana, Firenze.

4. See above, chap. 3, p. 86.

The Manifestation of the Breath of the Father and of the Son

In other representations still, the Father and the Son are the more substantial hypostases, depicted with the traits of human personhood, while the Spirit, almost always in the form of a dove, is both more aerial and less personal. This corresponds more closely to the specifically fluid nature of the third person. One of the most beautiful iconic interpretations of this model is the Divine Fatherhood, of the school of Novgorod (figure 7). Father and Son are very present, and both have human bodies and faces. Their difference, however, is underlined by the fact that the Father is an adult and he is much larger, while the Son is a child on his lap: this may indicate the relation between generator and generated. The Spirit, meanwhile, is a dove appearing inside the Son (and the Father), as though emerging from their depth, as their common heart. The unity of the three is established by fitting the Son and the Spirit in the frame of the Father's body, which means that the unity of substance is expressed differently according to the person: the Father is the source of unity, the Son inhabits the Father, and the Spirit inhabits both and perhaps binds them to each other. This is a good rendering of an "analogical Trinity."

Figure 7—"*The Fatherland with selected saints,*" School of Novgorod, beginning of the fourteenth century, State Tretyakov Gallery, Moscow.

THE BREATH OF GOD

Another quite similar representation, from the Lothian Bible, shows the Father and the Son as two men "sharing" the dove of the Holy Spirit between them (figure 8). The Father and the Son are united by common legs, but the first is a mature man, while the second is a beardless young man or even a teenager. Moreover, the difference of personhood between the Spirit and the two other hypostases is manifest. Along the same lines, underscoring the otherness of the third person, in the church of Urschalling in Bavaria (figure 9) the Holy Spirit is depicted as a woman, welling up so to speak from two masculine figures, an older one and a younger one. Interestingly, the Spirit has no visible hands of her own: she will need to act through the hands and works of the Father and the Son. Regrettably, in some extreme cases, the insubstantiality of the Spirit leads the artist to actually omit it. For instance, in Simone Cantarini's "Compassion of the Father" (figure 10), the third person disappears, with the effect of representing God as a Binity. However unfortunate this is, it is yet another confirmation of the elusive nature of the Holy Spirit.

Figure 8—"Trinity: Two Persons flanking Dove," Lothian Bible, c. 1220, The Morgan Library & Museum, New York.

The Manifestation of the Breath of the Father and of the Son

Figure 9—"The Trinity with a 'feminine' Holy Spirit," c. 1390, St. Jacob's Church, Urschalling, Bavaria.

THE BREATH OF GOD

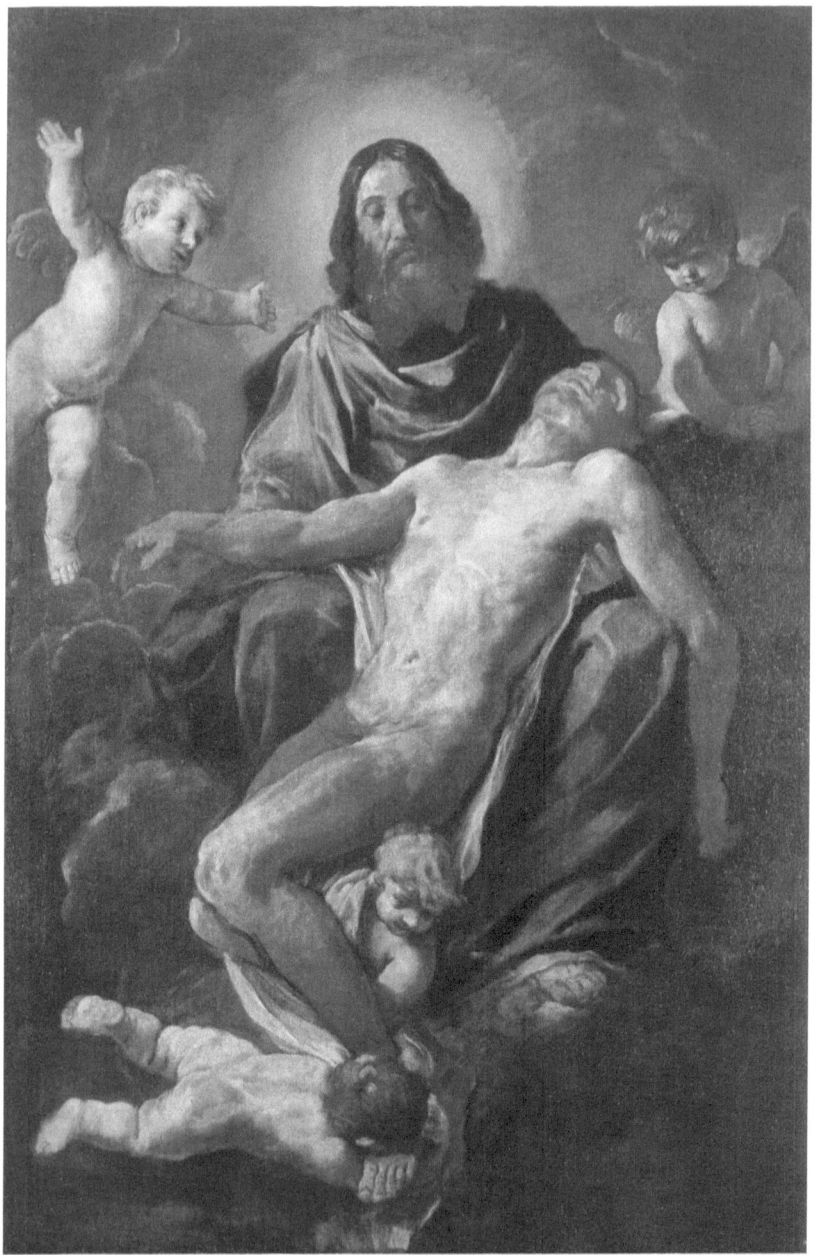

Figure 10—The Holy Trinity (unfinished), Simone Cantarini, 1640, National Gallery of Scotland, Edinburgh.

The Manifestation of the Breath of the Father and of the Son

Illustrations of the Trinity that present the second person as the Word are more rare. This "atmospheric" name of the Son is probably difficult to depict in the light of the human and material density he takes on in his incarnation. However, ancient representations of the Throne of God show how all three are mysterious and cannot be characterized as human persons: the Spirit is a dove, the Father is indicated by an empty throne, and the Word is depicted in the form of a scroll, which can only be read and thus listened to (figure 11). This expresses the fluid nature of all other trinitarian persons—as a corroboration of the analogical dimension of divine personhood, both in itself and in regards to the human person.

Figure 11—"The throne of God as a trinitarian image," early fifth century, St. Matrona's chapel, San Prisco (Naples, Italy).

Are there depictions of the third person as a Breath the Father breathes out into the Son? There are representations of the Spirit as breath or wind in the economy. Either the Holy Spirit itself blows out a creative wind, as in the late twentieth century painting by A. Kiefer (figure 12), or it is itself a powerful wind blowing down from the Father, depicted as an extended hand, as in the recent mosaic by M. Rupnik (figure 13).

The Breath of God

Figure 12—Send Forth Your Spirit, Anselm Kiefer, 1974, The Metropolitan Museum of Art, New York.

The Manifestation of the Breath of the Father and of the Son

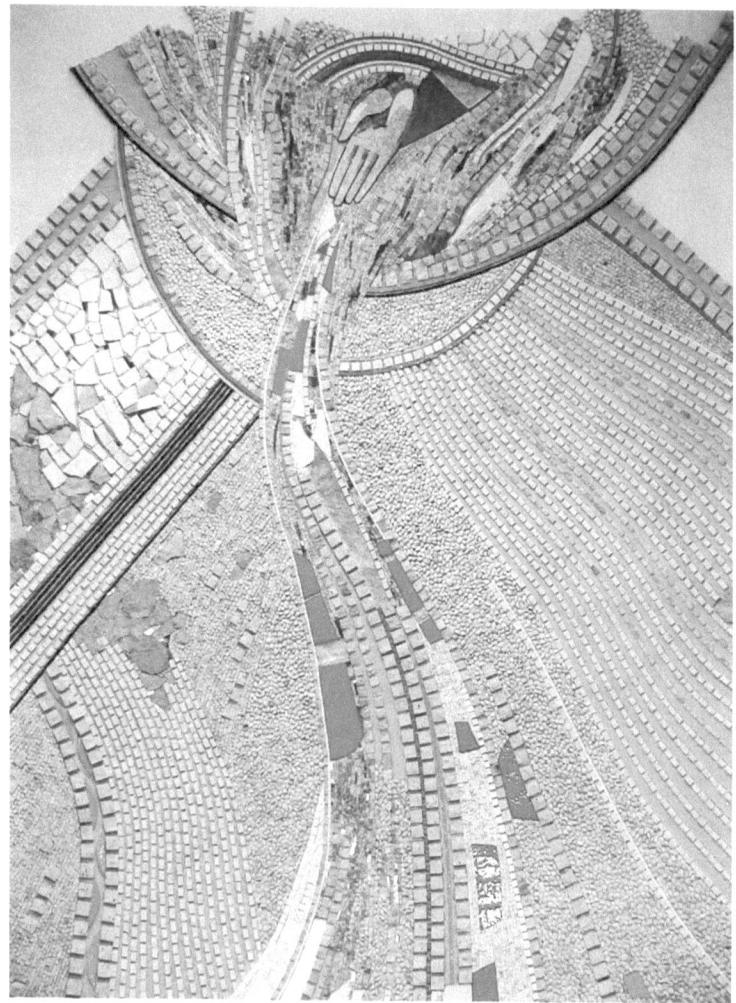

Figure 13—"The Hand of the Father and the Descent of the Holy Spirit on the Son," Marko Rupnik, 2004, Chapel of the Apostolic Nunciature, Damascus.

In chapter 2, I have allowed myself to compare the generation of the Son through the spiration of the Spirit to the creation of Adam through the breath of God. There are beautiful representations of this scene. Often the Creator is christomorphic, as in the stained-glass windows of Chartres (figure 14), but the sixteenth-century painting attributed to E. Delaune (figure 15) clearly portrays the Father breathing onto and into Adam. These may evoke the inner exhalation of the Breath from the Father to the Son, but do not do so explicitly.

THE BREATH OF GOD

Figure 14—"Creation of Adam," thirteenth century, Cathedral of Chartres.

The Manifestation of the Breath of the Father and of the Son

Figure 15—God creating Adam and breathing life into him, attributed to Etienne Delaune, sixteenth century, Louvre Museum, Paris.

The representations that are the closest to depicting the inner-trinitarian breathing of the Spirit are those where the Father and Son share a dove, which is so to speak "breathed" out by both. Figure 16 depicts this shared breath as a dove with wings that touch the lips of the Father and the Son and which thus provides a bond of unity between the two "breathers." Some *Gnadenstuhlen* offer a better representation of the *taxis*, as in figure 17: the Father, above the Son, seems to be the first source of the dove breathed out of his mouth down towards the Son. The Son also exhales the same dove, but he does so on the cross, as an economic expression of giving back the breath he receives.

THE BREATH OF GOD

Figure 16—"Celestial Hierarchy," Life of Saint Denis, 1317, Bibliothèque Nationale de France, Paris.

Figure 17—"Throne of Grace surrounded by the Tetramorphus," Cambrai Missal, c. 1120, Municipal Library, Cambrai.

The Manifestation of the Breath of the Father and of the Son

These last representations show how Christian iconography has truly perceived the need to consider the Holy Spirit as a breath and a wind, according to its revealed name: *Ruah-Pneuma*. They sometimes try to depict it as the common Breath of the Father and the Son. Nevertheless, they are unable to hold these together: the Spirit represented as Breath is an economic reality, while the eternal person is so to speak embodied in the more precise and substantial form of a dove. This confirms how difficult it is simply to represent the more fluid, interior, and anonymous nature of the divine Breath—and especially how difficult it is to fully take this into account to approach the third person in itself, in the inner life of the Trinity.

For this reason, it is useful to look at another art form, namely music. Although not even music will provide for an exact illustration of the third person as the Breath the Father inspires into the Son and receives back from him, it does have the potential to express some of the more specific characteristics of the Holy Spirit better than the more material arts, such as icons or paintings. I will just present a brief comment on one part of a piece from Bach, the *Kyrie* in the *Clavierübung III*, sometimes referred to as the *German Organ Mass*.[5] Bach is particularly relevant because he sets himself firmly in the Lutheran tradition that is wary of representing God through images, since this offers a risk of idolatry, while music is considered much more appropriate: it does not "objectify" God but introduces those who listen into a living relation with him.[6] Though the *kyrie* sung during a Eucharist is christological, the *Naumburg Kyrie* used here by Bach addresses the Father in the first verse, the Son in the second, and the Spirit in the third:

Kyrie, Gott, Vater in Ewigkeit,	O Lord, God, the Father for evermore!
Groß ist dein Barmherzigkeit,	Immense is your mercy,
Aller Ding ein Schöpfer und Regierer	Of all things you are Creator and Ruler.
Eleison.	Have mercy.
Christe, aller Welt Trost,	O Christ, Solace of the whole World,
Uns Sünder allein du hast erlöst,	Who alone we Sinners have redeemed;
O Jesu Gottes Sohn	O Jesus! Son of God!
Unser Mittler bist in dem höchsten Thron	Our Mediator before the highest Throne

---

5. I will closely follow the excellent musicological and theological commentary expounded in Charru and Theobald, *L'Esprit créateur*, 221–26.

6. See Charru and Theobald, *L'Esprit créateur*, 32–35.

The Breath of God

Zu dir schreien wir aus Herzensbegier,	Lord, to Thee in our need we cry,
Eleison.	Have mercy.

Kyrie, Gott heiliger Geist,	Holy Lord, God the Holy Ghost!
Tröst', stärk' uns im Glauben allermeist,	With faith console and sustain our heart,
Daß wir am letzten End,	That at the last we hence
Fröhlich abscheiden aus diesem Elend,	in joy depart.
Eleison.	Have mercy.

Now the first two verses give titles to the persons: "God, the Father for evermore" and "Christ, Solace of the whole world." Conversely, the third just calls out to "God the Holy Ghost." Charru and Theobald comment that this is an expression of the fact that the Spirit is "face-less" or "form-less" (*sans figure*). The text of the *kyrie* does not say who is the third person but only states what it does: it consoles, sustains, and gives joy.[7] Moreover, while in the first verse the believer is not mentioned and in the second the sinner cries out to Christ, as though at a distance, in the third it is in and through the believer that the divine person is present and at work: "The 'form-less' Spirit manifests itself *in* [the faithful], who is touched *in* his flesh by *the effects* of the inner 'consolation' and 'strengthening.'"[8]

The apparent absence of proper personal action of the Holy Spirit is also underscored by the fact that the third chorale does not offer a specific musical theme.[9] The first chorale to the Father (score 1) is made of two distinct themes, firstly in prime form and then in inverted form, which may indicate the Creator turning towards humankind in his mercy. The chorale to the Son (score 2) starts with the same prime form, which is beautifully unfurled under the words *Unser Mittler*, and ends with a brief appearance of the inverted form (measures 43–44): after the evocation of Christ's saving action the final inversion shows Christ turning towards the Throne of the Father as our Mediator.

---

7. Charru and Theobald, *L'Esprit créateur*, 222.

8. "L'Esprit 'sans-figure' se manifeste alors *en* lui, affecté *dans* sa chair *par ses effets* de 'consolation' et de 'fermeté' intérieures" (Charru and Theobald, *L'Esprit créateur*, 223).

9. See Charru and Theobald, *L'Esprit créateur*, 224–25.

The Manifestation of the Breath of the Father and of the Son

Score 1

Score 2

However, the verse addressing the Spirit joins together the two forms, inseparably, from the beginning to the end (score 3). The Spirit has no "title" or "form," it has no action of its own: it expresses itself in the form and works of the other two persons and brings them together.

Score 3

Nevertheless, the two themes are not exactly superimposed, but there is a slight counterpunctic tension between them. The authors explain that this introduces a "breath (*respiration*)," a movement of expiration and inspiration, of dilatation and contraction, according to the order in which the voices enter (score 4: the dilatation and contraction is indicated by the arrows that have been added to the score).[10]

---

10. See Charru and Theobald, *L'Esprit créateur*, 225–26.

The Breath of God

Score 4

Indeed, the Spirit is interior to the Father and the Son but is not identical to them. It is the open space in which they breathe. The Breath is this space itself.[11]

In the end, no pictorial or musical expression can offer an adequate representation of the mystery of the triune God and especially of the third person. Some present better than others the analogous dimension of divine personhood and of all aspects of trinitarian life. They stress the *maior dissimilitudo* between the divine persons, and between each of these and human persons. Paradoxically, the breath-metaphor will allow for a less anthropomorphic image of divine personhood and of the Trinity. If ever it

---

11. The triple fugue from the same *Clavierübung III* also expresses some of the traits of the Holy Spirit expounded here. Classically, each movement has been appropriated to one of the divine persons, with the idea that the third is referred to the Spirit as a wind: "The triple fugue . . . is a symbol of the Trinity. The same theme recurs in three connected fugues, but each time with another personality. The first fugue is calm and majestic, with an absolutely uniform movement throughout; in the second the theme seems to be disguised, and is only occasionally recognisable in its true shape, as if to suggest the divine assumption of an earthly form; in the third, it is transformed into rushing semiquavers as if the Pentecostal wind were coming roaring from heaven" (Schweitzer, *J. S. Bach I*, 277; see also Alain, *L'œuvre pour orgue de Jean-Sébastien Bach*, 37). Charru and Theobald, on the other hand, insist that here also there is no specific theme for the Holy Spirit but that all three fugues are fully trinitarian. Each has a main subject, which remains the same, and two counter-subjects: the theme of the Son is an embroidery or embellishment on the first, which is the theme of the Father, while the theme of the Spirit is inscribed into the same intervallic range: *G-C* and *F-B flat* (see Charru and Theobald, *L'Esprit créateur*, 260). The classical commentaries underline that the Spirit is a breath and a wind, but the relevance of the latter interpretation is that it presents a view of the Trinity in which the Father is the source and center, the Son comes forth from the Father and is relative to him, and the Spirit is interior to them and to their relation.

The Manifestation of the Breath of the Father and of the Son

was still necessary, this is yet a further confirmation of its value. However, all forms of representation stumble on the difficulty of expressing and respecting the characteristics of the *Ruah-Pneuma* of God. In the economy it sometimes is a wind or a breath, but when the eternal Trinity is depicted, the third person is either very similar to the other two, or it is a dove, or it simply disappears. The musical example confirms that the Spirit *qua* Spirit cannot be represented as the other persons can. This may be disappointing but it should have been expected. The Spirit manifests itself in its actions in and through others. This is why I will now turn to prayer, where the Spirit does precisely that, in relation to the Father and to the Son and in relation to the pray-er, and does so "in person."

Praying the Father through the Son and in the Breath

We will find prayer to be the most exact embodiment of all we have understood about the Holy Spirit and the Trinity in the previous chapters. I will offer a form of "phenomenology" of prayer; in other words, a descriptive analysis of prayer in the light of the pneumatological and trinitarian insights gained so far. A section of the first chapter was devoted to praying in the Spirit in a biblical perspective, but after having expounded the inner-trinitarian comprehension of the third person developed from that economic expression, it is now possible to come back to the economy with "new eyes," better equipped to understand the Spirit's action in our concrete lives of prayer. What does it mean to pray *en pneumati* if the Spirit is the eternal Breath of God? This question is closely linked with a wider one: what does it mean to pray *en pneumati* if each hypostasis of the Trinity is unique in its personhood? The "analogical Trinity" shows the way towards taking into consideration the difference between the Father, the Son, and the Spirit, so that prayer will imply a specific type of relationship to each divine name, where the Father is the Alpha and the Omega, the Incarnate Son the center, and the Spirit the inner breath that inspires and transforms the pray-er.[12]

Let us start with the Father. He is the source of the divinity. He utters the Word and breathes out the Breath. He does so in the eternal Trinity but also in the world and in our lives. As such he calls us and draws us to himself. He has the initiative in our prayer life: true prayer does not start

---

12. A reflection on this theme has previously appeared in a different form in Vetö, *Du Christ à la Trinité*, 452–58.

with our decision—our experience shows that our own will is anyhow rarely capable of truly settling us into prayer! Prayer begins and is made possible because we have been summoned: "No one comes to me," says Jesus, "unless drawn by the Father who sent me" (John 6:44). The Father is also the one we listen to when we pray: he is the one who spoke through the prophets and who, in these last days, speaks to us through his Son (see Heb 1:1–2). He is the one who addresses us and sends forth his Word. He is thus the one to whom the silent heart and inner ear of the pray-er is attuned. Not only does he speak to us but he is also the source of all gifts received in prayer—peace, joy, strength, a contrite heart or a transformed heart—as he is the source of life.

If the Father is the Alpha of prayer, he will also be its Omega, its term: "For us there is one God, the Father, from whom are all things and for whom we exist" (1 Cor 8:6). As such, he is the one to whom we orient ourselves principally to give thanks for all gifts received, just as Jesus did: "I thank you Father, Lord of heaven and earth. . . . All things have been handed over to me by my Father" (Luke 10:21–22). He is also the one we address our desires and petitions to. Let us not be too condescending towards prayers of petition: though they are less selfless and noble than contemplation and praise, they are in all religious traditions the basic type of prayer. They express our trust in God in the simplest way and testify to the way we let him play a concrete role in our lives.[13] Likewise, if the Father is the term, every offering of our self, every moment in which we entrust our lives to God, is in fact oriented towards the Father. Into the Father's hands we "commend our spirit" as Jesus did on the cross (see Luke 23:46). The beautiful prayer inspired by Charles of Foucauld says it all:

> Father, I abandon myself into your hands; do with me what you will. Whatever you may do, I thank you: I am ready for all, I accept all. Let only your will be done in me, and in all your creatures—I wish no more than this, O Lord. Into your hands I commend my soul: I offer it to you with all the love of my heart, for I love you, Lord, and so need to give myself, to surrender myself into your hands without reserve, and with boundless confidence, for you are my Father.[14]

---

13. See Chrétien, *L'Arche de la parole*, 21.

14. This prayer is a common possession of the spirituality inspired by Charles of Foucauld; it is a simplified version of a meditation written in 1896 by Br. Charles (Charles of Foucauld, "Prayer of Abandonment," lines 1–14).

The Manifestation of the Breath of the Father and of the Son

Fundamentally speaking, all Christian prayer is addressed, directly or indirectly, to the Father. Our daily model is the liturgy of the church, of course, which almost always addresses God the Father: "It is truly right and just, our duty and salvation, always and everywhere to give you thanks, Father most holy . . . "[15] This is rooted in the way Jesus himself prayed the Father and he taught his disciples to pray the Father: "Pray then this way: 'Our Father in heaven . . . '" (Matt 6:9). Historically speaking, the first generations of Christians did not even pray Jesus Christ, let alone the Holy Spirit: prayers addressed to Christ appear only during the second century, and prayers to the Spirit later still.[16] This does not mean we cannot pray the Son or the Spirit, but that all Christian prayer is ultimately related to the Father. It has the Father as its source and horizon.

In the previous chapter I have underscored the fact that from a certain point of view the Father, not only the Spirit, is "meta-personal" and fluid. He is an unfathomable, bottomless, gushing wellspring. As such, he also is faceless—or better, his "face" is veiled. This explains that the soul's desire rises towards the Father without ever fully embracing him. One hears his voice and receives his gifts but one never quite manages to perceive his face. For this reason, the prayer to the Father can, to a certain extent, be described as *adoration*. Without setting rigid boundaries it may nonetheless be helpful to distinguish between *contemplation* and *adoration*. To contemplate means to "look thoughtfully at something." Sometimes to contemplate is only to think and study something but it is in any case very much related to sight and is connoted as such. Rather than contemplate the Father we cannot see, we adore him. The pray-er stands in front of the Father, the all-powerful Creator and the Father of mercies, and expresses feelings and thoughts of love and respect. The pray-er stands in front of the Father's gaze and lets himself or herself be submerged by the "ocean of his love which knows no shores."[17] The pray-er cannot embrace the Father but

15. Common Preface VI (for masses with no proper Preface) in Socias, *Daily Roman Missal*, 762.

16. See Studer, *Durch Geschichte zum Glauben*, 39–42.

17. This expression originally comes from Gregory Nazianzen (*Oratio XXXVIII*, 7 [PG 36, 317]; see also John Damascene, *Expositio Fidei orthodoxae*, I, 9 [PG 94, 833]), to designate God as Being, but it is quite fitting to designate the Father, source of the Trinity and of all being. Thérèse of Lisieux uses it to express the immensity of the love of God in Jesus: "De même qu'un torrent se jetant avec impétuosité dans l'océan entraîne après lui tout ce qu'il a rencontré sur son passage, de même, ô mon Jésus, l'âme qui se plonge dans l'océan de votre amour attire avec elle tous les trésors qu'elle possède . . . " (Thérèse of Lisieux, *Œuvres complètes*, 281).

is embraced by him; he or she cannot truly contemplate the Father, but lets himself or herself be contemplated by him.

The Son is the center or the fulcrum of our life of prayer. As second hypostasis he receives and gives back the Breath in the eternal life of God and is thus so to speak the center or "pivot" of the divine relations. As Incarnate Word, he expresses the Father in the Breath and makes himself one of us. Therefore, if the Father is the source, the Son is the canal through which the source reaches us. Here we need to complete the quotation from 1 Corinthians about the Father with what Paul adds about the Son: "For us there is one God, the Father, from whom are all things and for whom we exist, and one Lord, Jesus Christ, through whom are all things and through whom we exist" (1 Cor 8:6). When the Father speaks to us, Jesus, as Word, is the teaching of the Father. This means that the best way to listen to the Father is to open our inner ears to the Word and to the words of the Word. These words, the teaching of Jesus, are the way the Father touches us. Of course we read the words of Jesus in the Scriptures to receive his encouragement, his exhortation, and his orientation. But, more fundamentally, through them we receive the Word (of the Father), the person of the *Logos* himself, into our hearts. In a way, more than the precise contents of the Scriptures, what stays are the taste and joy and nourishment of encountering the person of the Word: "Your words were found, and I ate them, and your words became to me a joy and the delight of my heart" (Jer 15:16; see Ps 119:24). And doing so we listen to the Father as he sends his Son, the Word, into our lives to communicate himself to us. The words are doubly tasty and nourishing because they are the Son and because they offer the Father's love and gifts.

Conversely, if the Father is not only the source but also the end or the term, the Son is the "way" (John 14:6) to the Father. Jesus himself says: "No one comes to the Father except through me" (John 14:6). When we orient our hearts and our minds to the Father, we do so through Jesus Christ. This means we turn to him, in order to turn to the Father. Or we turn to him in prayer, only to discover that he brings us to the Father. This happens in different ways. As "Emmanuel, . . . God is with us" (Matt 1:23), Christ is a master and a companion. He walks with us and guides us to the Father, who awaits us and who draws us to himself. Rather than an abyss or an ocean of love, the second person is a friend. The Father and the Spirit do not and probably could not say: "I do not call you servants any longer . . . but I have called you friends" (John 15:15). In prayer we share with Jesus and dialogue

The Manifestation of the Breath of the Father and of the Son

with him as with a trusted confidant, which we rarely do with the two other persons—and if we do, most often we do so through Jesus. Likewise Christ is the way insofar as he presents us a model to which we conform ourselves. I abandon myself to the Father, not to the Son; but so as to hand my life to the Father, I attach myself to the Son, I follow him, I put my steps into his. "Follow me . . . ," "take your cross . . . ," "take my yoke . . . ," says he.[18] Only through him are we able to give ourselves to the Father: "It is through him that we say the '*Amen*,' to the glory of God" (2 Cor 1:20). Praying will mean entering into Christ's love for the Father and filial attitude, so as to relate to the Father as sons and daughters do. It means entering into Christ's relation to the Father so as to become sons and daughters in the Son.

I argue above that we do not contemplate the Father, but we adore him. We do contemplate the Son, however.[19] The second person presents himself to the pray-er with a much more defined "figure" or traits, because he is eternally the "image of the invisible God" (Col 1:15), and because he is in the history of salvation the Word made flesh. In a way this corresponds to the model of the Trinity in which the second hypostasis is the most substantial, because it is the closest to a human person. The Son has assumed a humanity. And this calls for a contemplation of this humanity, since we are before him whom "we have seen with our eyes, [whom] we have looked at and touched with our hands" (1 John 1:1). Though the Breath has no face and the Father's face is inaccessible, I can rest my gaze on the face of Christ—on the "glory of God in the face of Jesus Christ" (2 Cor 4:6). He is approachable, attainable—even if I cannot "hold" him either (John 20:17). Indeed, many mystics have insisted on the importance of praying with the *humanity* of Christ. For Teresa of Avila, his humanity is the firm ground of our prayer: those who in prayer turn away from his humanity are "left floating in the air"; they are similar to "a bird flying about that doesn't know

---

18. "We actually relate to the Father in an analogous manner to that of the Son" (Weinandy, *Father's Spirit of Sonship*, 103; see also 35–38). Conformation to Christ is of course a classical theme in mystical life.

19. Of course, one could contend that we also adore the Son, as in the Roman Catholic practice of the "adoration of the Blessed Sacrament." However, the notions are not used in this case with exactly the same meaning as I do: there is a certain recourse to sight in adoration of the Blessed Sacrament that makes it a form of contemplation. More important still, these distinctions aim at offering orientations and not strict boundaries between dimensions of prayer to the one and same God.

where to light."[20] Ignatius of Loyola invites us very methodically to meditate on Christ's life and deeds through the application of each of our senses:

> It is profitable to use the imagination and to apply the five senses to the [Scriptural texts], in the following manner. *The First Point.* By the sight of the imagination I will see the persons, by meditating and contemplating in detail all the circumstances around them, and by drawing some profit from the sight. *The Second Point.* By my hearing I will listen to what they are saying or might be saying; and then, reflecting on myself, I will draw some profit from this. *The Third Point.* I will smell the fragrance and taste the infinite sweetness and charm of the Divinity, of the soul, of its virtues, and of everything there, appropriately for each of the persons who is being contemplated. Then I will reflect upon myself and draw profit from this. *The Fourth Point.* Using the sense of touch, I will, so to speak, embrace and kiss the places where the persons walk or sit. I shall always endeavor to draw profit from this.[21]

To pray the Son is first and foremost to humbly watch Jesus touch a sick person or a child, to observe his step on the dusty paths of Judea or Galilee, his tears and his weariness, his exultation of joy, his gaze full of compassion and love, forgiveness and expectation.

However, contemplating the Son is precisely a way for the pray-er to orient himself or herself towards the Father—or to be oriented towards him. "Whoever has seen me has seen the Father" (John 14:9): we cannot see the Father, but when we see Christ, through Christ, we have access to the Father (and the Spirit). On the "face of Christ" we truly see the "glory of God" (see 2 Cor 4:6). Turning towards the Father does not mean turning away from the Son in his humanity; on the contrary it means turning towards him and being brought to the Father. Likewise, contemplating Christ does not mean turning away from the Father; on the contrary, as I look at Jesus and listen to him, I discern the Father's loving gaze and word. As I come close to Jesus I receive the Breath, which fills him as well.

---

20. Teresa of Avila, *The Book of Her Life*, 148; *Interior Castle*, 405.

21. Ignatius of Loyola, *Spiritual Exercises*, 151. The doctrine(s) of spiritual senses is complex, because it does not deal with Christ's humanity alone, and there is a debate about whether these senses are different from the physical ones or are our five senses applied through grace and theological virtues to God. The contemplation of the humanity of Christ is one of its cornerstones, however. On this theme, see Bonaventure, *Journey into God*, 76–85; Rahner, "La doctrine des 'sens spirituels' au Moyen Age," 263–99; Balthasar, *Glory of the Lord I: Seeing the Form*, 365–425.

The Manifestation of the Breath of the Father and of the Son

Time has come to go back to the consideration of the Holy Spirit. I will not repeat all that has already been expounded in the first chapter, which of course remains valid and may be of some help in a life of prayer. I will concentrate on the fact that our relationship to the Breath of God is marked by how different it is from the Father and the Son. The Breath is interior to the two other hypostases and brings their intimate being together. It will likewise act inside of us to bring the Father and the Son into us, and to bring us into the Father and the Son.

Bringing the Father and the Son into us means helping us to listen to them, helping us let their words sink into our hearts and minds. To a certain extent, we do not listen to the Spirit itself, but to the Father, who speaks his *Logos*, and, from within, the Spirit turns the ear of our heart towards the Voice of the Father. It *in*-spires us by carrying the Word and opening its way into us. Or, if we do listen to the Spirit, it means we hear the whisper of the Breath that carries the Son, the Father's Word, and that enables us to recognize the Father and the Son.[22] It allows us to recognize that these human words in the Scriptures or these daily events in my life come from the Father and are his words in the Word. It allows us to understand that these words and events, which are general and for all, are also addressed especially to me at this precise moment. The Breath whispers and murmurs as do breath, wind, and water: "There is living water in me, which speaks and says inside me, 'Come to the Father.'"[23] It is the transparent "milieu," the "atmosphere" that we barely see, but that enables us to see and in which we relate to the Father and the Son.

This is why the Breath also brings us into the Father and the Son. I do not commend my life into the hands of the Breath as I do with the Father, but I abandon myself to the inner force of the Breath to be able to entrust myself to the Father—and it brings me much further into him than would any human desire or movement. As we have seen above, the Spirit is not more related to love than are the Father or the Son, but it is more related to kindling our love and passions and emotions from within. In this sense it awakens the desire that pushes us and draws toward the Father: the "water that lives and murmurs" in us is also a powerful wind and a burning fire.

---

22. We know that the Word from the mouth of the Father is carried by his Breath: "[The] prophesying by the Spirit necessarily contains the word which is from the Word, that is, the gift of the Spirit is dyadically accompanied by the revelation of the Word" (Bulgakov, *Comforter*, 232).

23. Ignatius of Antioch, *Letter of Ignatius*, VII, §2, 105.

I do not follow the Spirit, but I follow its inspiration, to follow Christ. I do not conform myself to the Spirit, but I let the Spirit conform me to Christ. We are able to conform ourselves or be conformed to Jesus precisely through the divine Breath who works in our innermost beings: "like the Son, the Holy Spirit has conformed us into sons."[24] Being interior to the Son, the Breath inserts us so to speak into Christ's mind and heart and desire.[25] It makes us enter, ontologically, into his mode of existence—into his Sonship.

For this reason, we do not address the Spirit in prayer exactly in the same way as we do the two other persons. We had begun to see in the first chapter that to pray the Spirit is to pray *in* it and *through* it. We do not converse with the Spirit as we may with the Father and especially with the Son. We call unto it and invoke it. Indeed, many of the prayers to the Holy Spirit are invocations: the *Veni Creator Spiritu* and the *Veni Sancte Spiritus* are well-known examples. I may well and I should address the third person and speak to it, but I do so to ask it to come pray in me, to inspire me to desire and speak as I should to the Father and the Son. I invoke *it* to nurture my conversation with *them*. I may of course thank and praise the Spirit, but mostly I thank the Father in the Spirit. And more fundamentally still, the Spirit of sonship, in turning us to the Father by conforming us to Christ, allows us to speak out our most important word, our true prayer: "Abba, Father!"

All this, however, does not mean we have no "personal" relation to the Spirit. It is simply a very specific type of personal relation. The Breath is not the source and the end; nor is it the way, "God-with-us," the visible companion. Instead, the Breath is the intimate, invisible companion. It is God as *intimior intimo meo et superior summo meo*.[26] The movement that turns me towards it in prayer is in a special way an inward one. I will "open up" to it as to something and someone immense and much wider than me, but this "opening up" will also be an "opening in." It will make me present to that which is hidden in me. As with the Father and the Son one does

---

24. Weinandy, *Father's Spirit of Sonship*, 103.

25. Let us recall how J.-Cl. Sagne considers the Spirit as the one who makes us enter into God's desire by transforming our *need* into true *desire*: "It is the role of the Holy Spirit to be the desire of God in God and the desire of God in us. The Spirit educates our desire, expands it and adjusts it to God's desire by giving it the same object" (Sagne, "Du besoin à la demande," 94; see above, chap. 1, 14–15).

26. See Sesboüé, "La personalità dello Spirito Santo," 57, quoting Augustine (*Confessionum*, III, vi, 11 [PL 32, 688]).

The Manifestation of the Breath of the Father and of the Son

need to "let go." With the eternal Breath, however, this means to let us be taken up by a current that propels us forward towards the Father and the Son. From another perspective, it means to let the living force of the Spirit well up in us and irrigate each recess of our being, to let down all barriers and dams to free an inner stream that taps into the deepest groundwater. Or, to use another type of image offered by the Scriptures, it means to let it fire up our love and passion, to make us vibrate for God and his project, as an inner furnace.

Paradoxically, this inward movement goes hand-in-hand with an outward one. To pray the Spirit, in the widest sense, means to be led not only into the depths of God but into the lives and worries of others. Here is why. Since the Breath brings the Father and the Son into us and us into them, it is so to speak an "indirect" person. It is also indirect, however, because it acts through others and makes them act. And this is true in our life as well: it acts by making us act, by transforming us and giving us the gifts we need. The divine Breath will thus be "experienced" through the faith, hope, and charity it gives rise to and through the virtues and gifts and charisms that flow from it. And our relationship to it will grow and flourish through the attention we pay to and the care we take of the gifts received. Now these gifts are also for others: the Father breathes the Breath into the Son to make it his and allow him to breathe back; in the same way, it is breathed into us to become ours, so that we may "breathe back out" to others. Our way of "breathing out" is to love God and to love others, especially the poor and the needy. We "breathe out" by employing the gifts for others. In this way, we relate to the Spirit in relating to others we minister and care for.

What now is the right term for the prayer to the eternal Breath of God? We *adore* the Father and *contemplate* the Son. Strictly speaking, we do not *contemplate* nor *adore* the Breath. Rather we ask it to be the light in which we adore the Father's glory, which we contemplate on the face of Christ. In a way, there is no other term: we adore and contemplate *in* the Spirit. We do, however, *invoke* the Spirit, while we rarely invoke the Father or the Son. The Breath is thus *invoked* as the one who gives us access to the *contemplation* of the Son and the *adoration* of the Father. Once again, one should not be too rigid and try to establish exclusive use of terms. All three divine names are worshiped and glorified, as the Nicene-Constantinople Creed professes, and adoration, contemplation, and invocation are three modes of worship, which are definitely porous to one another. However, each divine name is worshiped according to its mode of being and type of personhood. The words "adoration," "contemplation," and "invocation" help underscore these differences. Our life of prayer is at stake: many difficulties we have in praying to the third person come from the fact we try to reproduce a relationship modeled on the relationship we have to the Father and the Son, or even on human relationships. Understanding how different the Breath is frees us from these misleading models and opens us to the fresh way in which the divine Breath itself will lead us to relate to it as it is.

Indeed, the most beautiful prayers to the Holy Spirit contain the dimensions I have just expounded. The classical *Veni Creator Spiritus* is a powerful confirmation of all that has just been expounded and a perfect example of traditional saying: *lex orandi, lex credendi*, i.e., the rule of prayer is the rule of faith.

> Come, Holy Ghost, Creator, come
> from thy bright heav'nly throne;
> come, take possession of our souls,
> and make them all thine own.
>
> Thou who art called the Paraclete,
> best gift of God above,
> the living spring, the living fire,
> sweet unction and true love.
>
> Thou who art sevenfold in thy grace,
> finger of God's right hand;
> his promise, teaching little ones
> to speak and understand.
>
> O guide our minds with thy blest light,
> with love our hearts inflame;
> and with thy strength, which ne'er decays,
> confirm our mortal frame.
>
> Far from us drive our deadly foe;
> true peace unto us bring;
> and through all perils lead us safe
> beneath thy sacred wing.
>
> Through thee may we the Father know,
> through thee th'eternal Son,
> and thee the Spirit of them both,
> thrice-blessed three in One.

From first to last word, this hymn is an invocation to the third person, which asks it to come into the pray-ers' soul, into their intimate being. The

The Manifestation of the Breath of the Father and of the Son

Holy Spirit is a gift that is compared to water and fire. It illuminates, makes us understand God's teaching, inflames us with love, and confers strength and security. The only dimension that is missing is the aspect of being turned outward and toward others. The last paragraph is probably the most important: the divine Breath leads to the Father through the Son; it leads us into the life of the Trinity.

Before concluding with the Trinity, however, a difficulty needs to be addressed concerning our relationship to the divine Breath. Fundamentally, the Christian's relation to God is love: being loved and loving in return. Now, is it possible to conceive of a love of the Spirit for us if it is "but" a Breath? And is it truly possible to love "with all [our] heart, with all [our] soul and with all [our] might" (Deut 6:5) a Breath, a quasi-impersonal, fluid, and atmospheric mode of subsistence of God? It seems much easier to enter into a loving relationship to the Father and the Son. Of course, this brings us to a wider consideration than of just the life of prayer, but it stems from it, since prayer is desire and love.

"Dogmatically" speaking, we know that the Breath of God loves, insofar as it shares the numerically identical self-consciousness, intelligence, and will of the Father and the Son. As such it participates in the same fullness of love for us. However, it does so according to its mode of being, to its "position" in the trinitarian relations and *taxis*. In the inner life of the Trinity it loves in making the love of the Father interior to the love of the Son and the love of the Son interior to the love of a Father. Its love for the Father and the Son consists in communicating the love of each into the most intimate recesses of the being of the other. Thus, it loves us precisely in communicating the love of the Father and the Son, in making it penetrate into the utmost depth of our heart and enabling us to open to it and receive it. It loves us by communicating love and by communicating the Father and the Son. Indeed, to love is to communicate not only a feeling or a passion but also and before all to give oneself: it means offering oneself to the other and receiving the other. This is implied in Jesus' teaching: "No one has greater love than this, to lay down one's life for one's friends" (John 15:13). To offer oneself is the greatest gift one can give. The Breath does so fully, but in the same movement by which it gives itself, as always, it also "withdraws" before the Father and the Son, to give them as well. The greatest treasure we have to offer is our person; the greatest treasure the Holy Spirit offers is in a way the persons of the Father and the Son.

The Breath of God

Can we love the divine Breath? Yes, fully. It does offer itself to our love. However, its movement of withdrawal implies that in loving the Breath we are immediately brought to love the Son and the Father. To love the Spirit means to be so to speak propelled towards the other two persons. The more we love the Spirit the more intense is our love for Father and Son. And vice versa: since we love them in the Breath, in our love for them we love the Breath. We can truly love the Holy Spirit, but never without loving the Son and the Father in the same act of love.

Once again, there is an "indirect" quality both to the love of the Holy Breath for us and to our love for it. The presence of the Father and the Son always appears in the field of our relationship with the Spirit and, in fact, seems to cover the field—though the Spirit *is* the field, so it is clearly there as well. We do not enter into a dialogical, face-to-face loving relationship with the Breath as with a human person, nor into the same kind of love as with Father and Son. Nonetheless, it is not simply a relationship to an anonymous force, or else we would not even invoke it or ask it to work in us. It is a unique type of person, which calls for and indeed provokes in us a unique type of love. We are loved by the Breath and we love according to its being a "person-through-and-in-and-toward-other persons." This is precisely why, also, love of and for the Breath provokes in us love for others, as I have explained above.

Indeed, in the same way as an analogical conception of personhood in God can shed light on the different dimensions of the human person,[27] the polyhydric dimension of relationship of love for the three divine names can lead us to a better understanding of human love, obviously with the same limits and precautions. Love also may be a quasi-analogical notion. It is so when we consider our love for God and God's love for us: our loving relationship to Father, Son, and Spirit entails each time a profoundly different, though equally intense, type of love. It is love of and for the source and end of our existence; love of and for a master and friend; love of and for an inner transformative presence. It may well be the case in human love as well. It is a great help as we mature in life to understand there are many types of love, not only according to intensity and strength, but according to type: maternal, paternal, fraternal loves, friendship, and erotic loves are the obvious ones. Understanding the subtle differences help to find a path in the complex network of relations in our lives and many a failure in relationships come from not having perceived what type of relation was at stake.

27. See above, chap. 3, pp. 88–89.

The Manifestation of the Breath of the Father and of the Son

We can go even further, however. Indeed, we should probably not conceive of love as a pre-existing force or longing that simply "latches on" to a suitable "object." The longing is there, the force is there. But each and every love depends more on the persons in relationship than on the pre-existing propensity. Love is a relationship and a relationship is constituted and defined by its terms. Especially as love matures and deepens, it becomes more and more unique, it is marked by the two lovers' choices and common history, and thus corresponds always more faithfully to these lovers' person and being. In the end, it may well be that our love for each individual we love and the love of each one of those who loves us are radically unique and in many ways incomparable and unrepeatable.

A bit artificially, I have expounded our relation to each divine hypostasis one after another. In reality, however, everything developed so far has pointed quite consistently to the fact that they cannot be taken separately. Pope Leo XIII underscores this when he asserts that there should be no distinct feast for each person of the Trinity, lest one separates what in God is united. Even Pentecost is not a celebration of the third person in itself, but rather of the gift of the Spirit in an event of the history of salvation.[28] The present reflection on the specific traits of prayer to each divine person has in fact always been fully trinitarian. At the risk of repetition, to adore the Father means to listen to his Word, to travel the "Way" and conform ourselves to Christ—and to do so under the inner guidance and movement of the Breath. Likewise, the more I contemplate the Son in his humanity, the more intensely I see the glory of the Father and I am led to him—and I do so in the *dunamis* of the Spirit. Finally, when we invoke the divine Breath, it communicates the Father and the Son and brings us into their relation. The third hypostasis is "slippery" as soap for anyone who would wish to stop only with it.

---

28. "Our predecessor Innocent XII, absolutely refused the petition of those who desired a special festival in honour of God the Father. For, although the separate mysteries connected with the Incarnate Word are celebrated on certain fixed days, yet there is no special feast on which the Word is honoured according to His Divine Nature alone. And even the Feast of Pentecost was instituted in the earliest times, not simply to honour the Holy Ghost in Himself, but to commemorate His coming, or His external mission. And all this has been wisely ordained, lest from distinguishing the Persons men should be led to distinguish the Divine Essence" (Leo XIII, *Divinum illud munus*, 9 May 1897, 3 [DH 3325]). However, one should also remember the letter of Pope Hormisdas to Emperor Justin, *Inter ea quae* (26 March 521), which suggests that the Father, the Son and the Holy Spirit be "adored" without forgetting what is proper to each person (see DH 367).

It still is legitimate and even beneficial to pray one of the divine persons in particular. The prayer the Lord taught us addresses "Our Father in heaven . . ." And the last words of the Book of Revelation are a prayer to the Son: "Amen. Come, Lord Jesus!" (Rev 22:20). I believe it is crucial to be conscious of the differences between Father, Son, and Breath and to relate to each accordingly. However, once we are fully aware of this and keep it in mind, we need also to remember that in fact we are praying in the movement of the Three. Like the Trinity, our prayer should be truly one and truly distinct: three relations in one prayer, one prayer in three relations, so to speak. We know that, essentially, Christian prayer addresses the Father. But the Lord's Prayer is prayed in the Spirit and through—with and thanks to—the Son. When I ask Christ for forgiveness—*Kyrie eleison*—I am fundamentally asking for the forgiveness of the Father, and in some way, directly or indirectly, I am asking for the Holy Spirit to enable me to welcome it and let it transform me. When I invoke the Holy Spirit so that it may guide me, explicitly or not, I am essentially asking the Father to give me his Breath through the risen Lord, who breathes it into me. One doesn't simply *welcome* the divine Breath, one *receives* it, from the hands—or mouth!—of the Father, through the Son. Basil has beautifully expressed this movement: "The way to divine knowledge ascends from the one Spirit through the one Son to the one Father. Likewise, natural goodness, inherent holiness and royal dignity reaches from the Father through the Only-Begotten to the Spirit."[29] This means that praying separately and exclusively to one divine person is highly problematic.[30] I pray the Father, through the Son, in the Spirit—or in the Spirit, I pray the Father through the Son. However, because of the deep bond between the persons, praying each one in a truly trinitarian way does not necessarily ask for another step in prayer. Praying to one person is reaching out to the other two. Realizing this and making it explicit simply puts into light what is already there. It is not yet another prayer, but the same prayer, experienced in full consciousness.

In the end, Christian life in general and prayer in particular means to enter into the relation of the three divine persons, into their communion

---

29. Basil the Great, *On the Holy Spirit*, XVIII, §47, 74–75.

30. Ignatius of Loyola chose at one moment of his life to pray the Holy Trinity four times a day: a prayer was devoted to each divine person and a fourth one to the Trinity as a whole (Ignatius of Loyola, *Autobiography*, 79). This is problematic, because it risks considering each person autonomously and then the "Trinity" as the unique essence or a fourth reality—in effect a "quaternity" (see the Fourth Lateran Council [1215], chap. 2 [DH 804]).

The Manifestation of the Breath of the Father and of the Son

of love. The beauty of Rublev's icon of the three angels is that there is open space in the center, a space destined to be our "space" in the life of God. However, this needs to be understood very precisely, because it is not a neutral space, but a trinitarian one. Our truest "space" in the Trinity is Christ in his humanity, of which we are the members. The divine Breath envelops us as the atmosphere in which we live, it penetrates us to transform us and conform us to Christ in his filial relation to the Father. The focal point, however, the term of our longing and of our love is the source and the term of all, the Alpha and Omega of divine and human life: the Father. S. Coakley expresses it in a nutshell when she says:

> The "Father" (so-called here) is both source and ultimate object of divine longing in us; the "Spirit" is that irreducibly—though obscurely—distinct enabler and incorporator of that longing in creation—that which *makes* creation divine; and the "Son" *is* that divine and perfected creation, into whose life I, as pray-er, am caught up.[31]

The true reality of our present life and the full accomplishment of our desires and of our being in life-everlasting is to pray and to "exist" *towards* the Father, *through* and *with* the Son, *in* the Holy Breath, who is *in* us.

* * *

There are various manifestations of the Breath of God and of the Trinity in the economy. Art is quite relevant for the present reflection because it offers a field in which to apply the comprehension developed thanks to the breath-metaphor as a discerning factor, to verify to what extent different representations of the Trinity are coherent or not with the eternal relations in God. It also confirms the unique, elusive, non-representable nature of the third person. However, prayer is the truest manifestation, because it is the concrete expression of the Spirit's interiority in the Father and the Son and in the believer, as well as of the way it withdraws before them to unveil the forms of the Father and the Son in the believer's heart and worldly existence. Prayer (in the Spirit) is the fully concrete embodiment of the Breath of the Father and the Son. As such it shows itself to be the true goal and fruit of the present reflection.

---

31. Coakley, "Living in the Mystery of the Holy Spirit," 47.

Conclusion

This essay is in many ways merely a beginning. Certainly much needs to be nuanced and expressed more precisely, or even corrected. I have often worried about being too daring when expounding on the inner-trinitarian being of the Spirit. Nevertheless, this exploration of the mystery of the Breath in the depths of God has been motivated, step by step, by the wish to be as faithful as possible to the economy of the revelation and thus to the Scriptures. Indeed, it has been an attempt to be more faithful than we have been in the past. It truly is an essay, in the etymological meaning of the word:[1] I have tested a hypothesis, weighed it, and put it on trial. In the end, I believe that, though much may be fragile, its core has withstood the test. It is also an essay in the modern meaning of the word, because it never claims to be complete. It is not a full pneumatology and even less a complete exposition of trinitarian theology, even though it touches on both. It is the presentation and defense of one central idea. This idea necessarily implies an evolution in our vision of the Holy Spirit and of the triune God, it re-centers and reorients our comprehension, but does not replace it.

The core idea is that the third divine hypostasis is unique and profoundly different from the two others. This is expressed in its name, as revealed in the two Testaments: *Ruah* and *Pneuma*. Breath is not its only name, but it is the name that best defines the quality of its action in the world and in the believer's life, and synthesizes many of the traits of its other names. Breath is a name and a metaphor, and as such it can be expanded to depict the reality of the divine Spirit in a legitimate and indeed indispensable way. Notwithstanding all the limits to the status of our speech and comprehension imposed by the mystery we try to fathom, it truly does

---

1. "Essay" comes from the Latin *exigere*, to "weigh," through the Old French *essay*, to "put on trial" or to "try," and the Old English *assay*, to "test the quality of" (see Skeat, *Concise Etymological Dictionary*, 171).

Conclusion

illumine our understanding of the Spirit in the eternity of God, and thus illumines our understanding of the Father and the Son, of divine personhood and of some aspects of the life of the Trinity. The ultimate test and trial for a theological notion is that it corresponds to our relation to God and that it helps clarify and nourish this relation. To consider seriously the otherness of the third person as Breath helps to find the right attitude when praying the Spirit and praying in the Spirit. It helps welcome its unique type of love and love it in return. And this adjusts in the same way our prayer to the Father and to the Son.

I hope that this conception of the Holy Spirit and of the Trinity will generate in Christians a renewed comprehension and love of the Breath who lives and acts in the depth of our being, but also, in the same movement, of the Son who breathes it out to and into us and of the Father, the first breather, who communicates his intimate life and "heart" to the Son and through the Son to us.

>Father, through your Son Jesus Christ,
>pour out your Breath onto us,
>pour out the Breath of God!

Bibliography

Alain, Olivier, and Marie-Claire Alain. *L'œuvre pour orgue de Jean-Sébastien Bach*. Tours: Van de Velde, 1967.
Andresen, Carl. "Zur Entstehung und Geschichte des trinitarischen Personbegriffes." *Zeitschrift für die neutestamentliche Wissenschaft und die Kunde der älteren Kirche* 52 (1961) 1–39.
Anselm of Canterbury. *Monologion*. In *Complete Philosophical and Theological Treatises of Anselm of Canterbury*, translated and edited by Jasper Hopkins and Herbert Richardson, 1–87. Minneapolis: Arthur J. Banning, 2000.
———. *The Procession of the Holy Spirit*. In *Anselm of Canterbury* III, translated and edited by Jasper Hopkins and Herbert Richardson, 181–230. Toronto: Edwin Mellen, 1976.
Athanasius. *Epistola IV: De Spiritu Sancto*. Patrologia Greca 26. Opera Omnia 2. Edited by Jacques-Paul Migne. Paris, 1857.
———. *Epistolae ad Serapionem*. Patrologia Greca 26. Opera Omnia 2. Edited by Jacques-Paul Migne. Paris, 1857.
———. *Orationes Adversus Arianos*. Patrologia Greca 26. Opera Omnia 2. Edited by Jacques-Paul Migne. Paris, 1857.
Augustine. *Confessionum Libri XIII*. Patrologia Latina 32. Opera Omnia 1. Edited by Jacques-Paul Migne. Paris, 1861.
———. *Contra Maximinum*. Patrologia Latina 42. Opera Omnia 8. Edited by Jacques-Paul Migne. Paris, 1861.
———. *In Iohannis Evangelium tractactus*. Patrologia Latina 35. Opera Omnia 3.2. Edited by Jacques-Paul Migne. Paris, 1861.
———. *De Trinitate*. Patrologia Latina 42. Opera Omnia 8. Edited by Jacques-Paul Migne. Paris, 1861.
———. *The Trinity*. The works of Saint Augustine: A translation for the 21st Century 5. Translated by Edmund Hill. Edited by John E. Rotelle. Brooklyn: New City, 1990.
Aquinas, Thomas. "Commentary on 2 Corinthians." https://aquinas.cc/.
———. *Quaestiones disputatae I: De potentia*. Opera omnia 8. Parma: typis Petri Fiaccadori, 1856.
———. *Sententiarum magistri Petri Lombardi I*. Opera omnia 6. Parma: typis Petri Fiaccadori, 1856.
———. *Summa contra Gentiles*. Opera omnia iussu edita Leonis XIII 13–15. Rome: Typis Riccardi Garroni, 1888–1906.
———. *Summa theologiae*. Opera omnia iussu edita Leonis XIII 4–12. Rome: Typis Riccardi Garroni, 1918–1930.

Bibliography

———. *Super Epistolam ad Romanos Lectura*. In *Super Epistolas S. Pauli Lectura I*, edited by P. Raphaelis Cai, 5–230. Taurini: Marietti, 1953.
Balthasar, Hans Urs von. *The Glory of Lord: A Theological Aesthetics I: Seeing the Form*. Translated by Erasmo Leiva-Merikakis. Edited by Joseph Fessio and John Riches. Edinburgh: T. & T. Clark, 1982.
———. *The Glory of the Lord: A Theological Aesthetics VII: Theology: The New Covenant*. Translated by Brian McNeil. Edited by John Riches. San Francisco: T. & T. Clark-Ignatius, 1989.
———. *Mysterium Paschale: The Mystery of Easter*. Translated by Aidan Nichols. San Francisco: Ignatius, 2000.
———. *Skizzen zur Theologie III: Spiritus Creator*. Einsiedeln: Johannes Verlag, 1967.
———. *Theo-Drama: Theological Dramatic Theory II: The Dramatis personae: Man in God*. Translated by Graham Harrison. San Francisco: Ignatius, 1990.
———. *Theo-Drama: Theological Dramatic Theory III: The Dramatis personae: Persons in Christ*. Translated by Graham Harrison. San Francisco: Ignatius, 1992.
———. *Theo-Drama: Theological Dramatic Theory IV, The Action*. Translated by Graham Harrison. San Francisco: Ignatius, 2005.
———. *Theo-Drama: Theological Dramatic Theory V, The Last Act*. Translated by Graham Harrison. San Francisco: Ignatius, 2005.
———. *Theo-Logic: Theological Logical Theory II: The Truth of God*. Translated by Adrian J. Walker. San Francisco: Ignatius, 2004.
———. *Theo-Logic: Theological Logical Theory III: The Spirit of Truth*. Translated by Graham Harrison. San Francisco: Ignatius, 2005.
Balz, Horst, and Schneider, Gerhard, eds. *Exegetisches Wörterbuch zum Neuen Testament III*. Stuttgart: Kohlhammer, 1992.
Barth, Karl. *Church Dogmatics I.1: The Doctrine of the Word of God*. Translated by G. W. Bromiley. Edinburgh: T. & T. Clark, 1975.
———. *Church Dogmatics III.2: The Doctrine of Creation*. Translated by G. W. Bromiley et al. Reprint. Edinburgh: T. & T. Clark, 1968.
———. *Church Dogmatics IV.1: The Doctrine of Reconciliation*. Translated by G. W. Bromiley. Reprint. Edinburgh: T. & T. Clark, 1967.
Barth, Markus. *Ephesians 4–6*. The Anchor Bible 34A. Garden City, NY: Doubleday, 1974.
Basil the Great. *On the Holy Spirit*. Translated by David Anderson. Crestwood, NY: St. Vladimir's Seminary Press, 1980.
Bernard of Clairvaux. *Commentary on the Song of Songs*. Translated by Matthew Henry. Alternmünster: Jazzybee Verlag, 2016.
Bobrinskoy, Boris. "The *Filioque* Yesterday and Today." In *Spirit of God, Spirit of Christ: Ecumenical Reflections of the 'Filioque' Controversy*, edited by Lukas Vischer. London: SPCK-World Council of Churches, 1981.
———. *Le mystère de la Trinité: cours de théologie orthodoxe*. Paris: Cerf, 1986.
Boespflug, François. *Dieu et ses images: une histoire de l'Éternel dans l'art*. Montrouge: Bayard, 2008.
Bonaventure. *Breviloquium*. Opera Omnia 5. Ad Claras Aquas, Quaracchi: Typographia Collegii S. Bonaventurae, 1891.
———. *Journey into God: Itinerarium mentis in Deum*. Translated by Josef Raischl and Andre Cirino. Phoenix: Tau-Publishing, 2012.
———. *Sententiarum I*. Opera Omnia 5. Ad Claras Aquas, Quaracchi: Typographia Collegii S. Bonaventurae, 1882.

Bibliography

Botterweck, G. Johannes, and Helmer Ringgren, eds. *Theological Dictionary of the Old Testament V*. Translated by John T. Willis. Grand Rapids: Eerdmans, 1986.

———. *Theological Dictionary of the Old Testament XIII*. Translated by David E. Green. Grand Rapids: Eerdmans, 2004.

Boulnois, Marie-Odile. *Le paradoxe trinitaire chez Cyrille d'Alexandrie: Herméneutique, analyses philosophiques et argumentation théologique*. Paris: Institut d'Études Augustiniennes, 1994.

Bulgakov, Sergei. *The Comforter*. Translated by Boris Jakim. Grand Rapids: Eerdmans, 2004.

Calvin, John. *Calvin's New Testament Commentaries VIII: The Epistles of Paul to the Romans and Thessalonians*. Translated by R. Mackenzie. Edited by David W. Torrance and Thomas F. Torrance. Grand Rapids: Eerdmans, 1980.

Charles of Foucauld. "Prayer of Abandonment." http://www.brothercharles.org/wordpress/prayer-of-abandonment/.

Charru, Philippe, and Christoph Theobald. *L'Esprit créateur dans la pensée musicale de Jean-Sébastien Bach*. Sprimont: Mardaga, 2002.

Chrétien, Jean-Louis. *L'Arche de la parole*. Paris: Presses Universitaires de France, 1998.

Coakley, Sarah. "Charismatic Experience: Church of England Doctrine Commission." In *The Holy Spirit: Classical and Contemporary Readings*, edited by Eugene F. Rogers, 68–80. Oxford: Wiley-Blackwell, 2009.

———. *God, Sexuality and the Self: An Essay 'On the Trinity.'* Cambridge: Cambridge University Press, 2013.

———. "Living in the Mystery of the Holy Trinity: Trinity, Prayer and Sexuality." In *The Holy Spirit: Classical and Contemporary Readings*, edited by Eugene F. Rogers, 44–52. Oxford: Wiley-Blackwell, 2009.

Congar, Yves Marie Joseph. "Actualité de la pneumatologie." In *Credo in Spiritum Sanctum: Atti del Congresso Teologico Internazionale di Pneumatologia in occasione del 1600° anniversario del I Concilio di Costantinopoli e del 1550° anniversario del Concilio di Efeso, Roma 22–26 marzo 1982*, edited by José Saraiva Martins, 15–28. Vatican City: Libreria Editrice Vaticana, 1983.

———. *Je crois en l'Esprit-Saint*. Paris: Cerf, 1995.

———. *The Word and the Spirit*. Translated by David Smith. London: Chapman-Harper & Row, 1986.

Cyril of Alexandria. *Adversus Julianum*. Patrologia Greca 76. Opera Omnia 9. Edited by Jacques-Paul Migne. Paris, 1859.

———. *Commentarium in Ioannem*. Patrologia Greca 74. Opera Omnia 7. Edited by Jacques-Paul Migne. Paris, 1859.

———. *De Sancta et Consubstantiali Trinitate Dialogi*. Patrologia Greca 75. Opera Omnia 8. Edited by Jacques-Paul Migne. Paris, 1859.

Cyril of Jerusalem. *Catecheses*. Patrologia Greca 33. Edited by Jacques-Paul Migne. Paris, 1857.

Denzinger, Heinrich. *Compendium of Creeds, Definitions, and Declarations on Matters of Faith and Morals*. Edited by Helmut Hoping and Peter Hünermann for the original bilingual edition. Edited by Robert Fastiggi and Anne Englung Nash for the English edition. San Francisco: Ignatius, 2012.

Didymus. *De Trinitate*. Patrologia Greca 39. Edited by Jacques-Paul Migne. Paris, 1858.

Dillard, Victor. *Au Dieu inconnu*. Paris: Beauchesne, 1938.

Bibliography

Dragas, George Dion. "St. Athanasius on the Holy Spirit and the Trinity." In *Theological Dialogue Between Orthodox and Reformed Churches* II, edited by Thomas F. Torrance, 38–60. Edinburgh: Scottish Academic, 1994.
Ducoq, Christian. *Dieu différent*. Paris: Cerf, 1977.
Dunn, James D. G. *Romans 1–8*. Word Biblical Commentary 38A. Dallas, TX: Word, 1988.
Durand, Emmanuel. *Le Père, Alpha et Oméga de la vie trinitaire*. Paris: Cerf, 2008.
———. "Le Père en sa relation constitutive au Fils selon saint Thomas d'Aquin." *Revue Thomiste* 107 (2007) 47–72.
———. *La périchorèse des personnes trinitaires*. Paris: Cerf, 2005.
Durrwell, François-Xavier. *Holy Spirit of God: An Essay in Biblical Theology*. Tanslated by Benedict Davies. London: Chapman, 1986.
———. *Jésus, Fils de Dieu dans l'Esprit Saint*. Paris: Desclée, 1997.
Evdokimov, Paul. *L'Esprit Saint dans la tradition orthodoxe*. Paris: Cerf, 1970.
Fitzmyer, Joseph A. *First Corinthians*. The Anchor Bible 32. New Haven: Yale University Press, 2008.
———. *Romans*. The Anchor Bible 33. New York: Doubleday, 1993.
Fulgentius of Ruspe. *De Trinitate*. Patrologia Latina 65. Edited by Jacques-Paul Migne. Paris, 1861.
Gaybba, Brian P. *The Spirit of Love: Theology of the Holy Spirit*. London: Chapman, 1987.
Gregory Nazianzen. *Oratio XXXVIII*. Patrologia Greca 36. Opera Omnia 2. Edited by Jacques-Paul Migne. Paris, 1858.
———. *The Theological Orations*. In *Christology of the Later Fathers*, translated by Charles Gordon Browne and James Edward Swallow, edited by Edward Rochie Hardy, 128–214. Philadelphia: Westminster, 1954.
Gregory of Nyssa. *An Address on Religious Instruction (Oratio Catechetica Magna)*. In *Christology of the Later Fathers*, translated by Charles Gordon Browne and James Edward Swallow, edited by Edward Rochie Hardy, 268–325. Philadelphia: Westminster, 1954.
Gregory Palamas. *Capita physica, theologica, moralia et pratica*. Patrologia Greca 150. Opera Omnia 2. Edited by Jacques-Paul Migne. Paris, 1865.
Greshake, Gisbert. *Der dreieine Gott: eine trinitarische Theologie*. Freiburg: Herder, 1997.
Guillet, Jacques. "Spirito." In *Dizionario di teologia biblica*, edited by Xavier Léon-Dufour, 1229–32. Torino: Marietti, 1972.
Hilary of Poitiers. *De Trinitate*. Patrologia Latina 10. Opera Omnia 2. Edited by Jacques-Paul Migne. Paris, 1845.
———. *The Trinity*. Fathers of the Church Patristic 25. Translated by Stephen McKenna. Washington, DC: The Catholic University of America Press, 1968.
Ignatius of Antioch. *Letter of Ignatius: to the Romans*. In *Early Christian Fathers*, translated and edited by Cyril F. Richardson, 102–6. New York: Collier, 1970.
Ignatius of Loyola. *The Autobiography*. In *Spiritual Exercises and Selected Works*, edited by George E. Ganss, 65–111. New York: Paulist, 1991.
———. *Spiritual Exercises*. In *Spiritual Exercises and Selected Works*, edited by George E. Ganss, 113–214. New York: Paulist, 1991.
Irenaeus. *Against the Heresies I–III*. Translated by Dominic J. Unger. New York: Newman, 2012.
———. *Five Books of S. Irenaeus, Bishop of Lyons: Against Heresies*. Translated by John Keble. Oxford: Parker, 1872.

Bibliography

Jacob, Pierre. *Ignatian Discernment: A Commentary of the Rules of Discernment and the Autobiography of Ignatius of Loyola.* Anand, India: Gujarat Sahitya Prakash, 2001.
Jerome. *Commentarium in Isaiam Prophetam.* Patrologia Latina 24. Opera Omnia 4. Edited by Jacques-Paul Migne. Paris, 1845.
John Chrysostom. *The homilies of S. John Chrysostom: Epistle of St. Paul the Apostle to the Romans.* Translated by members of the English Church. Oxford: Parker-Rivington, 1841.
John Damascene. *Dialogus contra Manichaeos.* Patrologia Greca 94. Opera Omnia 1. Edited by Jacques-Paul Migne. Paris, 1864.
———. *Expositio Fidei orthodoxae.* Patrologia Greca 94. Opera Omnia 1. Edited by Jacques-Paul Migne. Paris, 1864.
Justin Martyr. *Dialogus cum Tryphone Judaeo.* Patrologia Greca 6. Edited by Jacques-Paul Migne. Paris, 1884.
Käsemann, Ernst. *Commentary on Romans.* Grand Rapids: Eerdmans, 1980.
Kasper, Walter. *The God of Jesus Christ.* Translated by Matthew J. O'Connell. London: SCM, 1984.
Kasper, Walter, and Gerhard Sauter. *Kirche-Ort des Geistes.* Freiburg: Herder, 1976.
Kilby, Karen. "Perichoresis and Projection: Problems with Social Doctrines of the Trinity." *New Blackfriars* 81/957 (2000) 432–45.
Koester, Craig R. *Hebrews.* The Anchor Bible 36. New York: Doubleday, 2001.
Kripke, Saul A. *Naming and Necessity.* Cambridge, MA: Harvard University Press, 1980.
Lacoste, Jean-Yves. "Zur Theologie des Geistes." *Communio* 15 (1986) 1–7.
Ladaria, Luis F. *Il Dio vivo e vero: il mistero della Trinità.* Casale Monferrato: Piemme, 1999.
———. *La Trinità, mistero di comunione.* Milan: Paoline, 2004.
Landes, Paula Fredriksen, ed. *Augustine on Romans: Propositions from the Epistle to the Romans; Unfinished Commentary on the Epistle to the Romans.* Chico, CA: Scholar, 1982.
Lémonon, Jean-Pierre. "L'esprit saint dans le corpus paulinien." In *Dictionnaire de la Bible: Supplément XI*, edited by L. Pirot and A. Robert, 192–327. Paris: Letouzey et Ané, 1991.
Leontius of Byzantium. *De sectis.* Patrologia Greca 86a. Edited by Jacques-Paul Migne. Paris, 1865.
Levering, Matthew. *Engaging the Doctrine of the Holy Spirit: Love and Gift in the Trinity and the Church.* Grand Rapids: Baker Academic, 2016.
Lévinas, Emmanuel. *Le Temps et l'Autre.* Paris: Presses Universitaires de France, 1979.
Lieggi, Jean Paul. *La sintassi trinitaria: al cuore della grammatica della fede.* Rome: Aracne, 2016.
Margerie, Bertrand de. *The Christian Trinity in History.* Translated by Edmund J. Fortman. Still River, MA: St. Bede's, 1982.
Maximus the Confessor. *Quaestiones ad Thalassium de Scriptura Sacra.* Patrologia Greca 90. Edited by Jacques-Paul Migne. Paris, 1860.
Meyendorff, John. *Byzantine Theology: Historical Trends and Doctrinal Themes.* New York: Fordham University Press, 1974.
Moltmann, Jürgen. *The Trinity and the Kingdom of God: The Doctrine of God.* Translated by Margaret Kohl. London: SCM, 1981.
Morales, Xavier. *Dieu en personnes.* Paris: Cerf, 2015.

Bibliography

Mühlen, Heribert. *Morgen wird Einheit sein: Das kommende Konzil aller Christen, Ziel der getrennten Kirchen*. Paderborn: Schöningh, 1974.

———. *Una Mystica Persona: die Kirche als das Mysterium der heilsgeschichtlichen Identität des Heiligen Geistes in Christus und den Christen: eine Person in vielen Personen*. Munich: Schöningh, 1964.

Orphanos, Markos A. "The Procession of the Holy Spirit According to Certain Later Greek Fathers." In *Spirit of God, Spirit of Christ: Ecumenical Reflections on the 'Filioque' Controversy*, edited by Lukas Vischer, 21–45. London: SPCK-World Council of Churches, 1981.

Pannenberg, Wolfhart. *Systematic Theology I*. Translated by G. W. Bromiley. Edinburgh: T. & T. Clark, 1991.

———. *Systematic Theology II*. Translated by G. W. Bromiley. Edinburgh: T. & T. Clark, 1994.

Pontifical Biblical Commission. *The Interpretation of the Bible in the Church*. Vatican City: Libreria editrice vaticana, 1993.

Pontifical Council for the Promotion of Christian Unity. *The Greek and Latin Traditions regarding the Procession of the Holy Spirit*. Vatican City: Typis Vaticanis, 1996.

Rahner, Karl. "La doctrine des 'sens spirituels' au Moyen Âge, en particulier chez Saint Bonaventure." *Revue d'ascétique et de mystique* 14 (1933) 263–99.

———. *Foundations of Christian Faith: An Introduction to the Idea of Christianity*. Translated by William V. Dych. London: Darton-Longman & Todd, 1978.

———. *The Trinity*. Translated by Joseph Donceel. New York: Crossroad, 1997.

Richard of Saint-Victor. *On the Trinity*. In *Trinity and Creation: A Selection of Works of Hugh, Richard and Adam of St Victor*, edited by Bob Taylor Coolmans and Dale M. Coulter, 195–352. Turnhout: Brepols, 2010.

Richards, Ivor Armstrong. *The Philosophy of Rhetoric*. Oxford: Oxford University Press, 1936.

Ricœur, Paul. *La métaphore vive*. Paris: Seuil, 1975.

Rogers, Eugene F. *After the Spirit: A Constructive Pneumatology from Resources outside the Modern West*. Grand Rapids: Eerdmans, 2005.

Rogers, Eugene F., ed. *The Holy Spirit: Classical and Contemporary Readings*. Oxford: Wiley-Blackwell, 2009.

Römer, Thomas Christian. *I lati oscuri di Dio: Crudeltà e violenza nell'Antico Testamento*. Translated by Fernanda Jourdan Comba. Torino: Claudiana, 2002.

Ross, David. *Aristotle*. London: Methuen, 1968.

Roussineau, Gabriel. "*Baptismus Flaminis*, A la recherche du baptême oublié." BA paper, Université Catholique de Lyon, 2008.

Rush, Osmond. *The Eyes of Faith: The Sense of the Faithful and the Church's Reception of Revelation*. Washington, DC: The Catholic University of America Press, 2016.

Sagne, Jean-Claude. "Du besoin à la demande, ou la conversion du désir dans la prière." *La Maison-Dieu* 109 (1972) 87–97.

———. "L'Esprit-Saint ou le désir de Dieu." *Concilium* 99 (1974) 85–95.

Scheeben, Matthias Joseph. *The Mysteries of Christianity*. Translated by Cyril Vollert. St. Louis, MO: Herder, 1946.

Schelling, Friedrich Wilhelm Joseph von. *Nachlass 8: Stuttgarter Privatvorlesungen (1810)*, Stuttgart: Frommann-Holzboog, 2017.

Schweitzer, Albert. *J. S. Bach I*. New York: Macmillan, 1962.

Bibliography

Sesboüé, Bernard. "La personalità dello Spirito Santo nella testimonianza biblica, nella teologia trinitaria recente e nell'esperienza storica della Chiesa e degli uomini." In *La personalità dello Spirito Santo: in dialogo con Bernard Sesboüé*, edited by Sergio Tanzarella, 21–60. Cinisello Balsamo: San Paolo, 1998.

Siffer-Wiederhold, Nathalie. *La présence divine à l'individu d'après le Nouveau Testament*. Paris: Cerf, 2005.

Skeat, Walker W. *A Concise Etymological Dictionary of the English Language*. Oxford: Clarendon, 1951.

Socias, James, ed. *Daily Roman Missal, Complete with Readings in One Volume*. Woodridge, IL: Midwest Theological Forum, 2012.

Soskice, Janet Martin. *Metaphor and Religious Language*. Oxford: Clarendon, 1985.

Soulen, R. Kendall. *The Divine Name(s) and the Holy Trinity: Distinguishing the Voices I*. Louisville: Westminster John Knox, 2011.

Staniloae, Dumitru. *Theology and the Church*. Translated by Robert Barringer. Crestwood, NY: St. Vladimir's Seminary Press, 1980.

Steeves, Nicolas. *Grâce à l'imagination*. Paris: Cerf, 2016.

Steinsaltz, Adin. *The Thirteen Petalled Rose*. New York: Basic, 1980.

Studer, Basil. *Durch Geschichte zum Glauben: zur Exegese und zur Trinitätslehre der Kirchenväter*. Rome: Pontificio Ateneo San Anselmo, 2006.

Tanzarella, Sergio, ed. *La personalità dello Spirito Santo: in dialogo con Bernard Sesboüé*. Cinisello Balsamo: San Paolo, 1998.

Teresa of Avila. *The Book of Her Life*. In *The Collected Works of St. Teresa of Avila I*, translated by Kieran Kavanaugh and Otilio Rodriguez, 1–308. Washington, DC: ICS Publications-Institute of Carmelite Studies, 1976.

———. *The Interior Castle*. In *The Collected Works of St. Teresa of Avila II*, translated by Kieran Kavanaugh and Otilio Rodriguez, 261–452. Washington, DC: ICS Publications-Institute of Carmelite Studies, 1980.

Tertullian. *Adversus Praxeam*. Patrologia Latina 2. Opera Omnia 2. Edited by Jacques-Paul Migne. Paris, 1844.

———. *Tertullian's Treatise Against Praxeas*. Translated and edited by Ernest Evans. London: SPCK, 1948.

Theophilus of Antioch. *Ad Autolycum*. Patrologia Greca 6. Edited by Jacques-Paul Migne. Paris, 1884.

Thérèse of Lisieux. *Œuvres complètes (Textes et dernières paroles)*. Edited by Jacques Lonchampt. Paris: Cerf-Desclée de Brouwer, 1992.

Thiselton, Anthony C. "Canon, Community and Theological Construction." In *Canon and Biblical Interpretation*, edited by Craig G. Bartholomew et al., 1–27. Grand Rapids: Zondervan, 2006.

———. *The Holy Spirit—In Biblical Teaching, through the Centuries, and Today*. Grand Rapids: Eerdmans, 2013.

Torrance, Thomas F. *Space, Time and Incarnation*. Oxford: Oxford University Press, 1969.

Turner, Max. *The Holy Spirit and Spiritual Gifts then and now*. Carlisle: Paternoster, 1996.

Vetö, Etienne. *Du Christ à la Trinité : Penser les mystères du Christ après Thomas d'Aquin et Balthasar*. Paris: Cerf, 2012.

———. "Foi et raison chez Thomas d'Aquin : Distinguer pour unir-Unir pour distinguer." In *La Vérité dans ses éclats. Foi et raison*, edited by Blandine Lagrut and Etienne Vetö, 89–110. Paris: Ad Solem, 2014.

Bibliography

———. "'Praying in the Holy Spirit': Spirituality and Pneumatology." *New Blackfriars* 97/1068 (March 2016) 157–72.
Wedderburn, Alexander J. M. "Some Observations on Paul's use of the Phrases 'in Christ' and 'with Christ.'" *Journal for the Study of the New Testament* 25 (1985) 83–97.
Weinandy, Thomas Gerard. *The Father's Spirit of Sonship: Reconceiving the Trinity.* Edinburgh: T. & T. Clark, 1995.
Welker, Michael. *Gottes Geist: Theologie des Heiligen Geistes.* Neukirchen: Neukirchener Theologie, 1992.

Index of Scriptures

OLD TESTAMENT

Genesis
1:2	10, 24, 56, 88
2:7	19, 24, 48, 52
8:8	19
18:1–15	102

Exodus
31:3	23
33:20	21

Leviticus
4:3, 5, 16	20

Numbers
11:25	19
24:2, 4	23
24:2	10

Deuteronomy
6:5	133
34:9	19

Judges
14:6	10
15:14	10

1 Samuel
9:16	20
16:13	10

1 Kings
18:45	56
19:12	56

2 Kings
2:9–15	19
2:16	10

2 Chronicles
15:1	10
20:14	10

Job
33:4	24

Psalms
19:2	54
29:3, 5, 7	56n81
33:6	49
51:10	26
51:13	34
104:29–30	24
119:24	126
139:7	25
147:18	49, 56

Index of Scriptures

Song of Songs

1:2	54

Wisdom

7:22–27	21
9:17	34

Isaiah

11:2	10, 23
11:4	49
14:21	56
26:9	33
30:27–33	56
40:13	23
63:10	34

Jeremiah

15:16	126

Ezekiel

13:13	56
27:26	56
36:26–27a	26
37:9–10, 14	23–24

Joel

2:28–29	10, 23
2:28	18
3:1	18

Haggai

2:5	20, 26

NEW TESTAMENT

Matthew

1:23	126
3:11	19, 61
3:16	10, 19
6:9	125
10:20	4
12:28	3
17:5	10
22:43	4

Mark

1:10	10, 19
9:7	10
12:36	4
13:11	5
14:36	25

Luke

1:35	10, 20, 88
1:41	3
2:25	10
2:26	4
2:27	3
3:22	10, 15, 19
4:1	3
4:4	3
4:14	20
4:18–19	20
4:18	10
9:34	10
10:21–22	124
10:21	6, 7, 8, 53
10:22	53
11:13	20
11:20	3
12:12	4
23:46	51, 124
24:49	3, 11, 20

John

1:18	21
1:32–33	10
1:32	10
1:33	11
3:5	19
3:35	5
4:10	20
4:14	24
4:23	6
4:24	57n86
6:44	124

Index of Scriptures

7:16	5
7:37–39a	19
7:38	24
8:26, 28, 38	5
12:45	5
14:6	126
14:9	5, 128
14:15–17, 26	20
14:17	23
14:26	5
15:13	133
15:15	126
15:26–27	20
15:26	5, 23, 69
16:5–15	20
16:7	69
16:8–12	26
16:13	5, 23, 51n70
16:14	5
20:17	127
20:22	19, 36, 43, 52

Acts

1:5	11
1:8	10, 20
2	8
2:2–3	10
2:2	57
2:3	19, 61
2:33	20
2:38	20
2:17–18	18, 23
4:31–32	27
8:17	19
8:20	20, 59
8:26, 40	57
10:37–38	20
10:44	10
10:45	20
11:12	4
11:15	10
11:17	20, 59
13:2	4
15:28	4
19:6	19
19:16	10
19:21	4

Romans

1:4	24
4:4	20
5:5	30, 62
8:9	47, 69
8:11	24
8:14	3, 8
8:15	6, 7, 13, 25, 26
8:16	15
8:26–27	14
8:26	6, 7, 14
8:27	7, 13
15:30	30

1 Corinthians

2:16	23
8:6	65, 77n10, 124, 126
12:2	8
12:3	6
12:4–31	30
13:12	21
14:14–17	14
14:14–15	7
14:14, 16	14
14:25	26

2 Corinthians

1:20	127
1:21–22	20
3:17	13
4:6	127, 128
13:12	55n78
13:13	30

Galatians

4:4	6
4:6	7, 13, 16, 25, 46, 52, 60, 69
5:16	3
5:18	3

Ephesians

1:13	20
2:18	6, 26–27, 30

Index of Scriptures

Ephesians (continued)

5:18–19	8
6:18	6, 13

Colossians

1:15	127

1 Timothy

2:5–6	77n10
6:13	77n10
6:16	86

2 Timothy

3:6	3, 8

Hebrews

1:1–2	124
6:4	20
9:14	26

1 Peter

2:5	26
3:18	58

1 John

1:1	127
2:20, 27	20
3:2	21, 21n61, 86n37
4:8, 16	30, 72, 100

Jude

20	6

Revelation

22:17	4, 16
22:20	136

Index of Names

Alain, Marie-Claire, 122
Alain, Olivier, 122
Andresen, Carl, 16
Anselm of Canterbury, 43, 43n50, 45,
 93, 93nn55-56
Athanasius, 32, 32n9, 50n65,
 65nn100-101
Augustine, vii, xi, xii, xxi, xxin6, 6,
 27n78, 30, 30n1, 31n3, 32n10, 35,
 36n21, 40, 40n41, 42, 43n49, 47,
 47n57, 78, 78n14, 80, 90, 90n48,
 92, 92n54, 107, 130n26

Bach, Johann Sebastian, ix, 119
Balthasar, Hans Urs von, xxii-xxiii,
 xxiiin11, 5, 5n10, 13n35, 16,
 16n46, 17n51, 21nn60-61, 22n63,
 25n74, 30, 31n5, 37, 47, 47n58,
 52, 52nn72-73, 58, 58nn89-91,
 77, 77nn5-8, 78, 80-81, 81n23,
 85, 86nn36-38, 89, 89n45, 90,
 90n46, 97n63, 128n21
Balz, Horst, 33n12
Barrett, Charles Kingsley, 13n36
Barth, Karl, xxii, xxiin9, 2, 2n4, 5,
 5n12, 17, 17n50, 37, 79, 80n19,
 85, 85n35, 89, 89n44, 97n63,
 97n64
Barth, Markus, 8n20
Basil the Great, 11, 11n30, 32, 32n9,
 36, 36n23, 40, 40n40, 59, 59n91,
 65nn100-101, 71n117, 78, 78n13,
 81, 81n24, 92, 92n51, 136, 136n29
Bernard of Clairvaux, 54, 54n76
Bobrinskoy, Boris, 64n99, 94n60

Boespflug, François, 102n2, 107n3
Bonaventure, 35n20, 37, 45, 80, 80n21,
 128n21
Botterweck, G. Johannes, 2n2,
 33nn12-13, 49n61, 49n63, 56n81,
 56n83, 57n87, 87n41
Boulnois, Marie-Odile, 78n11
Buber, Martin, 5, 16
Bulgakov, Sergei, 49-50, 50n64, 51n70,
 59n91, 85, 85n33, 91, 92n50,
 129n22

Calvin, John, 6, 6n15
Cantarini, Simone, viii, 110, 112
Charles of Foucauld, 124, 124n14
Charru, Philippe, ix, 119nn5-6, 120,
 120nn7-9, 121n10, 122n11
Childs, Brevard S., 1n1
Chrétien, Jean-Louis, 124n13
Coakley, Sarah, 9, 9nn24-26, 10n27,
 17, 18n54, 25n72, 26, 26n77,
 37n28, 62, 62n94, 63, 63n95,
 101n1, 102n2, 137, 137n31
Congar, Yves Marie Joseph, 14, 14n40,
 15n42, 15n44, 16n47, 17nn52-53,
 49n63, 50, 50n67, 87n40
Cyril of Alexandria, 36, 36n24, 44n52
Cyril of Jerusalem, 31n3, 32, 32n8

Delaune, Etienne, ix, 115, 117
Didymus, 32n10
Dillard, Victor, 78n11
Dragas, George Dion, 50n65
Ducoq, Christian, 17, 17n52

Index of Names

Dunn, James D. G., 3n5, 7n17, 8nn20–21, 13n36, 25n71
Durand, Emmanuel, 45n53, 98nn65–66
Durrwell, François-Xavier, 52, 52n71, 66n103, 70n114

Evdokimov, Paul, 64, 64n99

Fison, Joseph Edward, 13n36
Fitzmyer, Joseph A., 3n5, 7nn18–19, 25n71
Fulgentius of Ruspe, 53n75

Gaybba, Brian P., 50n65
Gregory Nazianzen, 22n62, 56, 92, 92nn52–53, 125n17
Gregory of Nyssa, 37, 50, 50n65
Gregory Palamas, 31n2, 48n59
Greshake, Gisbert, 64, 64n98
Guillet, Jacques, 56n84

Hilary of Poitiers, 79, 79n18, 85, 85n30
Hormisdas, Pope, 135n28

Ignatius of Antioch, 12, 77, 129n23
Ignatius of Loyola, 8, 9n23, 128, 128n21, 136n30
Irigaray, Luce, 17
Irenaeus, 12, 25, 25n73, 37, 77, 85, 85nn31–32, 107

Jacob, Pierre, 9n22
Jerome, 23n66, 88n42
John Chrysostom, 6, 6n15
John Damascene, 32n10, 48n59, 50, 50n66, 70n116, 125n17
Justin, Emperor, 135n28
Justin Martyr, 35n19

Käsemann, Ernst, 3n5, 8nn20–21
Kasper, Walter, 50n66, 53n74
Kiefer, Anselm, viii, 113–14
Kilby, Karen, 31, 31n6, 88n43
Koester, Craig R., 26n76
Kripke, Saul A., 39n38

Lacoste, Jean-Yves, 21n60

Ladaria, Luis F., 4n8, 5n13, 31n2, 47n56, 65n102, 68n108, 82n25, 85n34
Landes, Paula Fredriksen, 6n15
Lémonon, Jean-Pierre, 7n19, 14n41
Leo XIII, Pope, 135, 135n28
Leontius of Byzantium, 32n10
Levering, Matthew, 32n7
Lévinas, Emmanuel, 93, 94n59
Lieggi, Jean Paul, 69n112

Margerie, Bertrand de, 53n75
Maximus the Confessor, 32n10, 70, 70n116
McFague, Sallie, xiv
Meyendorff, John, 70n113
Mühlen, Heribert, 17, 17n53, 46, 46n55, 47n56
Moltmann, Jürgen, 50, 50n68
Morales, Xavier, 46n54, 66n103

Orphanos, Markos A., 31n2

Pannenberg, Wolfhart, xxii, xxiin8, 11, 11n31, 12, 12nn32–33, 13n35, 13n38, 24nn68–69, 25, 49n62, 56n82, 57, 58n88, 64, 64n97, 76, 76n4

Radner, Ephraim, 39n39
Rahner, Karl, xxii, xxiiin10, 2, 2n4, 18n56, 37, 76, 76nn2–3, 79–80, 80nn20–21, 84n29, 90, 90n48, 91, 91n49, 128n21
Rendtorff, Rolf, 1n1
Richard of Saint-Victor, 30, 36, 36n25, 44, 44n52, 45, 71, 71n117, 80n22
Richards, Ivor Armstrong, 35n17
Ricœur, Paul, 41, 41n44
Ringgren, Helmer, 2n2, 33nn12–13, 49n61, 49n63, 56n81, 56n83, 57n87, 87n41
Rogers, Eugene F., xxi, xxin7, 9n26, 10n29, 18, 18nn55–56, 48, 48nn59–60
Römer, Thomas Christian, 56n83
Ross, David, 41n46
Roussineau, Gabriel, 37n27

Index of Names

Rublev, Andrei, vii, 102–3, 137
Rupnik, Marko, viii, 113, 115
Rush, Osmond, 66n105

Sagne, Jean-Claude, 14, 15n42, 62, 62n94, 130n25
Sanders, James A., 1n1
Sauter, Gerhard, 53n74
Scheeben, Matthias Joseph, 36n22
Schelling, Friedrich Wilhelm Joseph von, 41, 41n47
Schneider, Gerhard, 33n12
Schweitzer, Albert, 122n11
Seitz, Christopher, 1n1
Sesboüé, Bernard, 4, 4nn8–9, 5n11, 11n30, 16, 16n48, 18n56, 21nn60–61, 22n63, 77, 77n10, 78, 78nn11–12, 82n25, 85n34, 130n26
Sheppard, Gerald T., 1n1
Siffer-Wiederhold, Nathalie, 12n34
Skeat, Walker W., 138n1
Socias, James, 125n15
Soskice, Janet Martin, 34, 34nn14–16, 35n18, 37, 37nn29–30, 38, 38nn31–36, 39n37, 41, 41n45, 42n48
Soulen, R. Kendall., 99n67
Staniloae, Dumitru, 22n64, 48, 48n59, 54n77, 55, 55n80, 94n60
Steeves, Nicolas, 37n28, 101n1
Steinsaltz, Adin, 90n47

Studer, Basil, 125n16

Tanzarella, Sergio, 77n9
Teresa of Avila, 127, 128n20
Tertullian, 15, 16n45, 37, 65nn100–101, 77, 85n30
Theobald, Christoph, ix, 119nn5–6, 120, 120nn7–9, 121n10, 122n11
Theophilus of Antioch, 12, 35n19
Thérèse of Lisieux, 125n17
Thiselton, Anthony C., 1n1, 2n3, 3nn6–7, 13n36, 17n49, 18n57, 20n58, 21n59, 24n67, 24n70, 26n75
Thomas Aquinas, 6, 6n16, 14, 14n39, 23n66, 27n78, 31, 31n4, 35n20, 36, 36n26, 37, 37n27, 40, 40n42, 41n43, 42, 45, 55n78, 60, 60n92, 62n93, 63n96, 68, 68n109, 78, 78n15, 79, 79n16, 80, 83n27, 90n47, 93nn57–58, 95nn61–62
Torrance, Thomas F., 11n31
Turner, Max, 21n59

Vetö, Etienne, 6n14, 23n65, 83n28, 123n12

Wedderburn, Alexander J. M., 10n28
Weinandy, Thomas Gerard, 50, 51n69, 66n104, 67n106, 68n110, 86n39, 99n67, 127n18, 130n24
Welker, Michael, 13, 13n37, 15, 15n43

www.ingramcontent.com/pod-product-compliance
Lightning Source LLC
Chambersburg PA
CBHW030113170426
43198CB00009B/613